Issues in Law and Economics

Issues in Law and Economics

HAROLD WINTER

THE UNIVERSITY OF CHICAGO PRESS   CHICAGO AND LONDON

The University of Chicago Press, Chicago 60637
The University of Chicago Press, Ltd., London
© 2017 by The University of Chicago
All rights reserved. Published 2017.
Printed in the United States of America

26 25 24 23 22 21 20 19 18 17   1 2 3 4 5

ISBN-13: 978-0-226-24959-9 (cloth)
ISBN-13: 978-0-226-24962-9 (paper)
ISBN-13: 978-0-226-24976-6 (e-book)
DOI: 10.7208/chicago/9780226249766.001.0001

Library of Congress Cataloging-in-Publication Data

Names: Winter, Harold, 1960– author.
Title: Issues in law and economics / Harold Winter.
Description: Chicago ; London : The University of Chicago Press, 2017. |
    Includes bibliographical references and index.
Identifiers: LCCN 2016027490 | ISBN 9780226249599 (cloth : alk. paper) |
    ISBN 9780226249629 (pbk. : alk. paper) | ISBN 9780226249766 (e-book)
Subjects: LCSH: Law—Economic aspects—United States. | Law and economics.
Classification: LCC KF379 .W56 2017 | DDC 349.73—dc23 LC record available at
    https://lccn.loc.gov/2016027490

TO ALL THE WINTERS (IN ORDER OF APPEARANCE):
SAM, PAM, ALAN, CHRIS, BRAD, CRAIG, JENN, AND THOMAS

AND TO THE MEMORY OF MY MOTHER
BERTHA WINTER
(1925–2015)

Contents

Preface

My introduction to the economic analysis of the law occurred in my last year as an undergraduate. I had just transferred from Trent University, in Peterborough, Ontario, to the much larger University of Western Ontario, in London, Ontario. At the time, you needed three years to earn a bachelor's degree in Canada, and a fourth year to qualify for a graduate program. With my bachelor's degree in economics in hand, my year at Western Ontario was to allow me to qualify for the PhD program there.

Being well trained in all the fundamentals of economics—micro, macro, econometrics, and mathematical economics—I decided to take what seemed to be, based on its description, a much less formal course than I was used to: Law and Economics. The course was taught by Stan Liebowitz and John Palmer, two economists who emphasized the less technical aspects of economic analysis. While I greatly enjoyed that course and was eager to pursue graduate courses in the field, I did not get that opportunity where I chose to earn my PhD—the University of Rochester. At the time, Rochester offered no graduate courses in law and economics. Instead, my main field of study was industrial organization/antitrust, but when I started my first teaching job I asked to teach law and economics. As of now, I've been teaching such a course for nearly thirty years.

One of the challenges I face teaching the course at Ohio University is that there is only one prerequisite—principles of microeconomics. As such, I tend to get a very interdisciplinary group of students, often with little background in economics, especially at an intermediate level, and with little background in statistics or math. Over the years, I have developed the course in a way to accommodate this particular group of students. It is still a very challenging course, not because I use a lot of graphs or math but because I expose students to economic reasoning in a way that is, at first, almost always alien to them.

Although I have used various texts over the years, I find that many students struggle with them. Of course, it is not that uncommon, in many fields, for the typical student to not "enjoy" reading the text. This is one reason why I have always preferred to prepare lecture notes from journal articles and working papers, using a text as a way to complement my lecture and not substitute for it. Over the years, as my lecture notes became more developed and comprehensive with respect to the issues I enjoy teaching, I moved away from formal texts, preferring to give my students readings made up of policy and opinion pieces, excerpts from case opinions, and a variety of online materials taken, for example, from economic and legal blogs.

The issues presented in this book represent the core of my approach to teaching law and economics. When I introduce a new issue, I like to give my students the brief facts of a case or a news story and have them discuss their personal views on the issue. Then I introduce either the court's views, or some public policy response, and after more discussion, I apply economic reasoning to the issue at hand. My main goal is to provide my students with a thorough economic analysis of the issue, with emphasis on what current researchers have to say about the theoretical, empirical, and policy aspects of it. The typical student in my class does not have the background to read academic journal articles that would be most relevant for the analysis, so I like to pull out the intuitive core of these articles and make the material more accessible to them.

Although I discuss many legal cases in this book, it is important to emphasize that in no way is this a casebook. Many of the important legal issues raised in these cases have little to do with the economic analysis. The cases and examples I present are only meant to motivate an economic analysis of an issue, not a legal analysis, and they are not necessarily chosen based on their legal or historical significance. Sometimes the case is an important part of the economic analysis that follows, and other times it simply introduces the issue but is not much further discussed.

The challenging aspect of writing a book of this length is to decide what issues to *exclude*. It wasn't difficult for me to reach my contractual word count threshold, so lots of interesting and important issues didn't make the cut. All professors have pet issues they like to teach, and undoubtedly many of these will not be included here. I didn't even include some of my own favorites, such as *droit de suite* in property and *attractive nuisance* in torts. Of course, there are certain key topics that must be included in any reasonable law and economics text, and that is why I decided to focus on the big four—property, contracts, torts, and crime.

In deciding what specific issues to include, I used a simple rule—go with what I know works best. All of these issues have been successfully used in a classroom environment, in some cases for many years, and in other cases just a handful of times, since I like to update my course on a regular basis. My class size is usually under twenty students, so I am fortunate to be able to have reasonable in-class discussions. My students generally find these issues highly interesting, especially as they are exposed to new ways of thinking about them. I have also had contact with a number of students who have gone off to earn a law degree, and they report back to me that my course served them well in law school.

One way I have tried to make the book include more issues without greatly increasing the word count is by putting serious thought behind the discussion questions that are included at the end of each chapter. The typical question asks students to go well beyond the analysis offered in the chapter. For example, in the chapter on copyright (chapter 4), I have purposely left out a discussion of an important issue—the doctrine of *fair use*. Instead, I leave it as a discussion question for students to think about. These discussion questions, then, can be used to motivate in-class discussion, be given as homework or exam questions, or be at the root of additional lecture material.

I have attempted to write this book so that it can accommodate a variety of teaching styles. Some professors like to prepare lecture material directly from the text, and if that text is a conventional one, my book can be adopted as a supplemental text. In this way, the professor can assign additional reading that matches the main text (in terms of topics covered) very closely, yet provides the students with some different cases and issues to consider. If a professor does not rely on a text for lecture notes but instead relies largely on scholarly articles, this book matches cases and issues precisely to such scholarly material. And if a course is designed as a seminar focusing on class participation, this book is specifically geared toward thoughtful discussion.

In addition, this book can accommodate a wide variety of student backgrounds. This allows a professor to decide how best to present lecture material. If the students have a sufficient technical background, a professor can use graphs, algebra, or calculus in presenting the more formal material and rely on my text for the more intuitive material. If the students are capable of understanding empirical analyses, the many scholarly empirical articles I discuss and cite can be delved into more deeply. Furthermore, if a professor leans more toward the institutional aspects of the law, this book can provide a succinct introduction to the economic aspect.

As with all my writing on the economics of public policy, I strive to make scholarly material interesting, intellectually challenging, and, most important, accessible to a broader audience, in this case undergraduate students. The economic analysis of the law is a fascinating field, and encouraging students to think about applying economic reasoning in ways they did not previously consider often leads to an exciting classroom environment. I hope not only that other professors find this book useful in their courses but that their students "enjoy" reading it as well.

Acknowledgments

My greatest debt of gratitude goes to my editor Joe Jackson. I had been thinking about this project for a long time, and initially attempted to place it with a large textbook publisher. While there was interest in the book, these publishers wanted me to provide a lot of electronic extras. I just wanted to write a book, not design a video game. Joe recognized this project for what it was—a book for students to actually *read*. Although it was a bit intimidating writing a law and economics book for the University of Chicago Press, Joe's encouragement and enthusiasm from the day I submitted my proposal, to the day I submitted my final draft, made this a highly pleasurable writing experience for me.

This is my third project with the Press, and I've always received excellent support from everyone there. On this project, I'd like to thank Leslie Keros, who did an exceptional job copyediting my manuscript, and Melinda Kennedy, who actually listened to some of my marketing ideas. And to the many others I have not personally spoken with or know by name, I thank you all for your dedication to this project.

Many of my best students over the past few years have provided me with research assistance. I'd like to especially thank Katherine Copas, Chris Denhart, Thomas Irwin, Dustin Kelly, Matthew LeBar, Fengyao Li, and Connor Swartz.

Only a handful of friends saw the manuscript in draft form, and they offered some encouraging comments. Thanks to Gwill Allen, Glenn Dutcher, and Thomas Ruchti. I also want to thank Steve Shavell for being generous with his time in answering several e-mails I sent his way.

And as always, I'd like to thank my family for their support, especially Thomas for letting me work at home while he played with his iPad, and Jenn for her unwavering encouragement and love.

Applying Economic Reasoning to the Law

One way to introduce the economic approach to the law (and social issues in general) is to think of economic analysis as involving three broad steps (see Winter 2013):

1. Identify the theoretical trade-offs of the issue in question.
2. If possible, empirically measure the trade-offs found in step 1.
3. Advise social policy based on steps 1 and 2.

Several brief examples from some of the issues presented in this book will help illustrate the key aspects of these steps.

Theory

For every social issue you can imagine, there will have to be trade-offs, or costs and benefits, to consider. Sometimes, the key trade-offs are fairly obvious. Increasing the size of a local police force has the benefit of reducing the crime rate, but involves the costs associated with hiring more police officers (see chapter 10). Copyright law's most important benefit is that it can encourage the creation of intellectual property by protecting the creator's financial gains from being eroded by pirated copies. On the other hand, copyright law's most important cost is that it grants the creator some amount of monopoly power, possibly leading to higher prices that can exclude some consumers from purchasing the good (chapter 4).

Other trade-offs are more difficult to recognize, especially for the layperson. The three-strikes law, which punishes third-time criminal offenders very harshly even for minor crimes, may lead to an increase in the murder rate (chapter 11). Medical malpractice law may induce doctors to increase the level of care they provide to their patients, even when this additional care does not improve health outcomes and is not recommended by the medical profession itself (chapter 9).

Step 1 is where economic analysis begins. Even for scholars who focus their research on the other two steps, there must always be some consideration of the trade-offs that are underlying the empirical work or policy analysis relating to whatever issue is at hand. Economists are trained to identify trade-offs that few others may ever consider. But how these trade-offs stack up against each other, and which ones are most relevant for whatever issue is being considered, ultimately requires some form of empirical verification and quantification. This leads us to the next step.

Evidence

Some of the most passionate debates in the economic analysis of the law (and in economics in general) involve disagreement over the interpretation of empirical evidence. It is not uncommon to find a substantial body of evidence that supports a particular hypothesis, only to discover an alternative substantial body of evidence that refutes the same hypothesis. In trying to determine if sharing computer files is significantly hurting the music industry, the evidence is mixed (chapter 4). In trying to determine if racial profiling is an efficient policing technique in reducing crime or merely an indication of racially biased behavior among police officers, the evidence is mixed (chapter 12). In trying to determine if the death penalty deters murder, perhaps the most substantial debate in law and economics, the evidence is mixed (chapter 10). Why is there such a severe lack of a consensus among these empirical studies? There are several reasons.

Empirical analysis requires data, which can come from several sources such as surveys, observable market information, and controlled experiments. Unfortunately, data collection is often difficult to do and, as a result, data are often measured inaccurately. There can also be alternative ways to measure a single variable, leading to the issue of which measure is most appropriate to use. Furthermore, the real world is a big and complicated place to study; that is, for any given issue, there may be a large number of variables that are relevant for the analysis. As such, a lot of data that would be needed to accurately measure trade-offs simply may not be available. Finally, and perhaps most important, there are many legitimate ways to approach an empirical analysis. Different statistical techniques and different ways to organize data can be used to test the same hypothesis. This variety of empirical methodologies inevitably leads to a variety of results.

There are also complications that are commonly found in empirical analyses that need to be taken into account. One such problem involves controlling for *confounding factors*. To determine if judges tend to sentence black men differently than they do white men, or sentence men differently than they do women, it is easy to compare average prison sentences across racial or gender categories (chapter 13). What you are very likely to find is that black men face longer sentences than white men, and men face longer sentences than women. But two obvious confounding factors (among several) that also influence the sentence length and must be taken into account are an offender's severity of offense and criminal history. If the group that faces the longer sentence also, on average, commits more severe offenses and has a more involved criminal history, it may be these factors that are the driving force explaining sentence length. It is important to note that these confounding factors do not preclude the possibility of judicial bias. Instead, controlling for these factors allows the researcher to have more confidence in attributing an effect to a variable of interest, such as judicial bias, as opposed to these other factors.

Another common problem found in empirical analyses is *reverse causation*. One simple prediction in combating crime is that if more police officers are hired, crime rates will fall (chapter 10). The causation, then, is that more police leads to less crime. On the other hand, it is also simple to predict that if crime rates increase, more police officers may be hired. The causation now is that more crime leads to more police. If this reverse causation isn't properly taken into account, a study that is trying to determine if the hiring of police officers is a sound approach to deterring crime may find that more police leads to *more* crime. Yet this result may be due to reverse causation, as opposed to a refutation of the prediction that more police leads to less crime.

These types of problems are well known to all but the least capable researchers, so they are rarely ignored in empirical studies. The real problem is that there can be disagreement as to which confounding factors matter most and need to be taken into account, and precisely how to correct for the problem of reverse causation. Along with the other problems discussed above, there are sincere differences in how researchers approach empirical analyses, routinely leading to mixed evidence relating to many, if not all, social issues. But it can still be worse. What if researcher bias is *insincere*?

Consider the following hypothetical situations:

1. The Recording Industry Association of America funds a study that ultimately finds that sharing music files is detrimental to the music industry.
2. The American Medical Association funds a study that ultimately finds that tort reform to alleviate the burden of medical malpractice liability improves health outcomes for patients.
3. A pro-death penalty group funds a study that ultimately finds that capital punishment reduces the murder rate.

How much confidence do you place in the results of these studies? Would you place more confidence in the results if they were *not* funded by these groups?

At times, empirical researchers are criticized for being influenced by their source of funding. But even without outside funding, researcher bias still has the potential to influence empirical research. If a nonfunded pro-death penalty researcher finds that capital punishment reduces the murder rate, should that result be ignored? If the same researcher finds that capital punishment does not reduce the murder rate, should that result be taken more seriously than if found by another researcher known to be neutral? How important is it to gauge researcher bias, for whatever reasons such bias exists, to determine the integrity of the empirical results?

The difficulty in considering researcher bias is not that it can be a problem, but that it has the potential to *always* be a problem. How can you ever be confident that a researcher is completely unbiased? Certainly, it may be prudent to require researchers to be transparent about their sources of funding if any exist, but what is even more important is for researchers to be transparent about their *data*. The key aspects of enhancing confidence in the results of empirical studies are to allow others to be able to verify the integrity of the data, to replicate results, and to test the robustness of the results to various statistical manipulations. To this end, it is important for researchers to *share* data.

Researchers have always had the opportunity to make their data available to others but, until fairly recently, they were rarely compelled to do so. Currently, given the ease of transmitting large computer files, many academic journals are now requiring researchers to make their data available as a condition of publication. For example, consider this statement by the editors of the *Journal of Law and Economics*, a leading journal in the field:

> It is the policy of the *Journal of Law and Economics* to publish papers only if the data used in the analysis are clearly and precisely documented and are readily available to any researcher for purposes of replication. Authors of accepted papers that contain empirical work, simulations, or experimental work must provide to the *Journal*, prior to publication, the data, programs, and other details of the computations sufficient to permit replication. These will be posted on the *JLE* Web site. The editors should be notified at the time of the submission if the data used in a paper are proprietary or if, for some other reason, the requirements above cannot be met. (*JLE* website.)

While this type of measure can help alleviate the problem of researcher bias, one thing it cannot do is help alleviate the lack of consensus empirical research commonly yields. It is important to note, however, that disagreement over step 2 does little to diminish the value of economic reasoning. There are legitimate and passionate disagreements in how to measure tradeoffs, but this simply is an unavoidable consequence of the nature of empirical work. Any academic discipline that attempts to apply empirical analysis to policy issues will have to confront these same problems.

Steps 1 and 2 are typically integral parts of step 3, the policy stage, but the converse is not true. Economic analysis, even of "real world" legal rules, does not have to include an explicit policy component. For example, let's say you are interested in determining if the death penalty can deter murder. You recognize that there are many costs and benefits to consider when analyzing capital punishment, but you only want to focus on its deterrence benefit. You begin with step 1.

In this case, step 1 is fairly straightforward. You assume that the death penalty is a more severe punishment than the next alternative (life imprisonment, for example), and then you predict that when criminals face an increased cost of their behavior as the severity of punishment increases, they will rationally respond by committing fewer crimes. Thus, your theoretical prediction is that the death penalty will deter murder. Step 2, the empirical verification of the deterrent effect of capital punishment, is a much more complicated process. But after you collect your data, and perform all the relevant statistical procedures, you do indeed find empirical verification that the death penalty deters murder. So now what do you do with this result? That depends on how you approach applying economic analysis to the law—*positively*, or *normatively*.

Positive economic analysis is primarily concerned with trying to explain *what is*, whereas normative analysis tries to argue *what should be*. We observe that only some jurisdictions enforce capital punishment. Can we explain why this is so? We don't have to have any particular interest in the policy aspects of capital punishment to want to identify, measure, and understand its costs and benefits. In addition, positive analysis can be used to examine questions such as *what has been* or *what can be*, again without any policy objectives in mind. Why has tort law relating to product liability dramatically changed over the past century? Can we predict how copyright law will change as copying technology continues to improve in quality and become less expensive?

Part of the confusion between the two approaches to economic analysis is that much positive economics, especially in a field like law and economics, leads to immediate normative implications. But as legal scholar Richard Posner (1979, 286–87) points out:

> The use of economics to support legal policy recommendations may seem to raise inescapably the issue of the adequacy of economics as a normative system, but it does not. The economist who demonstrates that criminals respond to incentives and hence commit fewer crimes when penalties are made more severe is not engaged in normative analysis. His demonstration has normative significance only insofar as the people who think normatively about criminal punishment consider its behavioral effects to the design of a just punishment system. In measuring economic costs and benefits, the economist *qua* economist is not engaged in the separate task of telling policymakers how much weight to assign to economic factors.
>
> I do not mean that this separate task is uninteresting or unimportant, but only that it is not part of economics as such . . . So long as it is accepted that the economist can measure costs and that costs are relevant to policy, economics has an important role to play in debates over legal reform.

And this "important role" of economics leads us to our last step.

Policy

Most economic research concerning public policy issues is meant to advise those in the position to implement policy. (In some cases, it is economists themselves who are in a position to implement policy, such as former chairman of the Federal Reserve Ben Bernanke). While some economists leave it to the audience of their research to determine its policy implications, others embrace the normative aspects of economic analysis and make explicit policy suggestions. The first task in advising public policy is to have a policy objective, and to this end economists typically favor the objective of *social welfare (or social wealth) maximization.*

The specific form of a social welfare function can vary across applications, but it always has one common feature—it posits an objective that is achieved when resources are used efficiently. As for the concept of efficiency, that may entail moving a resource to a higher-valued use (as in property law, discussed in chapter 1) or continued spending to reduce the accident rate as long as there is a return of more than a dollar in safety benefits for each dollar spent on resources used to lower the probability of an accident (as in tort law, chapter 7). Social welfare maximization, then, remains largely unconcerned with notions of fairness. According to some scholars, this is precisely why social welfare should be the guiding objective considered in policy settings:

> This article is concerned with the principles that should guide society in its evaluation of legal policy. We consider two fundamental approaches to such normative evaluation, one based on how legal rules affect individuals' welfare and the other grounded in notions of fairness . . . Our central claim is that the welfare-based normative approach should be exclusively employed in evaluating legal rules. That is, legal rules should be selected entirely with respect to their effects on the well-being of individuals in society. This position implies that notions of fairness like corrective justice should receive no independent weight in the assessment of legal rules. (Kaplow and Shavell 2001, 967)

Unsurprisingly, this view has been subject to various degrees of criticism from a number of other legal scholars, with the following excerpt presented as an illustrative example:

> The things people want and value are too complicated. What counts as good and bad, fair and unfair, just and unjust, and how much anyone cares about the answers to those questions—the content and extent, in other words, of our taste for fairness and distaste for injustice—are important to people; the answers to those questions are significant aspects of how we define ourselves. So long as this is true, no amount of argument ever is likely to show that debating

those questions and giving weight to the answers perforce will make people worse off. (Farnsworth 2002, 2026)

These normative arguments concerning what criteria should govern public policy are important and worthy of serious consideration, but are well beyond the scope of this book. Furthermore, if desired, they can be neatly sidestepped without losing much in terms of understanding the economic approach to law.

It may be tempting to conclude that when you see an economic analysis that uses a social welfare function, it must be a normative analysis. But that is not necessarily the case. The objective of social welfare maximization allows the economist to focus on a well-defined efficiency condition, thus facilitating the positive analysis. Certain tort-liability rules are efficient in the sense that they *minimize the social loss* of accidents (the flip side of maximizing social welfare). This allows for a metric to be used to compare liability rules (chapter 7). What isn't required is a statement justifying the objective because it is what policy makers actually do or should care about. A social welfare function may be nothing more than an analytical tool used to help understand and explain legal rules, even if it can also be used to advise public policy.

In cases where there is broad agreement over the use of social welfare to govern both positive and normative economic analysis, there may be disagreement over precisely what should be counted as social welfare. An excellent example of this can be found in the economic analysis of crime (chapter 10). To deter crime, society must use resources for the apprehension, conviction, and punishment of criminals. These costs are offset by the benefits in crime reduction. But should the benefits that accrue to individuals who commit crime be included in the definition of social welfare? After all, aren't criminals also *part* of society?

In theory, this can be an important issue. If criminal benefits are included in social welfare, this may suggest that fewer resources can be used to deter crime because crime itself has offsetting benefits. It may even imply that certain crimes should be *encouraged* when the benefit to the criminal more than offsets the cost to the victim. Notice, however, that it is a *fact* that a criminal reaps a benefit from committing a crime (or else why commit the crime), yet it is an *opinion* as to whether that benefit should be counted as social welfare. So what opinions do economists hold on this issue?

In his seminal paper, Nobel Laureate Gary Becker (1968) simply took it for granted that a criminal's benefit should be included as a variable in his model of crime and punishment. This matter-of-fact inclusion caught the attention of another Nobel Laureate, George Stigler (1970, 527):

> Becker introduces as a different limitation on punishment the "social value of the gain to offenders" from the offense. The determination of this social value is not explained, and one is entitled to doubt its usefulness as an explanatory concept: what evidence is there that society sets a positive value upon the utility derived from a murder, rape, or arson? In fact, the society has branded the utility derived from such activities as illicit. It may be that in a few offenses some gain to the offender is viewed as a gain to society, but such social gains seem too infrequent, small, and capricious to put an effective limitation upon the size of punishments.

This disagreement between two of the profession's greatest scholars illustrates the difficulties associated with determining what should be counted as social welfare.

In general, economists tend to be *inclusive* when considering what to count as social welfare, as explained by law and economics scholar David Friedman (2000, 230): "If instead of treating all benefits to everyone equally, we first sort people into the deserving and the undeserving, the just and the unjust, the criminals and the victims, we are simply assuming our conclusions. Benefits to bad people don't count, so rules against bad people are automatically efficient." But even an eloquent statement like this one does not change the fact that what counts as social welfare is always a matter of opinion, and that's assuming you care about the objective of social welfare maximization in the first place.

There is no denying that advising public policy based on economic analysis is challenging to do. Even if most economists agree on the objective of maximizing social welfare, there may still be disagreement as to what that actually entails. And if economists are in precise agreement over the policy objectives, the difficulties associated with empirically measuring trade-offs, as discussed above, may nevertheless still lead to a variety of policy opinions. As economists debate among themselves over appropriate policy measures, things can get more complicated for policy makers looking for advice when scholars from numerous other disciplines weigh in with their views.

The economic approach to law does not have to be thought of as more important, or more correct, than other approaches. Policy makers may find economic reasoning useful in thinking about which policies to enact, or they may choose to ignore it all together. Throughout this book, many examples will depict law and economic analysis (both positive and normative) as interesting, unique, and at times even a bit unusual. By the end, you will have to decide for yourself whether you find economic analysis to be important. But even if you find it to be unimportant, you will at least come to that conclusion with a better understanding of *why* you find it to be that way. In the highly contentious area of social policy analysis, the more views that are considered, the more rigorous the analyses become both theoretically and empirically, the more information policy makers can draw upon, the more likely the ultimate (and possibly naïve) goal of public policy—to try to improve the world in which we live—can be achieved, regardless of what the words "improve the world" mean to you.

References

Becker, G. S. 1968. "Crime and Punishment: An Economic Approach." *Journal of Political Economy* 76:169–217.

Farnsworth, W. 2002. "The Taste for Fairness." Review of *Fairness versus Welfare*, by L. Kaplow and S. Shavell. *Columbia Law Review* 102:1992–2026.

Friedman, D. 2000. *Law's Order*. Princeton, NJ: Princeton University Press.

Kaplow, L., and Shavell, S. 2001. "Fairness versus Welfare." *Harvard Law Review* 114:966–1388.

Posner, R. A. 1979. "Some Uses and Abuses of Economics in Law." *University of Chicago Law Review* 46:281–306.

Stigler, G. J. 1970. "The Optimum Enforcement of Laws." *Journal of Political Economy* 78:526–36.

Winter, H. 2013. *Trade-Offs: An Introduction to Economic Reasoning and Social Issues, Second Edition*. Chicago: University of Chicago Press

PART I

Property

CHAPTER ONE

Should Body Parts Be Salable?

Moore v. The Regents of the University of California *(1990) and the Market for Human Tissue*

Facts

In 1976, John Moore was diagnosed with hairy cell leukemia, a very rare form of cancer. He was referred to Dr. David Golde, a physician practicing at the Medical Center of the University of California, Los Angeles (UCLA). Golde recommended that Moore's enlarged spleen be removed, and Moore agreed and signed a consent form. Prior to the surgery, Golde arranged to use portions of Moore's spleen to conduct research.

The operation was successful, for both Moore and Golde. As Moore continued to recover, Golde continued to conduct research with Moore's cells. Furthermore, Golde insisted on Moore continuing to travel from his home in Seattle to UCLA to withdraw samples of blood, skin, bone marrow, and other material. As Moore became reluctant to continue making the trip, Golde offered to cover his expenses, and his generosity was amply rewarded. With Moore's cells, Golde's research eventually led to the commercial development of a cell line, and products derived from it, that had a market value estimated to be approximately $3 *billion.* Moore eventually became suspicious of Golde's behavior, and especially of his insistence on having Moore sign additional consent forms. Moore hired a lawyer, discovered the phenomenal market value of products derived from his cells, and filed a lawsuit against Golde and UCLA in an attempt to claim part of that value.

Court's Decision

The main issue the court faced was to determine who should be given the property right to the cells—Moore or Golde. The first appeals court assigned the property right to Moore and offered the following explanation:

> We are told that if plaintiff is permitted to have decision making authority and a financial interest in the cell-line, he would then have the unlimited power to inhibit medical research that could potentially benefit humanity. He could conceivably go from institution to institution seeking the highest bid, and if dissatisfied, would claim the right simply to prohibit the research entirely. We conclude that, if informed, a patient might refuse to participate in a research program. We would give the patient that right. As to defendant's concern that a patient might seek the greatest economic gain for his participation, this argument is unpersuasive because it fails to explain why defendants, who patented plaintiff's cell-line and are benefiting financially from it, are any more to be trusted with these momentous decisions than the person whose cells are being used. . . . If this science has become science for profit, then we fail to see any justification for excluding the patient from participation in the profits.

Thanks to the court's decision, Moore became a very wealthy man, but only on paper and only for a short time.

In the second appeal, the California Supreme Court reversed the previous court's ruling. They reasoned that giving the patient the property right over important research materials would make it more costly to obtain the materials and thus hinder such research:

> The extension of conversion law into this area will hinder research by restricting access to necessary raw materials. Thousands of human cell lines already exist in tissue repositories, such as the American Type Culture Collection and those operated by the National Institutes of Health and the American Cancer Society. These repositories respond to tens of thousands of requests for samples annually. Since the patent office requires the holders of patents on cell lines to make samples available to anyone, many patent holders place their cell lines in repositories to avoid the administrative burden of responding to requests. At present, human cell lines are routinely copied and distributed to other researchers for experimental purposes, usually free of charge. This exchange of scientific materials, which is still relatively free and efficient, will surely be

compromised if each cell sample becomes the potential subject matter of a lawsuit.

Moore was ultimately denied the property right over his cells. In a manner of speaking, the court ruled that Moore did not own his spleen.

Economic Analysis

Because the cells had already been developed into a commercial product line, the impact of the court's decision on the litigants would primarily be distributional: would the court allow Moore to share in the revenue generated by the spleen? But for similar future cases, the court's decision could affect the allocation of resources; that is, would the cells end up being used for medical research? So to analyze this case, let's put it into a slightly different perspective.

Let's say you have a diseased spleen and need to have it removed to save your life. Your doctor informs you that it is possible that your spleen may yield some material that can be used to develop pharmaceutical products worth a tremendous amount of money. If you are given the property right over the spleen, the doctor cannot use the spleen without your consent. If the doctor is given the property right over the spleen, you have no say in how it is used once it is removed. Of course, you have the right to refuse medical treatment, but let's assume you prefer not to die. So, with or without the property right, you have your spleen removed. Before any medical treatment is given, the court must assign the property right. What should it do?

Although there are many issues raised by this case—legal, ethical, moral, and so on—in property right cases a standard economic objective is to see that resources are moved to their highest-valued use. Ownership determines the value of a resource, and the higher the value the greater the social welfare. So, if the court is interested in pursuing this objective, the case boils down to a simple question: where is the spleen more highly valued, with the doctor or with the patient? While the lower court assigned the right to the patient, and the higher court assigned the right to the doctor, economic analysis offers a unique perspective in this case—*both* decisions are correct. How can this be?

What happens if the court awards the property right to the doctor? The doctor removes the spleen and keeps it for research purposes. The cells can be used to develop as many pharmaceutical products as possible, and the patient gets no financial compensation. What happens if the court awards the property right to the patient? The doctor removes the spleen and keeps it for research purposes. The cells can be used to develop as many pharmaceutical products as possible, and the patient becomes extremely wealthy.

But haven't we missed something? If the patient is given the property right over the cells, how does the doctor end up with them? To answer that question, all you have to do is answer this one: how long would it take you to sell your already-removed diseased spleen to the doctor, possibly for millions of dollars? Your answer to that question explains how the doctor ends up with the spleen.

An economist would predict that the spleen will end up being used for medical research because there are *gains from trade* that exist for that purpose. Whenever there is a consensual market transaction between two parties, gains from trade means that *both parties must benefit*. Imagine you have a car to sell, and you are willing to sell it as long as you get a minimum of $2,500. Anything less than that and you prefer to keep the car. A potential buyer shows up and begins negotiating with you. She values the car at $2,000, and that represents her maximum willingness to pay for your car. The two of you could negotiate for hours, but there are no gains from trade for you to sell the car to her. You need $500 more than she is willing to pay at a maximum.

Another buyer shows up to negotiate with you. He values the car at $3,500. If the two of you negotiate, eventually you will find a price between $2,500 and $3,500 that will have you sell the car to him. Let's say that price is $2,800. You sell the car and make $300 more than you need at a minimum, and he buys the car and pays $700 less than his maximum. You both gain from the sale, the total gains are $1,000, and the car ends up in a higher-valued use. It is important to note that regardless of what price the buyer pays for the car, when he takes ownership the value of the car increases from $2,500 to $3,500. Value has a subjective component, and this is why one specific object, such as a car, can increase in value when it changes ownership.

The great thing about this process is that you and the seller do not have to know anything about what the other is willing to accept, or willing to pay, for the car. You know how much you need at a minimum, and the buyer knows how much he will pay at a maximum. If those two values properly overlap, and negotiation can take place, trade will occur that is mutually beneficial. When gains from trade are exploited, resources are allocated efficiently.

The real issue in *Moore* is not where the spleen ends up. Whether the property right is given to the doctor or the patient, the gains from trade are so enormous that the doctor will end up with the spleen. We are talking about a market value in the *billions* of dollars. Unless the patient with the property right has a serious problem with allowing his removed diseased spleen to be used for medical research (and make no mistake, it must be a *very* serious problem), the lure of huge financial gains will have him gladly sell his spleen. The real issue seems to be distributional. Should the doctor have to pay for the spleen so that the patient is financially compensated? If the only objective is to move the resource to its highest-valued use, it doesn't matter if the doctor has to pay for it. The same financial lure that has the patient gladly sell his spleen, has the doctor gladly buy it.

There is one other point that is important to keep in mind when considering property right cases. Although it seems obvious in *Moore* that the highest-valued use of the cells is for medical research, in general it doesn't matter if the court knows this or not. As long as the parties are expected to negotiate, the key economic point is that it doesn't matter who gets the property right—*as long as a property right is assigned, the cells will end up in their highest-valued use.* This basic result is attributed to Nobel Laureate Ronald Coase (1960), and it is often referred to as the *Coase Theorem.* Simply stated, having well-defined property rights is the key to resolving property right issues, as long as the parties can transact. But what if the parties *cannot* transact, as in the case where a legal market does not exist?

As controversial as it appears to be to consider allowing a diseased spleen to be sold, how would you feel about allowing a healthy organ to be surgically removed and then sold? It is a fact that a person can live a fairly normal life with just one kidney. It is also a fact that the current system of supplying kidneys for transplant by donation only has led to a severe shortage of kidneys available for transplant. On their website, the National Kidney Foundation reports that as of 2014, more than 96,000 people in the United States are on a kidney transplant waiting list, yet fewer than 17,000 receive one each year. Approximately 13 people die each day waiting for a kidney. So why not allow someone with two kidneys to sell one to someone who requires a kidney transplant? Establishing a market for kidneys is an idea that is often championed by economists. Would the existence of gains from trade in the buying and selling of kidneys help alleviate the shortage?

It may be difficult to determine exactly how much a person in need of a kidney would be willing to pay for one, but determining the minimum (or competitive) price a kidney would sell for if such a market developed is more feasible, as demonstrated by one economic study (Becker and Elias 2007). To calculate the price of a kidney, the study assumes that there would be many potential sellers and that no individual seller would be able to set a price much higher than anyone else. The price must, at a minimum, cover the cost of supplying a kidney, and the study considers three main components of this cost: the risk of dying, the lost time during the recovery period, and the reduced quality of life. The next goal is to place a monetary-equivalence value on each of these components.

Without going into detail as to how the study comes up with these figures, it first determines that the risk of dying during a kidney transplant is approximately one in a thousand. Using a value (in 2005 dollars) of $5 million for a value-of-life estimate, the average (or expected) loss of life equals 1/1,000 (or 0.001) multiplied by $5 million, or $5,000. Second, the cost to an average person of a four-week postsurgery recovery period in terms of forgone earnings is determined to be $2,700. The last step is to place a monetary value on the reduced quality of life one may experience after having one kidney removed. For some, this may be quite low as you can typically lead a normal life with one kidney. But to the extent that you are physically active, and there is evidence that kidney donors may experience high blood pressure, there is likely to be some reduction in quality of life. The study determines this value to be $7,500. Putting all three values together, the total monetary cost to donors who give up a kidney is $15,200, suggesting that this would be close to the market-clearing price if a market for selling kidneys were to be established. (The study also allows for various assumptions on the figures used to calculate the price, and finds a likely *range* of prices as low as $7,600 and as high as $27,700.)

Regardless of what the price would be if a market for kidneys developed, there is no doubt that there would be an instant outcry concerning the morality of such a market. Unlike the kidney shortage, there is no shortage of examples of such outcries. Here is a representative one, written by ethics professor Katrina Bramstedt, concerning some of the consequences of allowing a market for kidneys:

> Patients consequently survive not due to the altruism of their fellow man—the long-time premise of organ donation—but because of their personal wealth. At the same time, a cohort of humanity is wiped out because they can't afford

the price of life. The sellers, too, are likely the poor. After a kidney, what do they sell next? Any system of organ selling makes the poor the clinical treasure trove of the rich. Values and ethics can and do underpin society and medical practice so health care structures that operate purely on economics—letting the wealthiest patients win at the literal expense of the poor—are inappropriate. (*New York Times* [online], August 21, 2014)

It is hard to imagine a better example of a perspective that is at odds with an economic one.

The most common line of attack against establishing a market for kidneys concerns how it will affect the poor. One argument is that the additional cost of the kidney would be a substantial financial burden on this group of people, making it more difficult (relative to the wealthy) for them to acquire a kidney. Or, as the above quote more colorfully states: "a cohort of humanity is wiped out because they can't afford the price of life." The problem with this argument is that it is substantially weakened when considered in the proper perspective.

Let's assume that the price of a kidney is around $15,000. Certainly, this amount on its own can be constraining, but it is only *part* of the cost of a kidney transplant. At the time the study estimated that price, the estimated cost of a kidney transplant operation (in 2005 dollars) was $160,000, not including the price of the kidney. This makes the total cost of a kidney transplant $175,000 under a market system, but only $160,000 under a donation system. What impact does the additional cost have on the type of people who can get kidney transplants?

For individuals who cannot afford the $160,000 (or, equivalently, do not have adequate insurance coverage), adding another $15,000 on top of that is irrelevant—they still can't afford a transplant. For those individuals who can afford the $175,000 total cost of the operation, the additional price for the kidney is also irrelevant—they still can afford a transplant. This leaves us with one last group: those who can afford the cost of the surgery, but not the additional cost of the kidney. These individuals are now excluded from getting a transplant only because of having to purchase the kidney. How do we evaluate the importance of this group?

This gap between $160,000 and $175,000 is unlikely to affect many people, but even if it does, what is the alternative? *Everyone* who cannot get a kidney through the current system will not be able to get a kidney if none are for sale. So even if there are individuals who are forever priced out of the kidney transplant market, how many more individuals will get kidneys due to the expected increase in supply? Ultimately, isn't this the most important point?

Furthermore, if you are worried about the poor having to pay $15,000 for a kidney, you should be even more worried about the cost of dialysis for many of those who remain on the waiting list. Just the monetary cost of dialysis is at least $75,000 per year, not even counting all the reduced quality-of-life costs a dialysis patient is subject to. Whoever is bearing the financial burden for those not able to get a kidney under the current system, will likely be thrilled with the potential to simply buy a kidney and have a transplant operation performed.

Another argument against establishing a market for kidneys that concerns the poor is that it would be these people who would be most tempted to sell their kidneys. Or, as the above quote states: "any system of organ selling makes the poor the clinical treasure trove of the rich." It's not difficult to believe that the poor will be the most likely suppliers of kidneys if a market develops, but will this be beneficial or detrimental to them? Don't the poor, or *anyone* for that matter, experience gains from trade when selling a kidney? In this sense, the poor prefer to be sellers of kidneys, as the concept of gains from trade necessarily implies that *both* buyers and sellers benefit from the market exchange.

Maybe a concern with the poor, or the less educated, as suppliers of kidneys is that they may not be well informed. Or perhaps, even if well informed, they may make impulsive decisions, especially if they are experiencing financial pressures. If these problems exist, especially for such an irreversible act as selling a kidney, they could experience much regret later on. A market for kidneys, however, would undoubtedly be well regulated. There easily could be safeguards put in place to try to keep suppliers of kidneys well informed and to perhaps give them a grace period in which to reconsider their decision. Still, these types of concerns make more economic sense than simply identifying the poor as the most likely suppliers. This fact tells us little about why a market for kidneys would be detrimental to them.

The criticism that a market for kidneys creates inequality among wealth classes is not likely to be widely embraced by economists. But that doesn't mean there aren't other economic issues to consider. First and foremost, while the expectation is that a market would increase the supply of kidneys available for transplant, this prediction would have to borne out in practice. Such a market would obviously be unusual, especially at first, and potential suppliers may simply be uncomfortable with the idea of selling a kidney. There would also tend to be severe criticism about such a market, possibly creating a social stigma that discourages participation. Also, markets require administrative costs to develop and be maintained, and these costs may be substantial. There may be other alternatives to the current system of donation only that could increase the supply of kidneys without creating as much of a public outcry or requiring as many resources to maintain.

Furthermore, it is often argued that a market for kidneys may lead to a *crowding-out effect* of donations. This means that some individuals may feel that the value of an altruistic donation is greatly weakened when a market for kidneys concurrently exists. One interesting experimental study (Mellstrom and Johannesson 2008) finds evidence (but only among women) that the number of subjects willing to be blood donors decreases by half when a monetary payment is offered (compared to the group of subjects not offered any monetary compensation). However, if instead of monetary compensation paid directly to the donor, the payment is offered to charity, this crowding-out effect disappears. Thus, the *form* of compensation, as well as the *gender* of the donor, may be important considerations in determining if an alternative method to increase the supply of organs for transplant can be effective.

In all, the main lesson from this discussion is that with well-established property rights, resources will move to their highest-valued use as long as transactions can take place. However, transactions may not always take place, such as when a market does not legally exist (as with kidneys), or when there are transactions costs that make it difficult for the parties to negotiate with each other. Market solutions are often where economists begin their analyses, even for unusual settings such as the selling of body parts, but it is not always where economists end their analyses. This will be discussed in the next chapter.

Discussion Questions

1. Any time there is a suggestion of developing a market for the selling of body parts, one of the first criticisms put forth is that such a suggestion is *repugnant*. Repugnance can be a motivating factor behind the illegality of many activities such as prostitution, pornography, slavery, and so on. How would you evaluate the criticism that the development of these types of markets is repugnant?
2. Kidneys for transplant can be harvested from cadavers, as well as donated by living donors. Discuss the challenges involved in developing and maintaining a market for cadaveric kidneys.

3. Besides a donation-only system or a market for buying and selling kidneys, what other ways can you think of to help alleviate the kidney shortage? How would you evaluate them?

References

Becker, G. S., and J. J. Elias. 2007. "Introducing Incentives in the Market for Live and Cadaveric Organ Donations." *Journal of Economic Perspectives* 21:3–24.
Coase, R. H. 1960. "The Problem of Social Cost." *Journal of Law and Economics* 3:1–44.
Mellstrom, C., and M. Johannesson. 2008. "Crowding Out in Blood Donation: Was Titmuss Right?" *Journal of the European Economic Association* 6:845–63.

CHAPTER TWO

Can Anyone Own the Sunlight?

Fontainebleau Hotel Corp. v. Forty-Five
Twenty-Five, Inc. *(1959) and the Assignment
and Protection of Property Rights*

Facts

In Florida during the mid-1950s, two luxury hotels facing the Atlantic Ocean had an interesting legal dispute. At issue was which hotel should be granted the property right over sunlight. The Eden Roc Hotel was constructed in 1955, just one year after the Fontainebleau Hotel. Soon afterward, the Fontainebleau decided to build a fourteen-story addition, and its location created a problem for the Eden Roc. From two in the afternoon until the end of the day, the addition would cast a shadow over the Eden Roc's cabana, swimming pool, and sunbathing areas. This shadow would reduce the enjoyment of these areas for the Eden Roc's guests, thus diminishing the desirability of staying at that hotel. The Eden Roc sued to prevent the Fontainebleau from continuing to build the addition.

Court's Decision

The Eden Roc got off to a great start with the lower court's decision: "[Our decision] is based solely on the proposition that no one has a right to use his property to the injury of another. In this case, it is clear from the evidence that the proposed use by the Fontainebleau will materially damage the Eden Roc." The Eden Roc prevailed, and the Fontainebleau was ordered to stop building the addition. The appeals court, however, soon after reversed that decision. That court offered the following argument: "There being, then, no legal right to the free flow of light and air from the adjoining land, it is universally held that where a structure serves a useful and beneficial purpose, it does not give rise to a cause of action . . . even though it causes injury to another by cutting off the light and air and interfering with the view that would otherwise be available over adjoining land in its natural state." Simply put, the appeals court did not believe that the Eden Roc had any right over the sunlight.

Economic Analysis

In the first decision, Eden Roc prevailed because the court found that the hotel was indeed harmed by the building of the extension. In the second decision, the Fontainebleau prevailed because the court did not believe that the Eden Roc had a legal right to sunlight. An implication of this ruling is that while the Eden Roc had no right over the sunlight, it did have the right to pay the Fontainebleau *not* to build the addition. Doesn't this mean, in effect, that the Fontainebleau "owned" the sunlight that the Eden Roc wanted access to?

Neither court explicitly addressed the key questions an economist would raise: what is the efficient outcome in this setting (that is, should the addition be built), and how do we achieve that outcome? To analyze this case, let's use a simple numerical example. Assume that the Fontainebleau values the addition being built at $3 million, and the Eden Roc values the sunlight reaching its pool area at $1 million. With these numbers, we can say that the socially efficient outcome is for the addition to be built, as this yields a net gain of $2 million. What can the court do to achieve the efficient outcome?

If the two parties can negotiate, this situation is identical to *Moore* from the previous chapter. Once a property right is assigned, regardless of which hotel gets it, the efficient outcome will be achieved. If the Fontainebleau gets the right, the Eden Roc could pay it not to build the addition, but it is only willing to pay up to $1 million at a maximum, and the Fontainebleau needs a minimum of $3 million. If the Eden Roc gets the right, it would need a minimum of $1 million to allow the building, and the Fontainebleau would be willing to pay up to a $3 million maximum. In either case, gains from trade between the two hotels will assure that the addition will be built. This, once again, is a demonstration of the Coase Theorem—the establish-

THE ASSIGNMENT AND PROTECTION OF PROPERTY RIGHTS 25

ment of a property right, not who gets that right, leads to the efficient outcome as long as the parties can negotiate.

The Coase Theorem is fundamentally a confirmation of Adam Smith's
invisible hand, or the principle of *laissez-faire*—a free market (with well-
defined property rights) can achieve a socially efficient outcome without
the aid of government intervention. To some scholars, this makes the theorem obvious, or tautological, or at least impractical, as it is explicitly applied
to a no-transactions-costs setting. But the Coase Theorem has an important
flip side—if there are transactions costs that make it difficult for the parties
to negotiate and exploit gains from trade, the assignment of the property
right *can* have an impact on the allocation of resources. Thus, resources
may not move to their highest-valued use in a positive-transactions-costs
setting. Coase himself was clearly aware of the "obviousness" of his original
insight and of the importance of considering alternative transactions-costs
settings, as he expressed years later in his Nobel Laureate lecture:

> If we move from a regime of zero transaction costs to one of positive transac-
> tion costs, what becomes immediately clear is the crucial importance of the
> legal system in this new world. I explained in *The Problem of Social Cost* that
> what are traded on the market are not, as is often supposed by economists,
> physical entities but the rights to perform certain actions and the rights which
> individuals possess are established by the legal system. While we can imagine in
> the hypothetical world of zero transaction costs that the parties to an exchange
> would negotiate to change any provision of the law which prevents them from
> taking whatever steps are required to increase the value of production, in the
> real world of positive transaction costs such a procedure would be extremely
> costly, and would make unprofitable, even where it was allowed, a great deal
> of such contracting around the law. Because of this, the rights which individu-
> als possess, with their duties and privileges, will be, to a large extent what the
> law determines. As a result the legal system will have a profound effect on the
> working of the economic system and may in certain respects be said to control
> it. (Ronald H. Coase, Nobel Prize Lecture, December 1991)

Perhaps the interesting aspect of the Coase Theorem is that it posits an
obvious and impractical no-transactions-costs setting, with the intention
of encouraging scholars to direct their attention toward the more interesting and practical positive-transactions-costs setting.

So now let's assume that the owners of the two hotels refuse to negotiate with each other; that is, this case now involves *high* transactions costs.

It may not seem realistic to assume high transactions costs when there are only two parties involved in the dispute. While it is true that, in general, transactions costs are likely to increase with the number of parties involved, it is also possible to have high costs with just two parties.

For example, in this case, evidence was presented that the Fontaine-bleau purposely, and with malice, chose the location for its extension to block the sun from areas of the Eden Roc. Under these conditions, it may very well have been the case that the owners of the two hotels would not be able to sit down and negotiate with each other. Transactions costs can be obvious at times, such as travel costs and time costs, and they can be more subjective at times, such as bad feelings between the parties. Whatever the case, we will assume that there will be no negotiation between these two hotels. How does this affect the analysis when compared to a no-transactions-costs setting?

In a high-transactions-costs setting, whether the addition is built depends on who is assigned the property right. If the court assigns the property right to the Fontainebleau, the addition will be built. If the court assigns the property right to the Eden Roc, the addition will not be built. In the latter case, even if there are gains from trade for the Fontainebleau to pay the Eden Roc for the right to build, the high-transactions-costs setting does not allow for that transaction to occur. The lesson here is that in this setting the allocation of resources depends on the assignment of property rights. So how can the court rule to achieve the efficient outcome in this setting?

Until now, our focus has been on the *assignment* of property rights. But how the court deals with these types of cases involves another step—the *protection* of property rights. One way to protect a property right is to use a *property rule*. What this entails, after the property right is assigned, is for the court to do nothing more. This is precisely what we have been talking about. A property rule is strongly noninterventionist. The court needs to decide which party will be assigned the property right, and then leaves it to the parties to resolve their own dispute. Is a property rule efficient?

What we have seen so far is that when there are no transactions costs, a property rule is efficient. Once the right is assigned, the parties will negotiate to exploit any gains from trade that exist, as predicted by the Coase Theorem. But when there are high transactions costs, a property rule will not guarantee the efficient outcome. If the court assigns the property right to the Eden Roc, the high transactions costs will prevent the Fontaine-bleau from negotiating to build the addition. Of course, if the court assigns the property right to the Fontainebleau, the efficient outcome will occur because the party with the higher-valued use has the property right. When this happens, there are no gains from trade to exploit, regardless of how high the transactions costs may be.

What this tells us is that a property rule can be efficient in a high-transactions-costs setting when the court knows the highest-valued use to begin with. If the Fontainebleau is given the right to build the addition, the Eden Roc would not be willing to pay enough to stop building, even if negotiations could take place. The problem here, however, is that the court has to know the highest-valued use before assigning the property right. This means the court needs to know two things—the Fontaine-bleau's value for the addition, and the Eden Roc's value for the sunlight. If the court doesn't know these two things, the best the court can do is guess. Or, the court can decide to protect the property right with a different rule.

Let's say the court does not know the efficient outcome but does have one piece of information—that the Eden Roc values the sunlight at $1 million. Without knowing the Fontainebleau's value, the court cannot use a property rule to guarantee the efficient outcome in a high-transactions-costs setting. But there is something else the court can do. The court can assign the property right to the Eden Roc, because this is where its information lies, and it can protect that right with what is known as a *liability rule*.

A liability rule involves further intervention beyond the assignment of a property right. The court now also sets a damages (or payments) schedule that the parties follow. In this example, the court can assign the right to the Eden Roc but allow the Fontainebleau to buy the right to build an addition for exactly $1 million. What will the Fontainebleau do? The Fontainebleau will pay $1 million to build the addition that it values at $3 million. The Eden Roc is assigned the property right by the court, but the Fontainebleau builds its addition *without* requiring the consent of the Eden Roc.

What a liability rule does is allow the parties to mimic a market trans-action without actually having one. The amount of the payment, however, is not negotiated by the parties but mandated by the court. But notice, as long as the court knows one side of the story, it can design a liability rule that guarantees the efficient outcome. In this example, the court does not know how much the Fontainebleau values the addition. With the payment set at $1 million, the Eden Roc's value, the Fontainebleau will only make the payment if it values the addition at greater than $1 million. If the Fon-tainebleau values the addition at less than $1 million, it will not make the payment and the addition will not be built. If the Fontainebleau's value is greater than $1 million, the efficient outcome will be for the addition to be built, and it will be. If its value is less than $1 million, the efficient outcome will be for the addition not to be built, and it won't be. In either case, this specific liability rule allows the court to achieve the efficient outcome without knowing what it is.

A liability rule has the advantage of allowing for flexibility, especially when transactions costs are very high. The party not given the property right can still influence the allocation of resources by following the court's payment schedule. The party with the property right has no say in the matter. If the court has the Fontainebleau's information but not the Eden Roc's, the court can give the property right to the Fontainebleau and have the Eden Roc pay $3 million to prevent the addition from being built. If the Eden Roc paid that amount, the Fontainebleau would not be allowed to build, even though it was assigned the property right. But in this example, the Eden Roc does not value the sunlight at $3 million, so the efficient outcome, the building of the addition, will occur.

It is not uncommon to see economists offer the following policy advice concerning the protection of property rights: in low-transactions-costs settings, use a property rule; in high-transactions-costs settings, use a liability rule. While this is often sound advice, relying on the level of transactions costs in choosing one rule over the other does raise some issues worth considering. For example, can the court actually determine what type of transactions-costs setting the parties are in?

As mentioned above, transactions costs tend to increase with the number of parties involved, but can still be high with just two parties. Actually, one common observation is that if there are only two parties, they must be in court precisely because they couldn't work out their own problems. Thus, simply being in court suggests a high-transactions-costs setting. This thinking, however, may be flawed.

Consider the hotels case. There certainly is a conflict of interest between the two hotels over the building of the addition. If it is a low-transactions-costs setting, why didn't the Eden Roc negotiate with Fontainebleau to stop building? Or, why didn't the Fontainebleau negotiate with the Eden Roc to continue building? Because neither of these events occurred and the parties ended up in court, we can conclude that there must have been high transactions costs discouraging negotiation. But ask yourself this question: before the hotels take their case to court, if they try to work out their own problem, which hotel should be the one to pay the other? Should the Eden Roc have to pay to prevent building, or should the Fontainebleau have to pay to continue building? At this point (before the case goes to court), this has little to do with transactions costs and everything to do with the lack of a well-defined property right.

Until a property right is assigned, the parties may be at a loss as to how to proceed. So it is crucial for *both* parties to clearly understand exactly who has the right before negotiations can begin. Ironically, the assignment of the right in and of itself may create a high-transactions-costs setting. Property rights are valuable, sometimes extremely valuable (think of the $3 billion spleen in *Moore* from the previous chapter). Once a property right is assigned, the party granted the right is made wealthier. In a sense, the assigning of the right creates a winner and a loser, and bad feelings may develop that can affect the ability of the parties to negotiate a mutually beneficial solution.

For the sake of argument, let's assume the court can determine the type of transactions-costs setting. In a truly low-transactions-costs setting, it doesn't matter if the court uses a property rule or a liability rule. If the parties can negotiate to exploit gains from trade, they will do so under either rule. With a property rule, we are simply in the setting of the Coase Theorem, so the efficient outcome will be reached. With a liability rule, however, it is the court that sets the payment schedule, and not the parties themselves. What happens if the court sets the wrong payment schedule? Let's use some numbers to show that it won't matter what schedule the court sets, as long as the parties can negotiate.

Assume the court assigns the property right to the Fontainebleau, but allows the Eden Roc to stop the addition from being built if it pays $500,000. This is clearly a gross underestimation of the Fontainebleau's true value of $3 million. The Eden Roc will pay $500,000 because it values the sunlight at $1 million, and the Fontainebleau will not be able to build. But is that true? Due to the court-determined payment schedule, the Fontainebleau cannot compel the Eden Roc to pay more than $500,000, but the liability rule says nothing about whether the Fontainebleau can turn around and pay the Eden Roc for permission to build. With low transactions costs, this is precisely what we can predict will happen.

For example, the Fontainebleau can tell the Eden Roc not only to hold on to its $500,000 but to accept an additional $1.5 million to allow the extension to be built. The Eden Roc will gladly ignore the liability rule, and the Fontainebleau will still gain by building its addition. All the liability rule does is place a maximum payment on the Eden Roc; it does not preclude the Fontainebleau from negotiating an alternative, mutually beneficial outcome.

In theory, then, a low-transactions-cost setting always allows for the efficient outcome to be achieved under a property or liability rule. In practice, though, even if we maintain the low-transactions-costs setting, a property rule is less costly for the court to administer. Both rules require the assignment of a property right, but only the liability rule requires an additional step—the setting of the payment schedule. Thus, recommending a property rule over a liability rule in a low-transactions-costs setting is generally sound economic advice.

Is it sound advice, however, to recommend a liability rule over a property rule in a high-transactions-costs setting? As we have seen above, in this setting the choice between the two rules depends on the information the court has. If the court knows the efficient outcome, a property rule can be efficient. The court can simply assign the property right to the highest-valued use. If the court does not know the efficient outcome, a property rule is no longer efficient, but a liability rule may be if the court has *some* information. If the court knows only one party's value, but not the other's, a liability rule can be designed that achieves the efficient outcome. If, however, the court has no knowledge of the values, neither rule can be efficient.

Thus, the efficient approach to protecting property rights depends not only on the transactions-costs setting but also on the available information of each party's value. The best that can be said is that a liability rule requires less information than does a property rule to achieve the efficient outcome, but that information still has to be available to the court.

While much scholarly emphasis is placed on the debate between property rules and liability rules, another way to protect a property right is to use what is known as an *inalienability rule*. An inalienability rule places what can be very strict restrictions on the use of property after a right has been assigned. For example, suppose the court in this case gives the Eden Roc an inalienable right over the sunlight. Unlike with a property or liability rule, there are now no conditions in which the Fontainebleau can build the addition. The right to the Eden Roc is absolute and cannot be transferred in any way.

Legal scholar Susan Rose-Ackerman (1985) identifies four cases concerning the transfer of property (examples in parentheses):

1. Pure property—sales and gifts are permitted (you can sell your car or give it away)
2. Modified property—sales are permitted but gifts are forbidden (a person who declares bankruptcy can sell assets at a fair market price but cannot give them away)

3. Modified inalicnability—sales are forbidden but gifts are permitted (you cannot sell a kidney, but you can donate one)
4. Pure inalienability—sales and gifts are forbidden (you cannot sell your vote or give it away).

While economists are typically, at a minimum, suspicious of rules that restrict the selling of property, Rose-Ackerman discusses several situations in which inalienability can be justified. For example, if the conservation of certain species of wildlife is a social goal, preventing the sale of animal body parts could reduce the incentive to hunt endangered species. Also, preventing the selling of blood may be an effective way to control quality, especially if it is costly to test blood or if there are imperfections in the way blood is tested. The belief here is that the altruistic motive for giving blood is not likely to attract donors who know that they suffer from an illness that taints their blood. And recall the argument from the previous chapter, claiming that allowing a market for kidneys would severely disadvantage the poor and suggesting that no such market should be developed. Finally, not many believe that allowing votes to be sold or given away would promote democratic ideals.

The harshest criticism of inalienable rights, especially from an economic perspective, is that they don't allow individuals to exploit gains from trade. And because gains from trade are defined as making *both* parties to a transaction better off, not allowing the transaction must make them both *worse off*. It must be noted, however, that the exploitation of gains from trade may be at odds with alternative social objectives. Just consider the issue of legalizing drugs. Should drugs be legally salable because there are gains from trade between buyers and sellers? Should they be illegal because they can be horribly debilitating to those who abuse them? Should they be illegal only if drug abusers harm others? There simply are no *correct* answers to these questions. Your answer will depend on what you perceive to be the appropriate social objective.

All in all, the strength of the economic approach to property rights is that it can advise judicial decision making when the courts take an interest in moving resources to their highest-valued use. Economic reasoning points not only to the importance of transactions costs, but to the information needed to protect property rights in a way that promotes efficiency. This doesn't mean that the courts *should* take an interest in the objective of moving resources to their highest-valued use, only that such an objective *can* be a legitimate concern in property rights cases. And to many economists and other scholars, it *is* a legitimate concern.

Discussion Questions

1. A 1982 case, *Prah v. Maretti*, had very similar facts to the hotels case. Prah's house had solar panels that required the sunlight as a natural source of energy. Maretti began constructing his house in a location that would block the sunlight from reaching Prah's solar panels. Prah sued Maretti to have construction halted. This court did not agree with the opinion written nearly twenty-five years earlier in the hotels case, and ruled in favor of Prah's having the right to unlimited sunlight. The court's reasoning, in large part, relied on the nature of the use of sunlight in this case: "Access to sunlight has taken on a new significance in recent years. In this case, the plaintiff seeks to protect access to sunlight, not for aesthetic reasons or as a source of illumination but as a source of energy. Access to sunlight as an energy source is of significance both to the landowner who invests in solar collectors and to a society which has an interest in developing alternative sources of energy." How would you use economic reasoning to evaluate the court's opinion in this case, especially when compared to the earlier hotels case?

2. The original intention of Coase's research was to reconsider a classic problem in economics—that of a *negative externality*. A negative externality exists when one party does something in its own selfish best-interest, but in doing so imposes an external cost upon another party. Pollution settings are the most common examples of negative externalities. How would you apply economic reasoning relating to the assignment and protection of property rights to the following negative externality scenarios: (a) secondhand cigarette smoke bothering non-smokers in a public restaurant, (b) noisy airport traffic bothering neighboring residents, and (c) a local movie theater showing pornographic films over the objection of the majority of residents?

3. A curious doctrine in property law is known as *adverse possession*. When a trespasser possesses land owned by someone else, after a certain amount of time and under certain conditions, title automatically transfers (without compensation) from the original owner to the trespasser. The original owner faces a statute of limitations (typically, but not always, seven years) to maintain title and remove the trespasser. If the statute of limitations runs out, the court will consider the following conditions of possession before transferring title to the trespasser: (a) *continuous* or regular and uninterrupted occupancy of the land throughout the statute of limitations time period, (b) *hostile* or in opposition to the interests of the true owner, (c) *open and notorious* so that the true owner is clearly aware that the trespasser is there, (d) *actual* occupation of the land

with the intent to keep it solely for oneself, and (e) *exclusive* occupancy so that there is no confusion as to who acquires title once the time has run out. Is there an economic sense to allowing title to transfer without compensation from the trespasser to the original owner? What other methods can be used to protect property rights in this setting?

Reference

Rose-Ackerman, S. 1985. "Inalienability and the Theory of Property Rights." *Columbia Law Review* 85:931–69.

CHAPTER THREE

Should Eminent Domain Power Be Available to Private Companies?

Poletown Neighborhood Council v. City of Detroit *(1981) and the Economics of Takings*

Facts

In the spring of 1980, General Motors Corporation (GM) decided that it was going to close its Cadillac and Fisher Body plants that were located within the city of Detroit. This decision by GM would have a tremendous negative impact on the city in terms of increased unemployment and reduced tax revenues. The city, however, was given an opportunity by GM to find an alternative site that would be suitable for the corporation's long-term plans. The new site needed to satisfy four criteria: an area between 450 and 500 square acres, a rectangular shape, access to a long-haul railroad line, and access to the freeway system. An appropriate site was found that occupied parts of Detroit and the city of Hamtramck (also known as "Poletown" for its high concentration of Polish residents). The city invoked its power of eminent domain to acquire the property and evict residents from their homes and businesses, and then transferred the land to GM, a private corporation. A Poletown neighborhood association, as well as other residents, challenged the legality of using eminent domain power in this manner.

Court's Decision

While there are slight variations across states and municipalities, the last sentence of the Fifth Amendment of the US Constitution succinctly states the common requirements controlling eminent domain power: "nor shall private property be taken for public use, without just compensation." In this case, the key issue the court had to determine was whether the "public use" requirement for eminent domain was indeed satisfied since the property ended up in the hands of a private corporation.

The Supreme Court of Michigan affirmed the trial court's decision that the city's use of eminent domain case was legal:

> In the instant case the benefit to be received by the municipality involving the power of eminent domain is a clear and significant one and is sufficient to satisfy the Court that such a project was an intended and legitimate object of the Legislature when it allowed municipalities to exercise condemnation powers even though a private party will also, ultimately, receive a benefit as an incident thereto.

> The power of eminent domain is to be used in this instance primarily to accomplish the essential public purposes of alleviating unemployment and revitalizing the economic base of the community. The benefit to a private interest is merely incidental.

Despite the Court's approval of this use of eminent domain power, the opinion clearly advised caution in using this decision as a precedent for future similar cases:

> Our determination that this project falls within the public purpose, as stated by the legislature, does not mean that every condemnation proposed by an economic development corporation will meet with similar acceptance simply because it may provide some jobs or add to the industrial or commercial base. If the public benefit was not so clear and significant, we would hesitate to sanction approval of such a project. The power of eminent domain is restricted to furthering public uses and purposes and is not to be exercised without substantial proof that the public is primarily to be benefited. Where, as here, condemnation power is exercised in a way that benefits specific and identifiable private interests, a court inspects with heightened scrutiny the claim that the public interest is the predominant interest being advanced. Such public benefit cannot

be speculative or marginal but must be clear and significant if it is to be within the legitimate purpose as stated by the Legislature. We hold this project is warranted on the basis that its significance for the people of Detroit and the state has been demonstrated.

While it was a 5–2 decision to approve the use of eminent domain, the two dissenting judges wrote separate, and scathing, dissenting opinions. In short, both judges did not see the "public use" aspect of this action as being fulfilled, and one of the judges did not mince words in expressing his disapproval:

> The evidence then is that what General Motors wanted, General Motors got. The corporation conceived the project, determined the cost, allocated the financial burdens, selected the site, established the mode of financing, imposed specific deadlines for clearance of the property and taking title, and even demanded 12 years of tax concessions.
>
> Eminent domain is an attribute of sovereignty. When individual citizens are forced to suffer great social dislocation to permit private corporations to construct plants where they deem it most profitable, one is left to wonder who the sovereign is.
>
> With this case the Court has subordinated a constitutional right to private corporate interests. As demolition of existing structures on the future plant site goes forward, the best that can be hoped for, jurisprudentially, is that the precedential value of this case will be lost in the accumulating rubble.

The total cost to the city of preparing the land for GM (including acquisition costs, relocation costs, demolition, the building of roads and rail, and other preparations) was approximately $200 million. The city was able to recoup some of these costs by requiring GM to purchase the land—at a price of $8 million. If GM was unhappy at having to pay this modest amount, it could take solace in the fact that it was also given the twelve years of tax concessions it asked for. It is no wonder that the facts in this case lead many scholars to ask if this was an appropriate use of the government's eminent domain power, or simply an abuse of that power.

Economic Analysis

Perhaps the first question to ask about eminent domain power is this: why do we allow the government to invoke such power? Why not require the government to purchase property in the same manner as private individuals, that is, through market transactions? As we have seen in previous chapters, gains-from-trade is a powerful concept that guarantees that both parties in a transaction benefit from the agreement. If the government wants to acquire a property, it can simply negotiate with the property owner to secure the property. If the government values the property more than the owner does, the transaction will occur. If the government's value is less, the transaction will not occur. In either case, the efficient outcome is achieved.

We have also seen, however, that markets don't always move resources to their highest-valued use. When this occurs, a nonmarket solution, such as eminent domain, may be necessary to facilitate the transfer. Let's consider a very specific, and admittedly narrow, hypothetical setting to illustrate some points about the possible value of eminent domain. Imagine that the government is interested in acquiring multiple adjoining parcels of land to build a new airport. Assume that *all* the parcels must be acquired or the airport will not be built. Furthermore, the government's value for the parcels exceeds the sum of the values of the individual landowners. That is, the highest-valued use for the land is to have the airport built. So why might the market not work in this setting?

Let's start with one of the most obvious potential problems—high transactions costs. If the government has to purchase many parcels of land, there are bound to be some individual cases in which the transactions costs can be high. Furthermore, even if the cost *per* transaction is modest, the aggregate transactions costs may be enormous. These costs can lead to market failure. This is a classic setting for a liability rule. The government gets to invoke its eminent domain power, and a nonnegotiated payment (just compensation) is mandated to be paid to each home owner. The government gets to circumvent all those transactions costs, the homes are taken, and the airport is built.

At first blush, transactions costs offer a strong justification for eminent domain. Upon more careful scrutiny, however, that justification is greatly weakened. Eminent domain power is not magically invoked—its use requires potentially substantial administrative costs. The process usually begins exactly the same way a market transaction begins—with negotiation. If that doesn't work, then other costs are incurred to move forward with the government taking. And if the taking is challenged, extremely costly court proceedings may be necessary to determine the final disposition of the property. So to rely on the transactions costs justification, it is important to consider the *relative* costs of using the market compared to using eminent domain.

Another argument in favor of using eminent domain (see Shavell 2010) also deals with the difficulties involved in transacting with a large number of landowners, but not those stemming from the transactions costs associated with negotiating. If, in our example, the government needs all the parcels of land to build the airport, even one landowner's refusal to accept a purchase offer can prevent the land from moving to a higher-valued use. Let's make the story very simple and assume that as long as each landowner gets an offer that is no less than his value (that is, his minimum willingness to sell), that parcel will be sold. All the government has to do is offer as low a price as needed to get each landowner to sell. But still, there may be a problem with using the market, even if there are no explicit transactions costs.

If the government has imperfect information on the distribution of values across the parcels, the more parcels there are, the more likely it becomes that at least one landowner will reject the government's offer because it is below his value. Of course, the government can then propose higher offers, but with a wide range of values that need to be met, there still is a good chance that at least *one* of those offers will be rejected. To the extent that eminent domain can avoid this difficulty in getting all landowners to accept the purchase offers, the parcels are more likely to be transferred. Furthermore, if the offer prices continually increase to encourage all the parcels to be sold, purchasing may become a costlier option than eminent domain. This can be an especially acute problem when there are social costs associated with the raising of funds to pay just compensation, as when the government must devote resources to the administration and collection of taxes.

Even in a low transactions costs setting with perfect information about the landowner's value, the government may still prefer eminent domain over purchasing for a very simple reason—just compensation may undercompensate the landowner's true value, thus saving the government money. In the story told above, the government was willing to meet each landowner's true value; the government just didn't know what each true value was. That is what led to high purchase prices and a possible advantage in using eminent domain. Now, however, we are considering the possibility of the government's benefiting by *not* having to meet a landowner's true value.

Just compensation is usually calculated by determining the *fair market value* of the property. Although there is plenty of wiggle room in how this is done, and different appraisers can estimate substantially different values for the same property, the basic approach is reasonably similar across jurisdictions. Here is a description that was provided by the House Research Department of the Minnesota House of Representatives (August 2006, 1) to aid lawmakers in understanding the approach:

> Just compensation is determined by looking at the fair market value of the property taken as of the time the commissioners make the award. Fair market value is what a person who is willing, but not required, to buy the property would pay a seller, who is willing, but not required, to sell it, taking into consideration the highest and best use to which the property can be put . . . Highest and best use is defined as the most profitable use for which the property is adaptable. A real estate appraiser will consider four criteria: legal permissibility, physical possibility, financial feasibility, and maximum productivity. *The owner's actual use, or intentions for use, is not relevant to determining the highest and best use* (emphasis added).

To an economist, when considering a seller "who is willing, but not required, to sell" a property at some price, that price would have to exceed a value based on whatever criteria is important to the seller. But that is typically not the case when determining fair market value.

For example, let's say you live in a house that has been in your family for several generations. In addition to its market value, there is a personal sentimental value you place on keeping it in the family. Considering your subjective value, you would need a minimum of $500,000 to sell your house. But you know that if you tried to sell the house, the highest offer you would get is only $300,000 because other buyers would not be willing to pay extra for the sentimental value. If the government were to buy your house, it would have to pay you at least $500,000. If the government were to take your house through eminent domain, just compensation is likely to be set much closer to the market value of $300,000. If this happens, the government can save $200,000 by taking your house rather than buying it.

A common belief among economists is that just compensation is far more likely to undercompensate true value rather than overcompensate for it, because true value often has a difficult-to-determine subjective component. On the other hand, the property may not have a sentimental or subjective value associated with it, as may be the case with commercial property. If this is true, just compensation determined by fair market value is more likely to approximate the true value of the property.

There are really two questions to address when considering whether just compensation saves the government money compared to having to purchase the property. First, does fair market value, however calculated, approximate true value? If fair market value falls short of true value, and just compensation is assessed at fair market value, eminent domain can save the government money. Second, if fair market value is a reasonable approximation of true value, is just compensation actually assessed at fair market value? If just compensation is assessed below fair market value, once again the government may be saving money by using eminent domain. Putting these two concerns together, it is possible that just compensation grossly underestimates true value.

One ambitious study (Chang 2010) examines takings in New York City between 1990 and 2002 to determine if payments made by the government to property owners are accurate representations of fair market value. The process begins when city administrators identify a property they wish to purchase for public use. Thus, it begins as a market transaction, but a transaction in which the city has an advantage—it can invoke eminent domain power if a voluntary exchange is not made. This is an important point to keep in mind because with a private transaction, the property owner cannot be compelled to sell.

The next step is for the city to solicit an independent appraisal of the property, and then make an initial offer. At this point, the property owner has three choices: accept the offer as payment in full, accept the offer but only as an advanced payment with more negotiation to come, or reject the offer. In the latter two cases, the city may invoke its eminent domain power. The second option is the most commonly chosen. If a settlement is not reached, either party can seek a remedy through the courts. If eminent domain power is eventually used, just compensation at fair market value will be, at least in theory, the required payment.

The study looks at eighty-nine cases in which the city tried to acquire residential property. In each case, the initial offer was rejected, but the case did not end up being decided in court—a settlement was eventually reached. The study develops a statistical technique to estimate fair market value for each property, and then compares that amount to the actual settlement amount reached. The study finds that in 53 percent of the cases, the settlement amount was less than the fair market value; in 40 percent of the cases the settlement amount was greater; and in 7 percent of the cases the two amounts were roughly equal. While New York City paid nearly $17.3 million for property estimated to have a fair market value of approximately $21.2 million, a savings of $3.9 million, keep in mind that in many cases the settlement offer was greater than the fair market value. This casts doubt on the notion that the city uses eminent domain, or more specifically in this setting the threat of eminent domain, *only* to save money.

Perhaps it is unusual that 93 percent of the cases had settlements that diverged from the fair market value, but the study offers some reasons for this. First, both the government and the property owners use appraisal techniques that, according to the study, are not as accurate as the technique the study uses to estimate fair market value. So even if both parties believe they are settling at a fair market value, the settlement may be higher or lower than the more accurate estimate. Second, the government may be willing to settle at a high amount, and the property owner may be willing to settle at a low amount, simply to avoid future litigation costs. Finally, even if both parties are willing to incur litigation costs, the outcome of the litigation may be too unpredictable to make it worth pursuing. To whom will the court award the property right? And if the government prevails, how will the court assess just compensation?

A related study (Chang 2011) examines the *court-determined* settlements in the same New York City eminent domain setting as in the previous study. The main result is that the courts usually set compensation closer to the city's offer than to the property owner's claimed value. Why do the courts tend to favor the city? While it may not be surprising to find that those whose property is being taken have an incentive to exaggerate the value of their property, this study argues that the city typically does *not* have an incentive to undercompensate with its offer. And if the courts are aware of this behavior, they may tend to favor the party claiming the least-biased value.

So why doesn't the city try to undercompensate the property owner? One explanation is that while undercompensation may appear to save the city money, just the opposite may be true. If the court determines that its award for compensation is "substantially in excess" of the city's offer, the court can rule that the property owner's litigation expenses must be paid by the city. This provides the city with the incentive to think carefully before conveying too low an offer. Furthermore, there may be political motivations for consistently not undercompensating property owners, such as maintaining a reputation for fairness that yields political support in the future, or having city officials who believe that fairness is ideologically sound. The results of this study do not seem to suggest that the city uses eminent domain power to save money.

Another economic justification for eminent domain is that it can prevent what is known as the *holdout problem*. Consider two adjacent tracts of land owned by separate owners. Each owner values a single tract at $50,000. The government requires *both* tracts and is willing to pay up to a total of $250,000 for the two tracts, or $125,000 on average. Thus, there are gains from trade for the owners to sell to the government. Let's say one owner sells a tract to the government before the other owner sells, and gets $75,000 for it. This leaves the government with a net willingness to pay of $175,000 for the second tract ($250,000 − $75,000). During negotiations with the second owner, that owner may realize that the remaining tract of land is now worth more than the initial average of $125,000. Thus, this owner may reap more gains from trade simply by being the last one to sell.

This may not seem like much of a problem if the second owner actually sells the property, even for a much higher price than the first owner received. After all, there are still gains from trade for the tracts to be sold to the government. As long as they are sold, the properties move to their highest-valued use, regardless of how the gains from trade are shared between the three parties. But the holdout problem is not just about the second owner reaping more gains from trade. It is about both owners wanting to be the *second* seller.

Each seller has an incentive to "hold out" to take advantage of being the last obstacle the government has to overcome to achieve its objective. Consider the airport example above, in which the government had to purchase many parcels of land. If every owner tries to be the last to sell, that can create a substantial delay in completing the project, and may even prevent the project from ever being realized. Note, however, that this is a different problem from the government's not having perfect information about the true values. In that setting, an owner only rejected an offer that was below his true value. With a holdout problem, an owner can reject an offer above his true value, in the hopes of gaining more payment in the future. Thus, eminent domain can be justified to avoid holdouts, facilitating the movement of property to a higher-valued use.

While preventing holdouts is often thought of as one of the strongest economic justifications for eminent domain power, there may be other ways to circumvent holdouts without invoking eminent domain. For example, the state may have alternative sites available for whatever use is being considered, reducing the potential for holdouts at any given site. Or perhaps individual property owners may not be aware that their tracts are being considered in tandem with other tracts, providing no indication that there is an advantage to being the last seller. But even if there is a potential holdout problem to overcome, whenever a market transaction is circumvented, there is always the potential for a resource to be transferred to a lower-valued use. This is especially a concern when just compensation is less than the subjective value of the original property owner.

Critics of eminent domain have a built-in consistency to their argu- ment—both the government and private companies should be required to use the market for transferring resources. Many supporters of eminent domain, however, lack a similar consistency—only the government, and not private companies, should be able to invoke such power. But if there is economic sense to allowing eminent domain power to be used to trans- fer resources to a higher-valued use (and, as argued above, situations can exist in which there is such sense), why shouldn't private companies get to invoke eminent domain power, at least in some settings?

If we are to argue that eminent domain only makes sense for govern- ment, but not private, takings, we need to think about the differences be- tween governments and private companies. Perhaps the most important difference has to do with their objectives. One can debate whether gov- ernments truly pursue social objectives when they invoke eminent domain power, but there is likely to be little debate that private companies are primarily concerned with their own *private* objectives. A private company concerned with profit maximization would use eminent domain power to reallocate property only when that is the least expensive way to do so, and this may very well lead to moving a resource to a lower-valued use. A gov- ernment concerned with social welfare maximization, on the other hand, may choose not to invoke eminent domain power in such a setting.

Or perhaps the types of projects governments pursue tend to have more obvious higher social value than the projects private companies pursue. It may be very difficult to determine to which use a resource is best suited, but if governments pursue "big" projects, like building highways or air- ports, there may be less concern with moving resources to lower-valued uses than with private company takings. Of course, private companies may also pursue "big" projects, like GM in *Poletown*, and governments may pursue "small" projects with less obvious social value, so there is no hard and fast distinction to universally apply. It could also be that many individ- uals simply distrust private companies, and endowing them with additional power is not thought of as being prudent. Of course, the exact same thing can be said about how some people view the government.

Maybe the way things currently are makes the most sense. If eminent domain power is justified in certain settings, yet private companies are not given that authority in such cases, the government can act as a middleman to facilitate the transfer of resources from one private party to another. To whatever extent the government pursues a social objective, this can help counter the potential for private companies to abuse eminent domain power (if they were to have it). But this is also not without potentially serious problems. Private companies may start devoting resources toward gaining government favor, and these resources can create an additional social cost to the eminent domain process. Furthermore, the attraction of private funds can easily undermine social objectives and possibly even encourage corruption among government officials.

From an economic perspective, perhaps the distinction should not be between public use and private use but between the conditions that warrant eminent domain and those that do not. If the ends justify the means, and the social objective is to move resources to their highest-valued use, *how* the resources move may not be as important as making sure that they do move. This being said, it still must be noted that any time a resource moves through a nonmarket mechanism, the potential exists for that resource to move to a lower-valued use.

Discussion Questions

1. If eminent domain power is used to transfer property to a higher-valued use, does just compensation have any role in promoting economic efficiency?

2. One argument against eminent domain power is that it may transfer property to a lower-valued use. But there is a counterargument to consider. If the government is taking property that is more highly valued elsewhere, there will be gains from trade for the original owner to pay the government *not* to take the property. Thus, eminent domain can't actually transfer a resource to a lower-valued use. How would you evaluate this counterargument?

3. When you think about the government taking property through eminent domain, the typical reason is to acquire land to build highways, airports, or other public works. But sometimes eminent domain power is invoked in unusual settings, such as the following:

    a. In the early 1980s, the owners of the Oakland Raiders professional football team decided to move the team to Los Angeles. The city of Oakland wanted to keep the team in Oakland because of the economic benefits the team brought to the city, and so the city invoked its power of eminent domain to do so.

    b. In 2004, the state of Rhode Island invoked its eminent domain power to take over a privately owned parking facility at Green International Airport.

The state owned a competing facility at the airport, and after the decline in demand for airport parking after the terrorist attacks on September 11, 2001, both parking facilities faced a substantial drop in revenue. The state used its power of eminent domain to eliminate the competition and increase its revenue.

How would you evaluate these uses of eminent domain power?

References

Chang, Y. 2010. "An Empirical Study of Compensation Paid in Eminent Domain Settlements: New York City, 1990–2002." *Journal of Legal Studies* 39:201–44.

———. 2011. "An Empirical Study of Court-Adjudicated Takings Compensation in New York City: 1990–2003." *Journal of Empirical Legal Studies* 8:384–412.

Shavell, S. 2010. "Eminent Domain versus Government Purchase of Land Given Imperfect Information about Owners' Valuations." *Journal of Law and Economics* 53:1–27.

CHAPTER FOUR

Will File Sharing Ruin the Music Industry?

A&M Records v. Napster *(2001) and the Economics of Copyright Protection*

Facts

The court's opinion in this important copyright case nicely lays out the facts:

> Napster facilitates the transmission of MP3 files between and among its users. Through a process commonly called "peer-to-peer" file sharing, Napster allows its users to: (1) make MP3 music files stored on individual computer hard drives available for copying by other Napster users; (2) search for MP3 music files stored on other users' computers; and (3) transfer exact copies of the contents of other users' MP3 files from one computer to another via the Internet. These functions are made possible by Napster's MusicShare software, available free of charge from Napster's Internet site, and Napster's network servers and server-side software.

> Napster provides technical support for the indexing and searching of MP3 files, as well as for its other functions, including a "chat room," where users can meet to discuss music, and a directory where participating artists can provide information about their music.

One other key fact in this case is that Napster's server was an integral part of the file-sharing process. Napster's central servers maintained an index of users and files, and users needed to log in to this server to access peer-to-peer file sharing. In short, if Napster were to shut down its servers, file sharing through the system would halt.

Court's Decision

Although the court needed to consider several issues in this case, one important focus of its opinion hinged on answering two questions: did the plaintiffs have copyright ownership over the music in question, and did the infringers violate the exclusive rights of the plaintiffs? The appeals court confirmed the finding of the lower court:

> Plaintiffs have sufficiently demonstrated ownership. The record supports the district court's determination that "as much as eighty-seven percent of the files available on Napster may be copyrighted and more than seventy percent may be owned or administered by plaintiffs."

> We agree that plaintiffs have shown that Napster users infringe at least two of the copyright holders' exclusive rights: the rights of reproduction and distribution. Napster users who upload file names to the search index for others to copy violate plaintiffs' distribution rights. Napster users who download files containing copyrighted music violate plaintiffs' reproduction rights.

The court required Napster to remove copyrighted music files from their system, and although they made a strong effort to do this, because of the phenomenal number of files that existed, they were not 100 percent successful. The court eventually ordered Napster to shut down, and soon after they declared bankruptcy.

Economic Analysis

As a general rule in the United States, for works created after January 1, 1978, copyright protection lasts for the life of the author plus an additional seventy years. So, copyright protection is a fairly long-term phenomenon. As a social policy issue, copyright protection offers an excellent example of an economic trade-off. The main benefit of copyright is that it provides an incentive for the creation of intellectual property. The main cost is that it grants the holder of the copyright monopoly power. Both of these factors need to be examined in more detail.

Imagine that you are an author and you are going to write a historical fiction novel. At first, you devote one year and a significant amount of
money to traveling and undertaking research so as to be historically accurate in your writing. Then, you devote one year to sitting at your desk and
writing your novel, and you have no concurrent source of income. Once all
this is done, you get a lucrative publishing contract for your book and will
collect royalties based on how many copies of your book are sold. From all
accounts, your book is expected to be a smash hit. You certainly hope the
accounts are accurate as you piled up a tremendous amount of debt in the
past two years.

What would happen if you lived in a world *without* copyright protection? Your book would be published, and immediately afterward other
publishers would copy the material and put out their own editions. Your
royalty payments would greatly diminish for two main reasons: you would
receive no payments from the pirated copies, and the increased competition among publishers would lower the price at which your book sells. So
even if your book is the biggest-selling book of all time, you may not make
back enough money to recover all the debt you incurred writing it.

Let's consider this problem more carefully. In writing your book, you
incur what is known as an *up-front cost*. That is, even before a single copy is
sold, you already have incurred costs that eventually need to be recovered.
Once the book is ready to be printed, then the publisher incurs what is
known as *incremental costs*. That is, each single copy of the book requires
a certain amount of paper and ink. (There will be other costs as well, such
as marketing and distribution costs, but these can be ignored without affecting the analysis that follows.) These costs, too, must eventually be recovered. Succinctly put, *all* costs must eventually be recovered to make it
worthwhile for this book to be written in the first place. Without copyright
protection, however, that may never happen.

If many firms decide to publish the book, the increased competition is
likely to lower the price of the book. In theory, as more firms enter the
market, the price of the book will fall until it reaches the incremental cost.
If this happens, any firm publishing the book, including your publisher,
will be able to recover its incremental costs. In the end, though, your up-
front costs may never be recovered. Unless your publisher has copyright
protection and can (at least legally) be the *only* firm that publishes your
book, there will be no way to raise the price above the incremental cost
to make enough money to cover those costs as well as your up-front costs.

So now, let's go back to the day when you are considering devoting
the next two years of your life to researching and writing a book. You look

ahead to the day it will be published, and you understand that there will be no copyright protection. Your publisher understands this also. You know that if any other publisher can pirate your book without having to compensate you in any way, you will never recover your up-front costs. Your decision is simple—you find some other way to make a living. The world will be deprived of your wonderful book.

This, then, is the benefit of copyright protection—it allows creators of intellectual property to eventually be compensated for all of their costs. It protects the financial motive that may be needed to encourage creators to devote their time, energy, and resources to creating books, movies, or music. Copyright protection can be thought of as allowing for the development of an artistically rich society, and it has the potential to greatly enhance social welfare.

As grandiose as that sounds, we still must consider the inevitable other side of the story. Copyright protection may create monopoly power, and that power is widely known as being detrimental to society. What isn't widely known, however, is precisely why monopoly power reduces social welfare. The usual argument is that it makes products more expensive for those who buy them. While this is true, it may not be important from a social welfare perspective. What is important is not necessarily who buys the monopoly product but who *doesn't* buy it.

There are two obvious types of consumers that can be identified: those who buy the product at the monopoly price, and those who don't. It is true that consumers prefer to pay a lower price rather than a higher price, but any consumer who actually buys at the monopoly price must be experiencing *gains from trade* to do so. The monopolist can't force consumers to buy a product. All it can do is set a price and sell to anyone who values the product more than that price. Every transaction must benefit the monopolist *and* the consumer, or else that transaction would not occur. Thus, those who buy at the monopoly price are enhancing social welfare by exploiting gains from trade.

Those who don't buy the product can further be divided into two groups: those who are properly excluded, and those who are improperly excluded. To produce a good requires, at a minimum, the incremental cost. If a consumer is not willing to pay at least that cost, there would be no gains from trade with that consumer. Even if we are talking about a competitive market with many firms producing, each unit of the product must be sold at no less than its incremental cost. From a social welfare perspective, then, these consumers are properly excluded from the market.

That leaves us with the other group of consumers. These consumers are not willing to pay the monopoly price for the product, so they are excluded from that market. But *if* the market were competitive, and the price was at the incremental cost, these consumers would purchase the good. In other words, consumers are improperly excluded if they would be willing to pay the incremental cost, but not the monopoly price, to purchase the good. From a competitive market perspective, there are gains from trade with these consumers, but the monopolist excludes them, thus reducing social welfare by not experiencing all the gains from trade that are possible.

So, how are we to resolve this copyright protection trade-off? Does the increased incentive to create intellectual property outweigh the monopoly power problem? There are some who argue that copyright protection is not needed to provide incentives to create. Instead, there are other factors that provide this incentive (for examples, see Landes and Posner 2003). If this is true, perhaps copyright protection only has a detrimental social welfare impact and, therefore, should be abolished. It is important, then, to consider these other factors:

Superior quality of originals. If the copying technology is not satisfactory to the consumers, firms that pirate the original product may not be able to successfully compete against the original. For example, consider a copier who sits in a movie theater and makes a video copy of a newly released movie (this is known as *audience camming*). The video is then transferred to DVD and sold on the street while the movie is still currently in the theater. Even if the DVD is priced well below the price of a movie ticket, it is likely to be a very poor substitute for the original (and also for the eventual authorized DVD).

First-to-the-market advantage. The original product will likely be the first to the market. The longer it takes for a copy to be produced, the longer the original producer can reap monopoly profit. This advantage may allow the producer to recover the up-front costs. For example, if the script of a play can be copied on opening night, the time it would take to develop a competing production would likely be longer than the staying power of the typical play. Another nice illustration of this principle can be found in patent law. A generic drug requires FDA approval before it can be made available to consumers. These drugs are approved on a "first in, first out" order, and there are no set standards for review times. Due to a huge backlog of applications, the current review time is between two and three years.

High production costs of copying. If there is a high cost to making a copy, firms that pirate the original may have a difficult time competing against it if the copy cannot enjoy a significant price advantage. These costs may be technological in nature, such as the costs of purchasing and using the copying equipment, or they may involve some form of original expression. For example, one publisher may copy the text of another publisher's book, but incur additional costs to add a review essay, annotations, editorial comments, and so on.

Technology designed to prevent copying. Owners of originals may be able to design their product to include technological impediments to copying. Computer software products can be protected with software encryption that, while not impossible to get around, may make it very costly to make copies of the original. Data can be added to a music compact disc that will not allow it to be read by a computer or allow the music to be converted to mp3 files. If technically possible, strong protection technology may completely eliminate the need for copyright protection for some products.

Alternative motives and alternative sources of funding for creating. Some creators of intellectual property may do so simply for the joy of being creative, or for the prestige, or for the celebrity. Also, publishing may yield monetary benefits not derived from sales of the original. For example, professors who publish scholarly books and journal articles may earn higher salaries. Furthermore, alternative funding sources, such as family support, private donations, or public subsidies, may provide enough of a financial incentive to encourage creativity.

Copying as enhancing the value of the original. How much consumers are willing to pay for the original may depend on their ability to make copies. This enhanced value for the original product can be *indirectly appropriated* by the firm through an increased price of the original. For example, one study (Liebowitz 1985) provides a nice illustration of this principle by looking at how publishers of academic journals were affected by the widespread provision of photocopy services in libraries. A library may purchase photocopy machines to make additional revenue or just to provide a valuable service to its patrons. In either case, if photocopying enhances the value of journal subscriptions to the library, the owners of the journals may charge higher subscription prices to libraries (relative to individual subscription prices). The study provides evidence that this is precisely what happened. Thus, journal publishers were able to enhance their revenue *because* of increased copying.

To see how these factors may affect the creation of intellectual property, let's apply them to *Napster.*

In the music industry, two of these factors may support the case against copyright protection. First, for every financially successful musician out there, how many more are there who create and perform music simply for the joy of it, or for a modest financial return? Local music scenes often thrive on part-time musicians who hold regular day jobs and perform at night. Certainly, some musicians who are in the business primarily to earn huge revenues may opt out of the industry if copyright protection was not enforced, but the quality and quantity of music produced may not suffer much. Second, sharing music files may greatly enhance the demand for additional products that are tied in to the original. For example, live performances, T-shirts, posters, and so on may all have enhanced sales as music is shared. Furthermore, file sharing may even enhance the demand for the original if consumers like to sample music before they buy it.

Some of the other factors, however, are not likely to be relevant in supporting a case against copyright protection in the music industry. The cost of copying music is extremely low (close to zero), and even if you want to burn songs to a compact disc, the cost is modest. Although you do need to incur the expense of a computer (or equivalent device), these are now so commonplace and versatile that it is unlikely consumers buy them specifically to download music. As for the quality of the copies, it is reasonably high, and perhaps equivalent in some cases (buying vs. copying mp3 files, for example). Finally, even if the music industry can put out product before it can be copied, it doesn't take long to be able to copy. In fact, copying may occur even *before* a product is released. For example, a California man, Kevin Cogill, was arrested by the FBI in 2008 for uploading nine Guns and Roses songs to his music site several months before the songs were officially released.

There is one other important point supporting copyright protection against sharing music files. With this technology, one copy can instantly be shared with millions of people worldwide. Back in the "old" days, it would take a long time and considerable expense to copy music onto cassette tapes to distribute pirated music to millions of people. Today, just one "click" allows for massive infringing to occur. And even with advances in technology that can prevent copies from easily being made, the technology required to "hack" the protection devices tends to advance just as quickly. In short, the technological breakthroughs in file sharing in terms of costs, quality, speed of access, and large-scale sharing ability strongly support, but do not prove, the case for continued copyright enforcement.

The music industry has, unsurprisingly, been concerned with the rapid change in copying technology. Consider the following statement issued by the Recording Industry Association of America (RIAA):

It's commonly known as "piracy," but that's too benign of a term to adequately describe the toll that music theft takes on the enormous cast of industry players working behind the scene to bring music to your ears. That cast includes songwriters, recording artists, audio engineers, computer technicians, talent scouts and marketing specialists, producers, publishers and countless others. While downloading one song may not feel that serious of a crime, the accumulative impact of millions of songs downloaded illegally—and without any compensation to all the people who helped to create that song and bring it to fans—is devastating. (Excerpt from *Who Music Theft Hurts*, RIAA website.)

Economists have spent a fair amount of time trying to determine if file sharing has had an adverse impact on the music industry. As is often the case with a body of empirical research, the results are a mixed bag. Before discussing some of these studies, however, at this point it may be tempting to just step back and say, of course there has been a reduction in revenue. After all, we are talking about *billions* of infringements. Why bother with the formal empirical analysis? In this case, that may be a legitimate point. The RIAA may simply be stating the obvious—the impact of file sharing is "devastating" to the music industry.

But what seems obvious to others may not be obvious to economists. There are many confounding factors that influence how much music is sold in a given year. Perhaps the decline in music industry revenue is due to worsening economic conditions, or to a perceived reduction in the quality of music. Maybe the younger generation has more of an interest in movies, video games, social networking, or other online activities. One study (Hong 2007) confirms this last point by presenting evidence that the growth of the Internet reduces the demand for recorded music. If these other factors are properly taken into account, file sharing may not be causing a loss in revenue. More important, if the goal is to quantify the impact of file sharing on revenue, other factors *must* be taken into account to determine how much revenue loss can specifically be attributed to file sharing.

Two economic studies provide good examples of how to achieve the goal of isolating the impact of file sharing on music industry revenue. The first study (Hong 2013) uses the advent of Napster to distinguish between two groups: one group of Internet users and one group of non-Internet users. The idea here is that whatever factors *other than file sharing* are affecting household music expenditures, the changes in expenditure across the two groups should be very similar. The main difference between the two groups, then, is that Napster's services should have little impact on non-Internet users but some impact on Internet users. Thus, the difference between the two groups' expenditures pre-Napster (June 1997 to May 1999) and post-Napster (June 1999 to June 2001) can largely be attributed to file sharing. The study's most reliable result is that 20 percent of the lost music industry revenue during the Napster period can be attributed to file sharing, with the bulk of this infringing driven by the downloading behavior of households with children ages six to seventeen.

The second study (Oberholzer-Gee and Strumpf 2007) addresses another complicating factor that empirical studies often have to overcome: *reverse causation.* The typical study on file sharing is concerned with the following issue—does file sharing affect album sales? But the causation can run the other way—do album sales affect file sharing? For example, let's say market conditions in the music industry lead to an increase in the price of recorded music and, as a result, to reduced album sales. As consumers purchase fewer albums, they may turn to file sharing. It is not file sharing in this case that is reducing album sales; it is reduced album sales increasing file sharing.

The study finds a clever and unusual way to break this reverse causation problem. The study examines the impact of German secondary school holidays on US downloading behavior. What is the link between German school holidays and US file sharing? Germans who share music files, on average, upload more songs than they download, and approximately one-sixth of all US downloads come from Germany. Thus, Germans, especially teenagers, provide a substantial source of music for American file sharers.

On school holidays, German teenagers not only have more time during the day to upload music, they may be able to stay up later at night, which (considering the time difference) corresponds to a popular time of day for file-sharing activity in the United States. In other words, German school holidays can be a factor that leads to more uploading of files in Germany, and that leads to more downloading of files in the United States. Furthermore, and importantly, German school holidays are not predicted to have any direct impact on music industry sales in the United States. For example, if file sharing did not exist, German school holidays would have no relation to US music sales. The causation, then, is from file sharing to music sales, and not the other way around.

The study looks at US downloading behavior for the period September 8 to December 31, 2002. In these seventeen weeks, the study observes 1.75 million downloads (or .01 percent of all downloads in the world). The main result is that file sharing did not have a significant negative impact on purchases of albums over the sample period. This result is further supported by other evidence accounting for reduced music sales, such as the fact that households without computers (and therefore less likely to be involved in substantial file sharing) reduced their spending on compact discs by a large amount in the early 2000s. The study also argues that the result extends past the 2002 sample period.

Taken together, these two studies (and others not discussed) find modest to insignificant impacts of file sharing on album sales. There is a body of research, however, that finds substantial negative impacts on music industry revenue. Consider the conclusion of a survey of this research: "The evidence here supports the current findings from almost all econometric studies that have been undertaken to date—file-sharing has brought significant harm to the recording industry. . . . Furthermore, analysis of the various possible alternative explanations for the decline in CD sales fails to find any viable candidates" (Liebowitz 2006, 24). While this is a strong statement, compare it to the conclusion of another survey published a few years later covering similar (but not identical) ground: "As our survey indicates, the empirical evidence on sales displacement is mixed. While some studies find evidence of a substitution effect, others, in particular the papers using actual file-sharing data, suggest that piracy and music sales are largely unrelated" (Oberholzer-Gee and Strumpf, 2010, 49).

Revenue loss is often the key metric on which economic studies focus, but revenue loss by itself does not necessarily tell us much about the continued incentive to create intellectual property. If copyright enforcement allows the firm to earn monopoly profit, it may very well be that this profit more than covers the minimum amount needed to recoup the up-front costs. The music industry may not be happy with a loss in revenue, but that loss may not have much impact on the amount of intellectual property created. Then again, it may. Music industry revenue is generated by sales, and this is a measure of the *quantity* of music sold. Another metric in which to gauge the impact of file sharing on the music industry is the *quality* of music produced. Does widespread file sharing reduce quality?

At first blush, it may seem that less revenue *must* lead to reduced quality. For example, the shrinking pie of music industry revenue will make it difficult for new artists to grab their share. Fewer new artists can be one indication of reduced quality. However, with more careful consideration, an interesting point can be raised: the changes in technology that have facilitated widespread and virtually costless file sharing have also lowered the costs of producing, promoting, and distributing music. And as one ambitious study (Waldfogel 2012) demonstrates, the reduced costs of creating music can enhance its quality, even if music industry revenue is shrinking.

The study develops three indices of music quality, and then compares each index for the period before Napster (1999) to the period after Napster. The first index is developed from critics' lists of best albums for some period of time (such as "best of the past decade" lists). This allows the study to measure the volume of high-quality music that is released for each year in the sample period (1960 to roughly 2009). The two other indices are based on service flow of music by *vintage*. The idea here is that if one vintage (for example, 1965 releases) is of higher quality than other vintages, that music should generate more radio airplay or sales (or both) over time. Music quality over time, then, can be tracked through usage changes as measured by airplay and sales.

For all three indices, the study does not find a drop in the quality of music post-Napster. That is, the advent of widespread file-sharing technology does not appear to negatively impact the quality of continued intellectual property creation in the music industry. In fact, the usage indices depict an increase in quality post-Napster. The usage measures concerning vintage tell a strong story: music depreciates rapidly over time. Using airplay (or sales), recent songs make up the largest share of what is played in a given year, and older songs continually receive less and less of a share. Quite simply, the music industry may have suffered a substantial drop in revenue post-Napster, but the importance of bringing new music to satisfy consumer demand has remained strong.

The technological advances that have harmed the music industry on one hand have helped the music industry remain viable on the other. The music industry may look different now than it did before Napster—more viable independent labels, digital distribution of product, and so on—but this study concludes that considering copyright protection based solely on loss in revenue may be misguided. A more complete social welfare analysis should consider how the changes in technology create benefits not only to consumers but to the music industry as well.

In all, the music industry may have indeed suffered a substantial loss in revenue due to the advent of Napster and other file-sharing technologies. But even if this is true, it is easy to forget one important point: the explicit goal of copyright protection is *not* to protect the revenue stream of copyright holders. Instead, it is to provide the incentive for the creation of intellectual property. Ideally, if copyright protection is needed, we would like to see the resulting monopoly power yield just enough revenue to cover the costs incurred to produce intellectual property. If more than this amount is being earned, and infringing behavior cuts into this excess, the hindering of creation may not be occurring.

There is one other point to consider. There is an often-used argument that if copyright infringing was not hurting the music industry, why would the industry be devoting so much time, energy, and money to fight such infringement? While this argument has strong intuitive appeal, one study offers an interesting observation concerning the entertainment industry's history of challenging new copying technologies: "The entertainment industry's opposition to file sharing is not *a priori* evidence that file sharing imposes economic damages. The industry has often blocked new technologies that later became sources of profit. For example, Motion Picture Association of America President Jack Valenti argued (in 1982) that 'the VCR is to the American film producer and the American public as the Boston Strangler is to the woman home alone.' By 2004, 72 percent of domestic industry revenues came from rentals or sales of videotapes and digital video discs" (Oberholzer-Gee and Strumpf 2007, 3n1). As for the question posed in the title of this chapter, it doesn't obviously appear that the music industry has been ruined by file sharing, at least not yet. Of course, it must be remembered that the industry has enjoyed considerable copyright protection, especially through favorable court decisions like *Napster.*

Discussion Questions

1. Copyright protection for the creation of music was unknown until the end of the eighteenth century. Famed Italian composer Giuseppe Verdi (1813–1901) was the first important composer to experience the new Italian copyright regime and devise strategies to derive maximum advantage of the protection. The substantial revenue Verdi earned from copyright protection had a strong impact on his creation of intellectual property—because he was now wealthy, it greatly *reduced* his composing effort. Thus, some claim, it is possible for copyright protection to give the creator of intellectual property less incentive to create, not more, as traditionally believed. How would you evaluate this claim?

2. In England, until recently, the copyright laws protected copyrighted material for fifty years from the date of release. This means that, for example, any copyrighted song released before the year 1965 goes into the public domain in the year 2015. However, with a phenomenal wealth of British popular music released in the 1960s, there was a strong lobby from the copyright holders to

extend the copyright protection from fifty years to seventy years. That lobbying was effective, and the law was accordingly changed. How would you evaluate this change in the copyright law?

3. In their case, Napster presented a defense known as *fair use*, which allows for copying of protected material to occur but *not* be deemed an infringement of the copyright laws. The courts consider four factors in determining if fair use applies in any particular case:

    a. the purpose and character of the use, including whether such use is of a commercial nature or is for nonprofit educational purposes

    b. the nature of the copyrighted work (for example, scholarly versus creative)

    c. the amount and substantiality of the material used in relation to the copyrighted work as a whole

    d. the effect of the use on a copyright owner's potential market for and value of his work

    Using these four factors, how would you evaluate Napster's claim that sharing music files constitutes fair use?

References

Hong, S. 2007. "The Recent Growth of the Internet and Changes in Household-Level Demand for Entertainment." *Information and Economics Policy* 19: 304–18.

———. 2013. "Measuring the Effect of Napster on Recorded Music Sales: Difference-in-Differences Estimates under Compositional Changes." *Journal of Applied Econometrics* 28:297–324.

Landes, W. M., and R. A. Posner. 2003. *The Economic Structure of Intellectual Property Law*. Cambridge, MA: Harvard University Press.

Liebowitz, S. J. 1985. "Copying and Indirect Appropriability: Photocopying and Journals." *Journal of Political Economy* 93:945–57.

———. 2006. "File Sharing: Creative Destruction or Just Plain Destruction?" *Journal of Law and Economics* 46:1–28.

Oberholzer-Gee, F., and K. Strumpf. 2007. "The Effect of File-Sharing on Record Sales: An Empirical Analysis." *Journal of Political Economy* 115:1–42.

———. 2010. "File Sharing and Copyright." In *Innovation Policy and the Economy, Vol. 10*, edited by J. Lerner and S. Stern, 19–55. Chicago: University of Chicago Press.

Waldfogel, J. 2012. "Copyright Protection, Technological Change, and the Quality of New Products: Evidence from Recorded Music since Napster." *Journal of Law and Economics* 55:715–40.

PART II

Contracts

Should the Courts Encourage Contractual Breach?

Acme Mills & Elevator Co. v. J.C. Johnson *(1911) and the Economics of Breaking Promises*

Facts

Johnson contracted to sell Acme Mills 2,000 bushels of wheat at $1.03 per bushel, to be delivered by a specific date. Acme Mills had to supply Johnson with 1,000 sacks (costing a total of $80) that would be used to transport the wheat. Instead, Johnson sold the wheat to Liberty Mills for a price of $1.16 per bushel, using the sacks provided to them by Acme. Acme sued Johnson asking for an award of $320—$240 in damages plus $80 for the cost of the sacks.

Court's Decision

There was no doubt that Johnson breached its contract with Acme. Johnson provided the excuse that it believed that Acme was going out of business and had no money to pay for the wheat. While the court did not accept this excuse, it still did not award Acme the damages sought. Instead, the court only required Johnson to pay Acme $80 for the sacks. Johnson was not punished by the court for breaching the contract.

In reaching its decision, the court relied on the following principle of law:

In contracts for the delivery of personal property at a fixed time and at a designated place, the vendee is entitled to damages against the vendor for a failure to comply, and the measure of damages is the difference between the contract price and the market price of the property at the place and time of delivery. This principle of law is so well settled, not only in this State, but in all the courts of this country, that it is no longer open to discussion. There is no reason why this rule should not apply to the facts of this case.

The court found that the market price for a bushel of wheat at the time and place designated by the contract did not exceed $1.00 per bushel. Thus, Acme actually benefited from the breach by approximately three cents per bushel. However, had the market price been higher than $1.03, Acme would have been awarded the price difference multiplied by the total number of bushels.

Economic Analysis

To introduce the economic analysis of contractual breach, we will start with a simple example that will illustrate the key terms and concepts that will be integral to the analysis throughout this chapter. Let's say that you are a book collector, and one day you are in an antiquarian bookstore and see a copy of a fairly rare book, in mint condition, that you have some interest in buying. The seller quotes you a price of $500, and you agree to pay that amount. Unfortunately, this seller only takes cash and you don't have enough money on you. So you and the seller work out an arrangement. The seller agrees to let you leave a $50 deposit, and he will hold the book until you can return tomorrow with the cash. After you give him the deposit, he writes out a receipt for you listing the title of the book, the edition, its condition, the amount of the deposit, and the amount of payment that remains.

The next day, on your way back to the bookstore, you pass an antique store and see a beautiful book stand that would be perfect for your new book. The antique dealer quotes you a price of $75 for the stand, and you buy it. However, the antique store is going out of business, so all sales are final. We will also assume that the only reason you want this book stand is to display your new book; that is, without that specific book, you place zero value on the stand. All that's left is for you to go back to the bookstore to complete the transaction.

Meanwhile, you are unaware that after you left the store yesterday, another potential buyer for the book showed up. She saw the copy of the book and was also interested. The seller, seeing an opportunity to make more money, quoted her a price of $600 for the book. After all, if she says no, what does it matter? He will still get $500 for it from you. But if she says yes, he can make an extra $100. Fortunately for the seller, and unfortunately for you, she says yes, actually has $600 in cash on her and buys the book. When you get back to the bookstore, the seller informs you he no longer has the book, he gladly refunds your $50 deposit, and you go home empty handed. Actually, not quite empty handed—you have a book stand that has no value to you now, and you can't return it.

When you get home, you look at the receipt that the seller gave you and you are angered that he, in effect, broke his promise to you. You decide to file a lawsuit against him for breach of contract. There is no doubt that it is costly to pursue a contractual breach lawsuit, but we are going to abstract away from those costs and assume that you are going to pursue your claim. You are seeking monetary damages to compensate you for the breach of contract, and the court decides to rule in your favor. This leaves the court with one last task—how to set damages?

There are a number of damage remedies the court can use, but we will focus on what are often considered to be the three most common ones (see Hermalin, Katz, and Craswell 2007, especially section 5.1.2):

1. *Expectations remedy*—leaves the breached-against party in as good a position as he would have been in had the contract been performed.
2. *Reliance remedy*—leaves the breached-against party in the same position he would have been in had he never entered the contract in the first place.
3. *Restitution remedy*—returns to the breached-against party any benefits he conferred on the breaching party.

The book example can be used to help explain how monetary damages are set under each of these remedies.

In the event of breach, leaving you in as good a position as you would have been in had the contract been performed is equivalent (in the example used here) to making you indifferent to the contract's being completed or breached. Thus, the expectations remedy must set damages to guarantee you whatever gains from trade you would have received had the transaction been completed. To set damages, then, the court needs to determine your value for the book. Obviously, this can be a very difficult amount to calculate accurately, especially when your value includes a sub-jective component. But this is a problem with implementing the remedy, as opposed to understanding how the remedy affects the behavior of the contracting parties when it is applied accurately. So for now, we will as-sume that the court can determine your true value for the book, and scru-tinize this assumption later in the discussion.

If the court is using the expectations remedy in this example, what amount of damages will be set? We know that you were willing to pay $500 for the book, so your value must exceed that amount. Let's say it can be determined that your value is $700. But this is not the end of the story. You also purchased the book stand, so the *enhanced* value of the book due to the stand must exceed its price of $75. Let's say this enhanced value is $100. Together, then, your value for the book is $800. Had you paid the seller $500, and you incurred the $75 cost of the stand, you would have received a net gain of $225 ($800 − $575). Also note, you paid $50 in ad-vance, but that amount has already been refunded to you.

When we put all this information together, the expectations remedy sets a monetary damages amount of $300. With that amount, less the $75 you paid for the stand, you are left with a net gain of $225. This is exactly what your net gain would have been had the contract been completed. Thus, the contractual breach leaves you no worse off than had the con-tract been completed.

If the court chooses to use the reliance remedy instead, that remedy leaves the breached-against party in the same position as if the contract had never been entered. Had you never walked into the bookstore, you would have had a net gain of zero, as no transaction would have occurred. After the breach, and with your down payment of $50 refunded to you, you have incurred a net loss of $75—the cost of the stand. Under the reli-ance remedy, then, the court would order the seller to pay you $75.

Finally, the restitution remedy has the breached-against party receive whatever amount was given to the other party. You gave the seller a $50 down payment. Had he not refunded that to you, the court would have required the seller to pay you back $50. But because he already paid that back to you, there is no additional benefit that you conferred upon the seller. In this case, under the restitution remedy the court will not require the seller to pay you any damages. This is precisely how the courts ruled in *Acme Mills v. Johnson*, as Johnson only had to pay back the $80 for the sacks supplied by Acme.

While these three remedies are well defined and commonly analyzed by legal scholars, the court typically enjoys a wide discretion in setting damages. After a breach occurs, the breached-against party and the breaching party are going to have opposing interests (that is why they are in court)—the former hoping for damages to be set high, the latter hoping for damages to be set low. But how the court sets damages is far more than just a distribution-of-wealth issue. It will also affect how the parties interact with each other, both prebreach at contract formation and postbreach in resolving their dispute. Furthermore, how damages are set will affect the allocation of resources. To compare damage remedies in an economic framework, then, the next step is to identify a social objective.

Efficient Breach

Breach of contract is typically thought of as being nothing more than a broken promise. If this is so, why not use the courts to impose damages in such a way as to discourage the breaking of promises? This wouldn't be difficult to do. In such cases, the court can simply set damages at an extremely high level. If the bookseller has to pay you $10,000 if he sells the book to another buyer, it is very unlikely that breach will occur. Discouraging breach sounds like a common-sense objective, but it does not always coincide with the social objective that economists typically favor—moving resources to their highest-valued use.

To allocate resources efficiently, it is still the case that a damage remedy must discourage breach, just not *all* breach. Instead, it must discourage breach that would move resources to a lower-valued use and *simultaneously* encourage breach that moves resources to a higher-valued use. When contractual breach does move resources to a higher-valued use, this is referred to as *efficient breach*. Is there a damage remedy that discourages inefficient breach and at the same time encourages efficient breach? Yes, the expectations remedy.

To see why the expectations remedy is efficient with respect to breach, we need to consider the second buyer's value for the book. The fact that she paid $600 for the book, while you were only going to pay $500, does not tell us that she values the book more than you do. Value is determined by the *maximum* amount a person is willing to pay, not by the price. Let's say, for the time being, that she values the book at $750, which is less than your value of $800. If the seller breaches to sell the book to her, this is an example of inefficient breach as it moves the book to a lower-valued use.

Under the expectations remedy, what price would the seller need from the second buyer to make it worth his interest to breach? When he sells the book to the second buyer for $600, it may seem that he makes an additional profit of $100, but this is not true. If he sells to you at a price of $500, he needs to make *at least* that much from breaching, but (as we have already seen) he will also have to pay you damages of $300. For it to be in his best interest to breach, then, he must make an *additional* $300 (on top of the $500) to cover both the price you were going to pay, and the damages he will be ordered to pay. Thus, he will only sell the book to the second buyer for a price no less than $800, which is exactly your value for the book. This means that if a breach occurs under the expectations remedy, the book must move to a higher-valued use because only a second buyer who values the book more than you do would ever be willing to buy it at that price.

To appreciate why the expectations remedy is efficient with respect to breach, it is instructive to compare it to a remedy that *isn't* efficient, such as the reliance remedy. Under the reliance remedy, if the seller breaches, he only has to pay you $75 in damages. If the second buyer is willing to pay $600 for the book, the seller can make an extra $25 by breaching ($100 additional revenue less $75 damages). As long as the second buyer is willing to pay at least $575, it is profitable for the seller to breach. This leaves a large range of values (between $575 and $800) the second buyer can have and still end up with the book, even though this moves the book to a lower-valued use. Using the same reasoning, the restitution remedy is also not efficient with respect to breach. In this example, the seller will not have to pay any damages to you if he breaches, so a second buyer who is willing to pay at least $500 can get the book, even if her value is less than yours.

Notice that while the expectations remedy is the only one of these three remedies that discourages inefficient breach, all three remedies encourage efficient breach. With the highest damage payment of the three being $300, if there is a second buyer who values the book more than $800, none of these remedies can discourage breach. The only way a damage remedy can discourage an efficient breach is if the payment is greater than under the expectations remedy. As argued above, a damage payment of $10,000 will be extremely effective at discouraging the bookseller from breaching, but this will keep the book out of the hands of a second buyer who may value the book well above your value.

So what should we make of the concept of efficient breach? Stepping back from the economic perspective, if a breach of contract is nothing more than a broken promise, so what if society benefits by having a resource move to a higher-valued use? You wanted that book, it was promised to you, you were going to uphold your end of the transaction, and yet the opportunity to get the book was taken away from you through no fault of your own. Furthermore, the breach did not occur due to some factor outside the control of the seller, such as a theft or fire. The seller breached opportunistically to increase his profit. Do we want to pursue a social objective that allows something like this to happen?

Legal scholar and philosopher Seana Shiffrin (2009, 1551–52) eloquently questions the morality of efficient breach:

> Morality . . . correctly regards *some* breaches of promises as morally wrong and as warranting not only compensation but the administration of morality's punitive remedies, including blame, criticism, recrimination, and avoidance. The contract law invokes promise as the fundamental component of a contract but, puzzlingly, does not subject gratuitous breaches of contract (and hence breaches of promise) to the distinctive measures endorsed and administered by law. . . .

> If the law's rationale for the bar on punitive damages is that the prospect of punitive damages might discourage efficient breach of contract . . . then the divergence between morality's response to breach and the law's response to breach is problematic in ways that morally decent citizens cannot accept.

It is not uncommon for economic arguments to be challenged on moral grounds (consider the moral outrage that would be associated with establishing a market for kidneys, discussed in chapter 1), so economists have had plenty of practice defending their ideas against such criticism. One approach is to simply dismiss the criticism, arguing that morality should play no role in the enactment of public policy. Another approach is not quite as dismissive in that it accepts competing objectives when considering public policy, but favors efficiency concerns over others. In this particular context of contractual breach, however, there is another approach that attacks the criticism head on by offering the following counter argument: efficient breach is *not* immoral.

Fully Specified versus Incomplete Contracts

Let's consider the book example in a slightly different context. You are negotiating with the bookseller to buy the book, and you are going to write out an explicit contract governing the terms of the transaction. You value the book at $800 (assume, for this example, that this is your value without considering the purchase of the book stand), and he quotes you a price of $500 (assume his minimum willingness to sell is $100). But before the transaction is completed, he tells you that there is a chance that an outside buyer may be interested in the book and he is hesitant about committing the book to you. To proceed with the transaction, you both decide to negotiate a *fully specified contract*.

A fully specified contract is one that deals with every possible contingency that can occur, and sets out specific terms for each contingency. Each contingency may be linked to a specific price for the good in question, or a specific damage remedy in case of breach. The important point is that there is no scenario, either leading to performance or breach, that is not explicitly accounted for. In other words, the two parties exploit gains from trade across every possible outcome that can occur.

For example, let's say there are only three contingencies: an outside buyer with a value of $750 may appear, an outside buyer with a value of $900 may appear, or no outside buyer may appear. When considering the terms for the contingency that no outside buyer appears, you will both benefit from trade and agree on a contract price between $100 and $800. When considering the terms for the contingency that the outside buyer who values the book at $750 appears, you will still find a contract price that leads to performance. But in this case, isn't there a potential for breach to occur if the outside buyer is willing to pay more than you pay? There is not, if you and the seller are looking to maximize the *joint value* of your contract.

Let's say at first you agree on terms that allow the seller to breach if this outside buyer appears. Without getting into the specifics of a numerical example, it can be shown that there exists another set of terms leading to performance that *both* you and the seller prefer over the initial terms that leads to breach. This occurs because the most the seller can get out of the outside buyer is $750, yet that still leaves an additional $50 up for grabs if the book goes to you. In general, for any outside buyer with a lower value than $800, there will be no contractual terms that allow for breach that both you and the seller prefer to some other terms leading to performance. The joint value of the contract is maximized when you get the book.

Now let's consider the terms for the contingency that the outside buyer who values the book at $900 appears. You first agree on terms that allows for performance of the contract, but it can be shown that there exists another set of terms leading to breach that both you and the seller prefer over the initial ones. For example, if you would have experienced $300 in gains from trade from performance, the seller can contract to give you $325 to be allowed to breach. In this case, you actually prefer breach (giving you a total of $825) to completion (giving you a total of $800), and the seller can tap into the extra $75 generated from the difference between the outside buyer's value of $900 and your total of $825. In general, for any outside buyer with a higher value than $800, there will be no contractual terms that allow for performance that both you and the seller prefer to some other terms leading to breach. The joint value of the contract is maximized when you do not get the book.

If this seems a bit confusing, the point that is really being made reverts to the Coase Theorem (from chapter 1): as long as you and the seller can transact, you will always exploit gains from trade and move the resource to the highest-valued use. The fact that the highest-valued use may involve a third party does not matter. If you have the highest value for the book, terms can be agreed on that always lead to performance. If an outside buyer has the highest value for the book, terms can be agreed on that always lead to breach. In other words, with a fully specified contract both parties exploit gains from trade from contractual completion, and both parties exploit gains from trade from contractual breach.

So now what can we say about the morality of breach? It is no longer an issue because with a fully specified contract, there is technically no such thing as breach that can occur. Up until now, we have been using the term *breach* to refer to the seller breaking the contract and selling the book to the outside buyer. But if the terms of the contract allow for the seller to sell to an outside buyer who values the book more than you do, and this contingency occurs, the seller is *fulfilling* the contract, not breaching it, when selling to the outside buyer.

Before you get too excited about how cleverly we did away with the issue of immoral breach, an immediate and correct criticism of fully specified contracts is that they rarely exist in the real world. Actual contracts tend to be *incomplete*, for a number of reasons (see Shavell 2006b). There may be many contingencies that need to be considered, and this can greatly increase the costs of contracting. Also, it will be difficult to anticipate every possible contingency, even if the parties are willing to consider each one. Some contingencies, even if anticipated, may occur with such a low probability that it won't be worth spending any time considering them.

Another reason why contracts may be incomplete is that the court may not be able to verify that a specific contingency occurred. Let's say your contract with the bookseller included a provision dealing with the possibility that the book could be stolen. If the court can't verify that the book was stolen, the seller could breach to sell the book to a second buyer but claim that it was stolen, introducing the possibility of a milder remedy. It is also possible that the parties decide that if there is an eventual problem with fulfilling an incomplete contract, they can decide at that point how to rectify it through renegotiation.

Finally, and importantly, because one of the roles of the courts in contractual breach cases is to decide on breach remedies, the contracting parties can rely on these remedies as a *substitute* for fully specified contracts. The parties may decide to contract quickly and with modest costs, allowing the court to sort things out later when necessary. This argument is especially compelling in situations where breach is a rare occurrence.

So, if real-world contracts are not fully specified, can we now accept the argument that breach is immoral? Not necessarily, as we still need to consider what is meant by "immoral breach" in the context of an incomplete contract. Legal scholar Steven Shavell, a leading proponent of the idea that breach can be moral, has this to say:

> To discuss the immorality of breach, one must, of course, state what constitutes moral behavior in the contractual context. I make two simple definitional assumptions. First, I presume that if a contract provides explicitly for a contingency, then the moral duty to perform in that contingency is governed by the contract. Second, I suppose that if a contract is incomplete in the sense that it does not provide explicitly for a contingency, then the moral duty to perform in the contingency is governed by what a completely detailed contract addressing the contingency would have stipulated, assuming that the parties know what this hypothetical contract would have stated. . . . The appeal of the foregoing definition of moral obligation derives from the observation that a contract that provides explicitly for a contingency is similar to a promise that provides explicitly for a contingency, and that there are well known grounds that individuals have moral obligations to keep such promises. (2009, 1570–71)

And what would the parties have agreed to in terms of contract completion or breach had they considered all the possible contingencies? While addressing a counterfactual question can be a wildly open-ended exercise, there is one damage remedy that can neatly tie everything together—the expectations remedy. If the bookseller breaches and is ordered to pay you your expectations damages, by definition you are indifferent to contract completion and contract breach and you are not harmed. Is this still an immoral breach? An economic argument can be made that it is not: "Under the expectation measure of damages for breach, the seller will fail to perform in the same contingencies as the seller would be permitted not to perform in a complete contract. Accordingly, breach should not be characterized as immoral under our assumptions" (Shavell 2006b, 449).

Thus, the expectations remedy is not only efficient with respect to breach, it allows for contractual breaches to be considered moral, at least in the economic context of contractual breach morality. So now, do we finally have a firm conclusion concerning the morality of contractual breach? Still not yet because we have to be concerned with the shortcomings of the expectations remedy, especially when compared to a breach remedy that simply rejects the possibility of breach.

Specific Performance

The efficiency of the expectations remedy is that it makes the breached-against party indifferent to contractual breach and contractual completion. There is a simple elegance to this remedy, but that simplicity quickly dissipates in the real world. How are the courts supposed to calculate expectations damages? In our first numerical example, your expectations damages are $800. To determine this value, the court must calculate your subjective value for the book and your subjective value for the book stand. Are such calculations even remotely possible to make? And to the extent that the court errs in calculating your true expectations, the efficiency of that remedy no longer holds.

As discussed in chapter 2, in addition to liability rules there are property rules, and the same is true in contract law. The remedy of *specific performance* is one such property rule. With specific performance, the breaching party is ordered by the court to complete the contract, as opposed to having to pay monetary damages. This has the same effect as the expectations remedy in making the breached-against party indifferent to contractual breach and contractual completion because, when the issue is finally resolved, the contract is never actually breached.

To place specific performance into our book example, we have to change the facts a little. Suppose that the seller has agreed to sell the book to the second buyer, but the book has not actually changed hands yet. For example, perhaps the order request came to the seller through e-mail, so there is a delay between when the seller decides to breach and when he will deliver the property. When you return to the store to pick up the book, the seller informs you that the book has been promised to another buyer, and he returns your $50 deposit. Let's assume that at this point, you have an opportunity to get an injunction prohibiting the seller to complete the breach until the court has sorted out what remedy it wants to apply to this case. And that is where our analysis begins: what factors are relevant for the court to consider in choosing between specific performance and the expectations remedy?

In one of the first significant analyses concerning the efficiency aspects of specific performance, legal scholar Anthony Kronman (1978, 357–58), quoting contracts scholar Arthur Corbin, points to the *uniqueness test* as a justification for the courts' use of that remedy: "If the 'subject matter of a contract is unique in character and cannot be duplicated' or if obtaining 'a substantial equivalent involves difficulty, delay, and inconvenience,' a court will be more apt to compel specific performance. 'The fact that such a duplicate or equivalent cannot be so obtained does not necessarily show that money damages are not an adequate remedy, but is a fact that tends strongly in that direction.'" This approach to awarding specific performance would likely fit well in our book example, as the book is assumed to be rare and in mint condition, and may be difficult to replace. Furthermore, using Kronman's approach, the unique character of the book makes it likely that you would have tried to negotiate such a remedy into the contract to begin with, perhaps paying the seller a higher price to secure performance and avoid a monetary damage payment in case of potential breach. Thus, the courts' use of specific performance in cases of unique goods substitutes for prebreach contractual negotiation costs.

Legal scholar Thomas Ulen (1984, 375–76) accepts Kronman's idea that the uniqueness test is a useful way to approach specific performance, but only as a starting point. Ulen argues that protecting subjective value with specific performance is important for a much wider group of contracts:

If contracting parties were free to specify *any* remedy that was mutually agreeable, they would likely opt for specific performance rather than damages where the promise attached some particular *subjective valuation* to the promisor's performance. The key difference here is the insertion that it is subjective valuation rather than uniqueness that makes specific performance attractive. Clearly, there is a relationship between uniqueness and subjective valuation: someone is more likely to attach a greater value than market value to a rare, one-of-a-kind item than to a highly fungible item. However, the class of things to which someone attaches a subjective valuation is greater than the class of unique items. Once (Kronman's) category is expanded to include all promises to which there is a subjective valuation, then the rest of Professor Kronman's analysis stands.

Yet Ulen takes his argument even one step further, suggesting that specific remedy should be the default remedy the courts use in *all* contractual breach cases.

Ulen's analysis relies on a basic idea discussed in chapter 2: when there are low transactions costs, the court should use a property rule; when there are high transactions costs, the courts should use a liability rule. Ulen sees most contractual settings as involving low transactions costs, since a contract in and of itself requires successful negotiation. Thus, as a property rule, specific performance fits well into these settings. The fact that the parties initially negotiated a contract, however, does not tell us much about how well they will transact with each other *postbreach*. There is bound to be some ill will based on the act of breach in the first place, and the fact that they are pursuing a resolution in court rather than privately renegotiating may suggest that transactions costs are high. But all this actually *strengthens* Ulen's argument about using specific performance as the default remedy.

If the court has a default remedy it *always* uses, this should reduce the postbreach transactions and court costs, compared to the situation in which the court could adopt any remedy at any time. The parties will benefit from knowing what the court will do because eliminating that uncertainty can only save additional costs in resolving the breach. So now the question is, which remedy is best as a default? Let's begin with using the expectations remedy as the default, but allow the parties to negotiate around the default when they specify their contractual terms. In other words, if they desire, the parties can include their own remedy in the contract that the courts will eventually uphold in case of breach. If they don't specify a remedy, the court will use the expectations remedy as the default.

As previously discussed, the expectations remedy itself can be very difficult for the court to accurately apply. How do the courts determine the amount that makes the breached-against party indifferent to contractual beach and contractual completion? Furthermore, if the parties can never know for sure how the court will calculate the expectations value, they might have to negotiate their own damage remedy *or* specific performance, as opposed to simply deciding on specific performance or the default. As a default remedy, then, the expectations remedy likely involves significant prebreach and postbreach costs, especially when compared to the default of specific performance.

With specific performance as the default remedy, the courts are not likely to face significant postbreach costs. Specific performance is defined as having the contract completed as initially written, so the courts do not have to "calculate" anything, as they would with a damage remedy. There may, however, be costs in applying specific performance that increase post-breach court costs, such as when the seller has already conveyed the prop-erty to a third party. If the parties want to negotiate around the default, they will have to incur prebreach costs, but at least they will only have to consider how to specify a damage remedy, not choose between damages or specific performance, as we just argued they might have to with the difficult-to-predict expectations remedy as the default. For these and other reasons, Ulen presents a strong intuitive case for making specific perfor-mance the default remedy in contractual breach cases.

Shavell (2006a) expands on the debate by explicitly distinguishing be-tween two types of contracts: contracts to *convey property* and contracts to *produce goods*. Up until this point, our analysis has focused on contracts to convey property—a rare book in our example—and Shavell agrees with Ulen about the desirability of specific performance over the expectations remedy in such cases. Although their analyses differ, they both see the con-tracting parties preferring specific performance if they were to fully spec-ify their contract. The difference is, however, that Shavell does not see spe-cific performance as *universally* superior to the expectations remedy for a broader class of contracts.

Consider a contract to produce a good where the buyer and seller ne-gotiate the terms before production begins. Assume the buyer values the good at $25,000, and the seller is willing to produce and sell the good for a minimum of $15,000. What if after the contract is signed there is a pos-sibility that something can go wrong with the production process and, if this high-cost contingency occurs, the seller can only produce and sell the good for a minimum of $60,000? Notice, the seller can perform under either contingency, but there are only gains from trade to produce if the high-cost contingency does *not* occur. If the parties are contracting under these conditions, which remedy would they *mutually* prefer?

It may seem that the buyer, to secure delivery of the good and guaran-tee its value, would prefer specific performance regardless of the seller's production-cost predicament. After all, the buyer's gains from trade are established when the final price is negotiated before the high-cost contingency occurs. There is no doubt, however, that the seller prefers the expectations remedy since that entails *at most* a payment of $10,000 (if the negotiated price is at the minimum of $15,000). Under specific performance, on the other hand, the seller has to incur a cost of $60,000 to produce a good the buyer values no more than $25,000. Thus, the price the seller can get has to be less than $25,000, making his loss *at least* $35,000.

While in the high-cost contingency there are no gains from trade to produce, there certainly are gains from trade *not* to produce. That is, both the buyer and the seller can negotiate contractual terms that make it mutually beneficial for them not to have the good produced in the high-cost contingency. For example, at whatever negotiated price for the good that would exist under specific performance, the seller can offer the buyer a lower price to accept the expectations remedy instead. The expectations remedy, as with specific performance, makes the buyer indifferent to contractual completion and contractual breach, but the buyer reaps more gains from trade by being offered a lower price to accept the expectations remedy. And the seller gets to avoid having to specifically perform at a hugely disadvantageous production cost. This suggests that if the courts are considering adopting a remedy that the parties themselves would have adopted had they fully specified their contract, it is not the case that specific performance universally achieves that objective.

But why does Shavell's argument matter? In Ulen's analysis, making specific performance the default remedy allows the parties to still choose to privately specify the expectations remedy in their contract. Ulen doesn't argue that specific performance is always the remedy contracting parties prefer, only that it is likely to be less costly to use specific performance as the default than it is to use the expectations remedy as the default. But Ulen does contend that if the parties typically prefer one remedy over the other, having that remedy as the default saves on contracting costs—the parties efficiently rely on the court's remedy when breach occurs. With contracts to produce, Shavell advances the strong argument that the parties will prefer the expectations remedy over specific performance, so allowing for the damage remedy to be the default will save on contractual costs.

In choosing a default remedy, it is important to consider the complete contractual costs picture: from transactions costs to administration costs, and from prebreach to postbreach costs. It is also important to predict what the contracting parties would choose if they were in the position to fully specify their contract. With all this in mind, the key point is to determine if the expectations remedy is more efficient than specific performance. In actuality, both Ulen and Shavell are asking the same type of questions, but coming up with slightly different answers. Ulen's answer is to universally use specific performance as the default. Shavell's answer is to use the expectations remedy as the default for contracts to produce goods, and specific performance as the default for contracts to convey property.

In the end, how you feel about contractual breach remedies may depend on how you feel about the morality and efficiency of breach (as well as other things, such as how the remedies facilitate contract formation in the first place). If you think breach, especially opportunistic breach, should be strongly discouraged, you favor strict remedies like specific performance or punitive damages. If you feel that efficient breach should be encouraged but inefficient breach should be discouraged, you favor the expectations remedy. If you feel that the expectations remedy is impractical and difficult to apply correctly, you may favor encouraging the parties to more fully specify their contract to include whatever remedies they agree on. But in this last case, another problem arises. When private parties stipulate their own remedies, the possibility exists that the courts will *not* uphold these remedies. Why the courts may do this is the topic of the next chapter.

Discussion Questions

1. In the book example used throughout this chapter, assume the seller breaches the contract and transfers the book to the third party. Kronman (1978, 377–78) considers three ways in which the courts deal with this type of situation:

   > Not infrequently, they simply limit the promisee to his damages remedy, on the ground that specific performance is no longer possible since the property has been conveyed to an innocent third party. Sometimes, however, a court will impose a constructive trust for the promisee's benefit on the profit realized by the resale (that is, the difference between the resale price and the original contract price), even though this may exceed the damages the promisee has suffered. And finally, on rare occasions, a court will require the good faith purchaser to retender the property and then compel specific performance of the original contract.

   How would you evaluate each of these approaches?
2. Identify and evaluate situations in which it would be quite costly for the courts to uphold the remedy of specific performance.

3. Some legal scholars propose that specific performance should be awarded whenever the breached-against party requests it. Evaluate this proposal.

References

Hermalin, B. E., A. E. Katz, and R. Craswell. 2007. "Contract Law." In *Handbook of Law and Economics, Volume 1*, edited by A. M. Polinsky and S. Shavell, 3–138. Amsterdam: North-Holland.

Kronman, A. T. 1978. "Specific Performance." *University of Chicago Law Review* 45:351–82.

Shavell, S. 2006a. "Specific Performance versus Damages for Breach of Contract: An Economic Analysis." *Texas Law Review* 84:831–76.

———. 2006b. "Is Breach of Contract Immoral?" *Emory Law Journal* 56:439–60.

———. 2009. "Why Breach of Contract May Not Be Immoral Given the Incompleteness of Contracts." *Michigan Law Review* 107:1569–81.

Shiffrin, S. 2009. "*Could* Breach of Contract Be Immoral?" *Michigan Law Review* 107:1551–68.

Ulen, T. S. 1984. "The Efficiency of Specific Performance: Toward a Unified Theory of Contract Remedies." *Michigan Law Review* 83:341–403.

CHAPTER SIX

Should the Courts Void a Contractual Clause They Deem Unfair?

Williams v. Walker Thomas Furniture Co. *(1965)* *and the Paradox of Stipulated Damages*

Facts

In April 1962, Ora Lee Williams purchased a stereo from the Walker-Thomas Furniture Company. The price of the stereo was $514.95, and it was to be paid in monthly installments. Shortly after her purchase, Williams defaulted on her payment. The purchase contract allowed for the stereo to remain the property of Walker-Thomas until the stereo was paid for in full. Thus, Walker-Thomas had the right to repossess the stereo as a penalty for the default in payment. This in itself was not that unusual. But this was just the start of Williams's troubles.

The contract had an additional stipulation, known as an *add-on clause*. Between 1957 and 1962, Williams had purchased several items from Walker-Thomas. When she purchased the stereo, she still had a balance of $164 owed to them. Because she had not reduced her balance to zero before purchasing the stereo, a default in payment allowed Walker-Thomas to repossess *all* items previously purchased. Even though Williams had paid nearly $1,400 in total over the years, she never brought her balance down to zero. Thus, because of the add-on clause, Walker-Thomas maintained ownership of every item she had purchased. With just one default, Walker-Thomas had the contractual right to repossess everything, and that is what it tried to do, until the court intervened.

Court's Decision

The lower court made it clear how it felt about this contract: "We cannot condemn too strongly [Walker-Thomas's] conduct. It raises serious questions of sharp practice and irresponsible business dealings." The court did not feel that the contract violated any law, however, and left it as a problem for the legislature to correct.

The appeals court faced no such dilemma. The appeals court was appalled by the facts in this case, as was the lower court, but believed it had an obligation to intervene on Williams's behalf. The court relied on a concept known as *unconscionability* to rule against Walker-Thomas:

> Unconscionability has generally been recognized to include an absence of meaningful choice on the part of one of the parties together with contract terms which are unreasonably favorable to the other party.... Did each party to the contract, considering his obvious education or lack of it, have a reasonable opportunity to understand the terms of the contract, or were the important terms hidden in a maze of fine print and minimized by deceptive sales practices? Ordinarily, one who signs an agreement without full knowledge of its terms might be held to assume the risk that he has entered a one-sided bargain. But when a party of little bargaining power, and hence little real choice, signs a commercially unreasonable contract with little or no knowledge of its terms, it is hardly likely that his consent, or even an objective manifestation of his consent, was ever given to all the terms. In such a case the usual rule that the terms of the agreement are not to be questioned should be abandoned and the court should consider whether the terms of the contract are so unfair that enforcement should be withheld.

Quite simply, the unconscionability doctrine allows contracts deemed to be unfair (as determined in each particular case) to be voided by the court.

Economic Analysis

An add-on clause certainly has the appearance of being very severe. After all, Williams had paid the vast majority of her debt to Walker-Thomas when she defaulted, yet she still did not own the property she had purchased over the years. The problem with considering the impact of the clause on

Williams *after* she defaults on her payment is that it ignores the benefit of the clause to Williams *at the time* the contract was signed. An add-on clause may facilitate the buyer's ability to purchase the goods in the first place.

Epstein (1975) discusses the role of the add-on clause in allowing buyers and sellers to exploit gains from trade. Consider Walker-Thomas's situation. They are trying to sell goods to people of limited means. Without credit, there are many sales that will not occur. Using the good purchased at the time (the stereo in *Williams*) as the only collateral is not likely to be adequate to the seller. The value of some goods can depreciate very rapidly, especially when there is the potential for consumer misuse. Furthermore, if Williams only loses the stereo when she defaults, she may not have a strong incentive to avoid defaulting. Walker-Thomas may not be interested in selling the stereo without some additional security.

It may be the case that the typical customer has no other goods to put up for collateral, or that goods they do possess still have their own liens on them. So, what makes good collateral for a furniture and appliance store? Furniture and appliances. Walker-Thomas has substantial expertise in selling these items. The store likely has a strong sense of the resale value of used items, and has a sales record of items purchased. The store is also dealing with return customers, so there is some customer loyalty that has built up. All of these factors suggest that the add-on clause is an efficient method for allowing customers the opportunity to buy items on credit, thus benefiting both the buyers and the seller.

After a default occurs, however, the analysis of an add-on clause takes on a different tone. The thought of a moving van parked in front of Williams's home, men removing her furniture and appliances, children crying at having their house emptied, is not an image most people care to see or even consider. Indeed, the add-on clause is harsh, as the court clearly argued. But what if Williams was denied the opportunity to purchase these items because she could not pay in full up front, or did not have the collateral to secure the loan? This too must be considered, not only in the type of situation that arose in *Williams* but in all cases where these types of clauses are used to facilitate trade. One other mitigating factor concerning the add-on clause is that it typically only allows the creditor to recover what is owed (plus interest and possibly repossession costs), so its objective is restitution, not punishment. In all, to dismiss the add-on clause as being nothing more than "sharp practice and irresponsible business dealings" is not delving into the issue deeply enough.

But then again, arguing that the add-on clause benefits *both* the buyer and the seller assumes that the buyer actually understands the clause. That may not be the case. Here is the clause that was in the Walker-Thomas contract:

> The amount of each periodical installment payment to be made by the pur-
> chaser to the company under this present lease shall be inclusive of and not in
> addition to the amount of each installment payment to be made by the pur-
> chaser under such prior leases, bills, or account; and all payment now and here-
> after made by purchaser shall be credited pro rata on all outstanding leases,
> bills, and accounts due the company by purchaser at the time each such pay-
> ment is made.

It certainly wouldn't be surprising if many people found that to be a difficult clause to understand.

Typically, two parties signing a contract are doing so in their own best interest. If one of the parties is not well informed, or doesn't understand part of the contract, there are mechanisms (such as lawyers) that can be used to rectify these problems. Still, if one of the parties doesn't want to put forth the effort to fully understand the terms of the contract, they are purposely choosing to save on contractual costs by being casual about the terms. Under these conditions, the justification for the courts' voiding a contract is weakened.

However, perhaps Williams read the contract but didn't understand the add-on clause, which is not difficult to believe given its arcane wording. Or, because this wasn't her first contract with Walker-Thomas, she wasn't anticipating anything different from her past experience to occur, so she did not carefully consider the full ramifications of defaulting on a payment. Whatever the case, is signing a contract without understanding it justification enough for the courts to void that contract? Lack of understanding may be important, but it may not be enough. The more appropriate issue is to try to determine what Williams would have done *had she understood the contract*. If, with perfect understanding, she would have signed the contract, the fact that she didn't understand it is not necessarily a strong justification for voiding it.

As discussed in chapter 5, one role for the courts is to hold parties to the terms of a contract they would have agreed on had they both been fully informed and the contract been fully specified. If these conditions can be determined, prebreach negotiation costs are minimized, and only when a breach occurs do the courts need to step in and make a postbreach determination. If it can be determined that most people would accept an add-on clause *if* it were understood, it may be inefficient for the courts to prohibit such clauses. But if people were not likely to accept an add-on clause if understood, but accept it only because of their lack of understanding, this may be a sound justification for the courts to prohibit such clauses. It may be very difficult to determine what people would do with a full understanding of the clause, but it is a scenario that is well worth considering.

In general, the doctrine of unconscionability allows the court great freedom in interpreting contractual terms and deciding what is fair well after the fact. While this has the advantage of protecting parties who appear to be in weak bargaining positions, it also has the potential to stifle contracting in the first place. Epstein argues that the doctrine should be used to complement other factors that more obviously allow a court to void a contract—such as duress, fraud, or incompetence—in cases where explicit proof of these factors may be too costly to develop, but they nevertheless seem to be present. However, the doctrine should not be used to undercut the private right of contract in a way that, on net, will reduce social welfare.

Legal scholar Eric Posner advances a completely different argument *in favor* of the courts deeming certain contracts unconscionable. Posner (1995, 185) argues that in addition to moving resources to their highest-valued use through property and contract law, the state may also be concerned with reducing poverty by guaranteeing all citizens some minimum welfare level: "The minimum welfare level is a standard of living, not simply a net worth, and comprises the consumption of shelter, food, medical care, and other 'basic necessities.' The state maintains the minimum welfare level by transferring cash and other benefits to anyone who falls beneath it." It is important to note that Posner is not putting forth an argument in favor of the state maintaining a minimum welfare level of its citizens; instead, he is merely claiming that it is a common objective that the state is likely to pursue. And if this is the case, the question he asks is, how might the unconscionability doctrine (and other restrictive contract rules) help achieve this objective?

Posner identifies two problems associated with the objective of maintaining a minimum welfare level: *welfare opportunism* and *welfare circumvention*. With welfare opportunism, because each individual is guaranteed a minimum level of welfare, some individuals may make riskier investments than they would without the "safety net" of the welfare system. In other words, failed investments involve a lower cost than they would if there were no guaranteed minimum level of welfare provided by the state, and so too many risky investments may be undertaken. With more failed investments occurring *because* of the welfare system, the cost of sustaining the system increases as more people enter it.

With welfare circumvention, individuals who receive welfare benefits may use those benefits to maintain a lifestyle that is not in accordance with the policy objective of the welfare system. As stated above, Posner defines the minimum welfare level as involving a specific bundle of goods and services. Individuals who have the opportunity either to use direct welfare cash payments or to trade other welfare benefits for cash may purchase goods and services that do not belong in that bundle. For example, if individuals use welfare benefits to purchase cigarettes, alcohol, or drugs (or expensive stereo equipment, as in *Williams*) instead of food or other basic necessities, they are circumventing the stated goals of the welfare system.

There are many ways for the state to discourage welfare opportunism and welfare circumvention, but in instances in which specific regulations are not binding, Posner sees the courts' use of the unconscionability doctrine as a legitimate way to promote the goals of the welfare system. What is interesting about Posner's (1995, 297) approach is that it provides a rationale for unconscionability that completely sidesteps more traditional rationales, such as protecting the poor from unfair contractual terms or disadvantaged bargaining positions: "The minimum welfare theory is not in itself paternalistic. The welfare opportunism and welfare circumvention problems are merely logical outgrowths of the assumption that the state is committed to the free market and to the minimum welfare level. The theory is indifferent as to the source of the assumption about poor relief, which could be derived from paternalistic motives (people should be protected against themselves), compassion (poor people should be helped), or entirely self-regarding concerns such as fear that poverty produces disorder."

Whatever benefits can be identified with the doctrine of unconscionability, its application is also likely to increase the costs of contracting. For the type of specified clauses that are most likely to be subject to heightened scrutiny, either the parties will have to bear the uncertainty of these clauses not being upheld by the courts, or they will have to incur prebreach costs to establish clauses that will be more acceptable to the courts. In Epstein's (1975, 303) own words, "The difficult question with unconscionability is not whether it works towards a legitimate end, but whether its application comes at too great a price." Protecting consumers who enter contracts from very weak bargaining positions is a legitimate goal for the courts to pursue, but deciding the best way to achieve this goal requires careful consideration not only of those who are protected by the policies but of those who are burdened by them, be they firms or other consumers.

Penalty Clauses

One of the great paradoxes of contract law is that the courts, in certain circumstances, do not uphold damage remedies that the contracting parties *themselves* include in the contract. For example, let's say you are interested in having a building contractor build your new house. After considering several options, you are leaning toward hiring a contractor who has a good reputation for doing high-quality work at a reasonable price. You do have one reservation: you have heard that this contractor sometimes has difficulty completing projects on time. You express your concern about this issue, and the contractor tries to convince you that this will not happen in your case. Still, you have your doubts and begin considering other options.

To gain your business, the building contractor agrees to pay monetary damages for each day beyond the contractual deadline the house is not complete. When damages are stipulated in the contract, they are known as *liquidated damages*. In this case, the liquidated damages clause may be the key component in convincing you to hire the contractor. Thus, one obvious benefit of liquidated damages is that it can help a seller secure a contract by providing an incentive not to breach, and this incentive can clearly be identified by the buyer. The problem is, however, liquidated damages may sometimes be considered by the court to be a *penalty clause*, and in this case the court may refuse to uphold the clause. As a matter of fact, that is exactly what happened in the case this hypothetical example is drawn from.

In *Muller v. Light* (1976), the following clause was included in the building contract: "Time being the essence of this contract, contractor shall pay to the owners or deduct from the total contract price One Hundred and No/100 ($100.00) per day as liquidated damages for each day after said date that the construction is not completed and accepted by the Owners and Owners shall not arbitrarily withhold acceptance." The building contractor (Light) completed the contract fifty-seven days after the agreed-on completion date, and owed the owner (Muller) $5,700 in liquidated damages. The Texas Supreme Court did not uphold the liquidated damages clause:

> In order to enforce a liquidated damage clause, the court must find: (1) that the harm caused by the breach is incapable or difficult of estimation, and (2) that the amount of liquidated damages called for is a reasonable forecast of

just compensation. The issue of the enforceability of liquidated damages in any given case is one of law for the court to decide.

In our judgment the clause in question fails by each standard. . . . First, damages for delay in construction of a building are usually predictable as the rental value of the building during the delay. Second, there is no reasonable relationship between appellants' damages, that is, the loss of the use of the house during the period of delay, and the amount of damages computed under the liquidated damages provision. Testimony established the rental value of the home at $400–$415 per month. The liquidated damages clause would establish damages of $3,000 per month. Such a disparity leads one to the conclusion that appellants, who drafted the liquidated damages provision, intended the provision to serve as an in terrorem device to insure prompt performance by the builder, rather than as a reasonable estimate of actual damages.

While the court clearly saw the sense in not upholding the penalty clause, is there an *economic* sense to the ruling?

It is not difficult to find reasons why the parties themselves may agree to include penalty clauses in their contracts (see De Geest and Wuyts 2000 for a concise survey of the pros and cons of penalty clauses). In the hypothetical building contract above, the seller encouraged the inclusion of a penalty clause to allay the buyer's fear of delay. Thus, a penalty clause can be used by a seller to signal quality or reliability to the buyer. In *Muller v. Light*, it appears that it was the buyer who encouraged the use of a penalty clause to enhance the incentive of the seller to complete the project in time. A classic example of the use of a penalty clause to encourage contractual completion arises when a buyer hires a baker to prepare and deliver a wedding cake on the day of the wedding. If the baker breaches and does not deliver, specific performance has little value in this setting as the day of the wedding has already passed. Certainly, monetary damages can be assessed, but the usual problems associated with postbreach negotiation or court costs arise. Or, perhaps the parties can agree on the inclusion of a penalty clause prebreach (*regardless* of which party is more insistent on its inclusion), with the sole purpose of greatly increasing the probability that breach will not occur.

There are also several reasons that have been identified for why the courts should not uphold penalty clauses. Some follow along the same lines as the typical justifications for the unconscionability doctrine—one of the parties may not fully read or understand the contract, and would not have agreed to a penalty clause otherwise. It is also possible that a penalty clause may be enforced incorrectly due to judicial error, placing undue burden on the breaching party. One group of law and economics scholars (Clarkson, Miller, and Muris 1978) argues that there is another compelling reason for the courts not to enforce penalty clauses—they may lead to breach of contract being *induced.*

When liquidated damages significantly exceed those that would be assessed under the expectations remedy, the breached-against party actually *prefers* contractual breach to contractual completion. This can lead to the unusual situation where the breached-against party purposely tries to prevent the completion of the contract by inducing breach. Furthermore, if the other party is aware of the possibility of breach inducement, he may try to protect himself from this occurrence to avoid having to pay a large penalty.

From a social welfare perspective, resources used to induce breach and to discourage the inducement of breach are wasted. Breach inducement is not an activity that leads to the production of any real goods and services, and it does not promote the objective of moving resources to a higher-valued use. To whatever extent penalty clauses do enhance social welfare, breach inducement works in the opposite direction. Thus, the authors argue that careful thought must be given to weighing the benefits of penalty clauses against their costs, and to how legal rules can be implemented that are, for the most part, efficient. Should all liquidated damage clauses be enforced? Should none (that are considered penalties) be enforced? Or, should some be enforced and others voided?

The authors conclude that if choosing between the extremes—all clauses enforced versus none enforced—all clauses should be enforced. Whatever costs are associated with breach inducement, it is likely that the benefits of liquidated damages far exceed those costs. This is not a surprising conclusion given that economists, as already mentioned, tend to believe in the efficiency of fully specified contracts. In general, however, the authors favor a more nuanced approach: "When contracting parties can covertly increase the probability of breach and when they might have incentive to do so, the courts should closely scrutinize the relation of the amount of the stipulated damage clause to damages from the breach. . . . When contracting parties clearly cannot overtly increase the probability of breach or when they have no incentive to do so, stipulated damage clauses should be enforced regardless of reasonableness" (Clarkson, Miller, and Muris 1978, 375, 377). Not only do the authors suggest that this approach is worth considering, they argue that courts adopt it in many contractual settings, even if judges don't explicitly state that this is what they are doing.

In settings in which it is difficult to induce breach, the authors argue that the courts often enforce penalty clauses. For example, when parties stipulate damages *after* a breach has occurred (so that breach can no longer be induced), the courts often enforce liquidated damages without concern over the reasonableness of the amount of damages. With contracts involving a covenant not to compete, courts also often enforce liquidated damages. With these particular contracts, inducing breach would require *encouraging* performance, as opposed to discouraging or delaying performance. Inducing someone to compete against you is obviously a difficult task to accomplish.

In settings in which it is not difficult to induce breach, the courts generally do not enforce penalty clauses. For example, construction contracts routinely involve joint decisions between the parties to be made during construction. This may provide an opportunity for the purchaser to induce delays and increase the probability of breach. With some contracts, one of the parties must pay a deposit that will be forfeited if a breach occurs. This too provides an incentive for the other party to induce breach. In both of these settings, the courts typically do not uphold unreasonable liquidated damage clauses.

While the problem of breach inducement is a thoroughly thought-out argument against penalty clauses, it does raise another question. If the parties are aware of the possibility of breach inducement, which is especially likely when one of the parties considers devoting resources to preventing inducement, why did they agree to a penalty clause in the first place? One explanation is that during the prebreach contractual negotiations, they agreed that breach inducement was a potential cost of using a penalty clause but that this cost was outweighed by other benefits, making it in both parties' best interest to include the clause. If true, this weakens the breach-inducement argument against penalty clauses. So, it is not simply the possibility of breach inducement that matters, but whether both parties were aware of this contingency when they agreed to the penalty clause.

Recall that economists tend to favor contracts that are as fully specified as possible. Allowing the parties to work out their own remedies for various contingencies typically guarantees that breach, if it occurs, will be agreeable to *both* parties. The strongest reason for not encouraging fully specified contracts is not that they may include penalty clauses, but that they increase prebreach negotiation costs. To minimize these costs, contract negotiation may be facilitated by allowing for postbreach remedies to be used in the rare instances that breach occurs.

We are still left with the key question: if both parties agree to penalty clauses, should the courts always uphold them? The courts can always void a contract if duress or fraud is deemed to be present, or if they find the contract to be unconscionable. Furthermore, the unconscionability doctrine can be applied to penalty clauses that are believed to be the result of an unfair bargaining process, but even penalty clauses that have no appearance of being unconscionable can nevertheless be voided by the courts. Is this behavior by the courts truly paradoxical? Without a doubt, that depends on whom you ask.

Discussion Questions

1. One fact that upset the appeals court in *Williams* is that the furniture store was aware that Williams received a stipend of only $218 a month from the government, and she had to support herself and seven children on that amount, yet they still sold her a stereo that cost more than $500. How does this fact affect your analysis of the case?

2. Consider the facts in *Jones v. Star Credit Corp.* (1969). In August 1965, Clifton Jones, a welfare recipient, agreed to purchase a home freezer from a door-to-door salesman. The base price for the freezer was $900, but there were additional charges for time credit, credit life insurance, credit property insurance, and sales tax, which brought the full price of the freezer to $1,234.80. At the time of the court's decision, March 1969, Jones had paid a total of $619.88. The defendants claimed that a balance of $819.81 was still due, and this amount included various additional charges related to an extension of time to repay that was granted to the plaintiffs. The court claimed that, "the uncontroverted proof at the trial established that the freezer unit, when purchased, had a maximum retail value of approximately $300." The court ruled that the contract was unconscionable and that no further payments were owed the defendants. How would you evaluate this decision?

3. Here are two other arguments that can be used in favor of allowing the courts to void penalty clauses:
   a. Penalty clauses discourage breach; therefore, they discourage *efficient* breach.
   b. Penalty clauses lead to increased litigation because for such clauses to be enforced, the breached-against party will have to sue the breaching party.
   Evaluate each of these arguments.

References

Clarkson, K.W., R. L. Miller, and T. J. Muris. 1978. "Liquidated Damages v. Penalties: Sense or Nonsense?" *Wisconsin Law Review* 1978:351–90.

De Geest, G., and F. Wuyts. 2000. "Penalty Clauses and Liquidated Damages." In *Encyclopedia of Law and Economics*, edited by B. Bouckaert and G. De Geest. Cheltenham: Edward Elgar.

Epstein, R. A. 1975. "Unconscionability: A Critical Reappraisal." *Journal of Law and Economics* 18:293–315.

Posner, E. A. 1995. "Contract Law in the Welfare State: A Defense of the Unconscionability Doctrine, Usury Laws, and Related Limitations on the Freedom of Contract." *Journal of Legal Studies* 24:283–319.

PART III
Torts

CHAPTER SEVEN

Should Tort Liability Be Governed by Fault or No-Fault Rules?

Indiana Harbor Belt Railroad v. American Cyanamid *(1990) and the Economics of the Great Debate in Tort Law*

Facts

In January 1979, American Cyanamid Company (Cyanamid), a major manufacturer of chemicals, loaded 20,000 gallons of liquid acrylonitrile into a leased railroad car for shipment from a plant in Louisiana to a plant in New Jersey. Along its journey, the railroad car would have to switch from the Missouri Pacific railroad line to the Conrail line, and this would occur at a switching line owned by Indiana Harbor Belt Railroad (Indiana Harbor). The switching line was located just south of Chicago in the village of Riverdale, part of the Chicago metropolitan area.

Shortly after the car arrived at the switching line, a leak was discovered. Because acrylonitrile is a highly toxic and possibly carcinogenic chemical, an evacuation of the surrounding area was ordered. When the car was moved to a remote location in the railroad yard, and it was calculated that only about a quarter of the tank had emptied, the evacuation was lifted. There was still a concern about soil and water contamination, however, and the Illinois Department of Environmental Protection ordered Indiana Harbor to take decontamination measures that cost nearly $1 million. Indiana Harbor brought a lawsuit against Cyanamid, hoping that the court would hold the chemical manufacturer liable for the cleanup costs that Indiana Harbor had to incur.

In this chapter, instead of next discussing the court's opinion and then moving on to the economic analysis, we are going to reverse that order. The opinion in this case was written by Judge Richard Posner, a pioneering scholar in the field of law and economics. His opinion explicitly uses economic reasoning, and it will be easier to understand and appreciate the court's decision if a thorough discussion of the economics of tort law comes first. Then the court's opinion, and a discussion of that opinion, will follow.

The Economics of Tort Liability Rules

The easiest way to discuss an economic model of tort liability is to set up a simple, yet highly instructive, numerical example. Once the basic results are explained, the model can be expanded to include more complicating factors. Consider the following tort scenario. A person (the potential injurer) has to decide if she should salt the sidewalk in front of her house when it gets icy during the winter months. She only has two possible actions to take: do nothing, or salt the sidewalk. It will cost her $3 to salt the sidewalk, but cost her nothing if she doesn't. If she does nothing, the probability a person (the potential victim) slips on the sidewalk is 10 percent. If she salts, that probability is reduced to 2 percent. Finally, if the victim slips on the ice, he will suffer a damage of $100. These are all the numbers you need to begin analyzing the role of tort law in promoting efficient behavior.

The Tort Social-Loss Function

The first step is to define precisely what is meant by *efficient behavior* in a tort setting. The typical social objective economists favor in these settings is to minimize the social loss of the accident. What are the components of the social loss? If an accident occurs, the victim suffers a damage of $100, but this only occurs probabilistically (which is why we refer to it as an *accident*). If the injurer does nothing, the probability of the accident is 10 percent, so the *expected damage* (that is, the average damage) is 10 percent of $100, or $10. If the injurer salts, the probability of the accident falls to 2 percent, so the expected damage is 2 percent of $100, or $2. Is it efficient for the injurer to salt the sidewalk? Yes, because by incurring a $3 cost of care, the expected damage is reduced by $8.

In a *unilateral* accident setting, only one party, in this case the injurer, has the potential to influence the probability of the accident occurring. So in this example, there are only two components of the social loss—the injurer's cost of care, and the expected damage. When the injurer does nothing, the social loss is made up of only the expected damage of $10. When the injurer salts, the social loss is made up of the $3 cost of salting and the $2 expected damage, for a total social loss of $5. To minimize social loss, then, it is efficient for the injurer to salt the sidewalk. In the language of economics, we refer to salting the sidewalk as *due care*.

It is important to recognize that due care has nothing to do with the way the injurer will *actually* behave. How much care the injurer takes is different from how much care society wants her to take. The liability rule will determine what the injurer actually does, and if the goal is to have her take due care, the rule will have to give her the incentive to salt the sidewalk. Also, due care does not necessarily imply a positive level of care, but will vary with each tort setting being considered. For example, if the cost of salting is changed from $3 to $11, the cost of salting the sidewalk will exceed the victim's expected damage of $10 when the injurer does nothing. In this case, it would be efficient for the injurer to do nothing.

While there are a number of liability rules that can be considered, in this simple example we will consider only three—no liability, strict liability, and negligence. Each of these rules has advantages and disadvantages relative to the others, but where an economic analysis of a tort liability rule usually begins is with one question: does the rule provide the injurer with the incentive to take due care?

No Liability

Under a rule of no liability, the injurer is *never* liable for the victim's damages, regardless of the situation. This rule does not provide the injurer with the incentive to salt the sidewalk. If she does, she will incur a salting cost of $3. If she doesn't, she will bear no costs at all. If the injurer is concerned with minimizing her personal loss, she will not salt the sidewalk. In this setting, a rule of no liability is not an efficient liability rule.

It should be noted that even with a rule of no liability, the injurer may nevertheless take due care for other reasons. For example, perhaps she is concerned about the victim's well-being, and does not want to be partly responsible for his slipping and hurting himself. Or maybe she feels that if she salts the sidewalk in front of her house, her neighbors may be inspired to salt the sidewalk in front of their houses, making the neighborhood safer for everyone. As we will discuss in the next chapter, liability rules do not exist independently of other forces that influence behavior. This can be a crucial point when deciding which liability rule to apply in any given setting.

Strict Liability

Under a rule of strict liability, the injurer is *always* liable for the victim's damages. One common misperception about strict liability is that it does not provide the injurer with the incentive to take due care because if she always has to pay damages, why should she incur any additional costs by taking care? It is true that if an accident occurs, the injurer will be liable for damages of $100 *regardless* of how much care she takes. However, the amount of care she takes will affect the probability of the accident occurring, and this will affect her *expected* damages.

What does the injurer gain if she spends $3 to salt the sidewalk? She lowers her expected damages from $10 (that is, 10 percent of $100) to $2 (that is, 2 percent of $100), for a savings of $8, which is a good deal for her. Notice how strict liability makes the injurer's personal-loss calculation identical to the social-loss calculation. It is in society's best interest to have the injurer spend $3 to save $8. And while the injurer does not have to care about what is in society's best interest, strict liability makes her behave *as if* she does care. In this setting, strict liability is an efficient liability rule.

Negligence

Under a rule of negligence, the injurer is liable for the victim's damages only if she takes *less* than due care. Compared to the previous two rules, which are both *no-fault* rules, negligence is a *fault* rule. What this means is that the injurer's liability will be determined by how much care she takes. With no liability, the injurer is never liable, so her care level is not an issue. With strict liability, the injurer is always liable, independent of her care level. The negligence rule allows the injurer to avoid liability by taking due care, thus demonstrating that the accident is not her fault.

In this example, will it be in the injurer's best interest to take due care? If she doesn't take due care she will be liable for the expected damages of $10. If she takes due care, it will cost her $3, but then she completely avoids liability so she bears no additional cost. It certainly is worth it for her to spend $3 to save $10. In this setting, the negligence rule is an efficient liability rule. Comparing across all three liability rules, if the goal is to provide the injurer with the incentive to take due care and minimize the social loss of the accident, only strict liability and negligence achieve that goal; no liability does not.

Here's one question that the current example cannot address: will the injurer ever have an incentive to take *more* than due care? In the icy sidewalk example, the injurer only has two possible levels of care to take, and due care is already at the higher level. There simply isn't a "more than due care" level to consider. So let's change the example. We will keep everything the same, except give the injurer one more option: after she salts the sidewalk, she can clear the ice with a shovel. If she does this, the probability that the victim slips on the ice is reduced to zero, but she must incur an *additional* cost of $9 (for a *total* cost of $12—$3 for salting and $9 for clearing).

From a social-loss perspective, clearing the ice is not efficient. The total social loss only includes the cost of care of $12, since there are no expected damages when the probability of the victim's slipping is reduced to zero. Both other care levels have lower social-loss values ($10 for doing nothing, and $5 for salting), and the due care level remains at salting the sidewalk. Quite simply, although clearing the ice eliminates the possibility of the victim's slipping, it does so at too great a cost. Lowering the probability from 2 percent to zero lowers the expected damages from $2 to zero, but it costs an additional $9 to do so. It is not in society's best interest to use $9 of resources to save $2.

This is a good opportunity to briefly discuss the importance of understanding precisely what the social objective is. Due care is not a fixed concept; it depends on the social objective being pursued. For example, assume the social objective is to minimize the probability of the accident's occurring. Due care would now be for the injurer to clear the ice off the sidewalk. You can argue that it is not worth spending $9 to save $2, but the counter to that argument is that society no longer is concerned with how much it costs to reduce the probability to zero, as long as the new objective is achieved. It is doubtful that many economists would embrace this new objective, but that doesn't mean there aren't others who would. In fact, when it comes to safety issues, it is not uncommon to see regulations proposed and enacted that often cost far more than their dollar worth in terms of safety improvements.

Let's stick with the objective of minimizing social loss as defined above. The due care level is for the injurer to salt the sidewalk but not to clear the ice. Under a rule of negligence, the injurer avoids liability if she salts. What does it cost her to clear the ice—an additional $9. What does she gain if she clears the ice—absolutely nothing. Once liability is avoided by salting, the injurer has no further incentive to increase her care level. The negligence rule does not give the injurer the incentive to take more than due care.

Under a rule of strict liability, the injurer can never avoid liability *unless* she can reduce the probability of the accident to zero. But as mentioned above, strict liability makes the injurer behave as if she cares about the social loss, even though she only cares about her personal loss. She can reduce the probability to zero and save the expected damages, but it would cost her an additional $9 to do so. Just as it makes no sense for society to want to spend $9 to save $2, it makes no sense for the injurer to want to do that either. The strict liability rule does not give the injurer the incentive to take more than due care.

The above numerical example, while depicting a simple tort setting, illustrates some of the key concepts that can be applied to much more general settings. In a unilateral setting, where the injurer is the only one who can affect the probability of the accident, both strict liability and negligence are efficient liability rules. There is, however, a slight difference as to *why* each rule is efficient. With strict liability, the injurer takes due care to *optimize on the margin*. This means that the injurer will continue to spend one dollar on care as long as it lowers expected damages by more than one dollar. When she reaches the due care level, one more dollar on care will lower expected damages by less than one dollar (this must be true by the definition of due care). Although she can never avoid liability, she will eventually reach the point where it simply is not cost effective for her to take any more care.

With the negligence rule, it isn't exactly optimizing on the margin that explains the injurer's behavior. As she increases her care level and approaches due care, each dollar spent on care is reducing expected damages by more than a dollar. But once she reaches the due care level, she is not spending that last dollar just to save a dollar; she is spending a marginal dollar to save the *total* liability. These slight differences in how the two rules create incentives to behave will become more important when we look at other tort settings in the next two chapters.

If both strict liability and negligence are efficient rules, how do we distinguish between them when considering which one to apply in tort settings? While providing the incentive to take due care is of primary concern to economists, it is not the only dimension in which the rules can be compared. Let's consider some other issues.

Claims Costs

Under strict liability, every time an accident occurs the victim has a legitimate claim. Whether the case goes to court or is settled beforehand, there are costs to bringing claims forward for every case. Thus, strict liability is often associated with a tremendous amount of claims costs. This is often considered one of the most serious shortcomings of strict liability. The negligence rule, on the other hand, is not predicted to lead to many claims. The rule itself gives the injurer the incentive to take due care to avoid liability. To the extent that victims (or their lawyers) understand this, successful claims are only likely to be made against injurers who take less than due care. One of the strongest advantages of the negligence rule is that it is efficient in terms of care *and* does not create a lot of claims costs.

Information Costs

Claims costs deal with the total number of claims that are made against injurers. Information costs, on the other hand, deal with the *per claim* costs of applying a liability rule. Strict liability has very low information costs. The court basically needs to determine two things: did an accident occur, and is there an identifiable injurer? Because strict liability is a no-fault rule, the court does not have to address the level of care the injurer was taking. But this is not the case with the negligence rule.

Critics of the negligence rule usually first and foremost point to the incredible difficulties in applying it. Two important pieces of information are needed for the court to apply this rule: the due care level of the injurer, and her actual care level. These can be very difficult to determine, especially with a high degree of accuracy. Even in a simple example like the icy sidewalk, the court needs to know the costs of care to determine due care. And although that example has simple dimensions of care to consider—do nothing, salt, or clear the ice—a slightly more realistic example can quickly become more complex.

For example, what is meant by "salting" the sidewalk? How much salt is enough? Does it depend on how thick the ice is, or what the weather forecast is? And what about determining the cost of clearing the ice? Does that depend on the age or physical condition of the injurer? Should she be responsible for hiring someone to do it if she's not physically capable? Can the court determine how good a job was done salting or clearing the ice? Now imagine the questions that need to be addressed for far more complex tort settings, such as those dealing with product defects or medical malpractice, the topics of the next two chapters. Can we ever rely on the court to establish the correct due care and actual care levels in these settings?

On top of these information costs, or because of them, there is another potential problem with the negligence rule due to its complexity: if the court makes a mistake using the rule, either in estimating due care or actual care, this can affect the behavior of the injurer. An improperly applied negligence rule can affect the efficiency of the rule, leading the injurer to take either too much or too little care. This is no small problem, as it works against one of the original strengths of the rule—its ability to provide the injurer with the incentive to take due care. We will study this particular problem in more detail in chapter 9.

One last point should briefly be mentioned concerning the no-liability rule. Although it falls short of the strict liability and negligence rules because it does not provide the injurer with the incentive to take any care, it does have one phenomenal advantage over both of those rules—it is a *costless* rule to use. Under no liability, there are no claims costs and no information costs. And if, as mentioned above, there are other forces that create incentives for the injurer to take care, a costless rule is one that must seriously be considered, at least in certain tort settings such as product liability, discussed in the next chapter.

Victim's Care Levels

In many accident settings, not only does the injurer have the ability to affect the probability of an accident's occurring, so does the victim. These are known as *bilateral* accident settings. Suppose that in the icy sidewalk example, the victim can wear boots to reduce the probability that he will slip on the ice. Now the victim has two care levels to consider—wear boots or not wear boots. Without using numbers, let's assume that the due care levels in this case are for the injurer to salt the ice *and* for the victim to wear boots. By definition of due care, this combination of care levels minimizes the social loss of the accident. Do the liability rules provide the incentives for the injurer and the victim to *simultaneously* take due care?

Let's first think about the strict liability rule and the victim's behavior. From a social perspective, we want the victim to wear boots. This means that whatever it costs him to wear boots, that cost is less than the reduction in expected damages. Assume that he has no interest in wearing boots other than to reduce the probability of slipping on the ice. Does it make sense for him to incur the cost of wearing boots under a rule of strict liability? It does not.

What does it gain him to incur the cost? It gains him nothing at all because he will be fully compensated for his damages by the injurer regardless of his wearing boots. You may be tempted to argue that he will still wear boots to lower his probability of slipping, but this is not the case. When the victim is fully compensated for damages, he is technically indifferent to the accident occurring and the accident not occurring. In simple terms, he no longer cares if he slips on the ice and hurts himself.

Economic reasoning can seem quite strange at times. Does it make sense to think of someone not caring about being hurt? It all depends on how you think about the meaning of "being hurt." If the victim's full damages can be monetized, and that amount is, for example, $100, the victim is considered *made whole* when he is compensated exactly $100. The concept of "made whole" means that the victim is in the same position *as if the accident never occurred*. This is why full compensation makes the victim indifferent to the accident occurring and not occurring. If this still seems strange to you, that's because it is, but in a specific way.

The result that the victim has no incentive to take care under strict liability is perfectly sound from a *theoretical* perspective. He never suffers any net damage when compensation is taken into account, so he has no reason to spend even one dollar on care. From a real-world perspective, however, this is highly unlikely to be true. Compensation rarely makes a victim whole. There may be costs associated with the accident that are not included in tort damages. For example, perhaps the court awards damages to cover medical bills and lost wages from time missed at work, but not for any pain and suffering the victim incurs. This undercompensation would leave the victim worse off after the accident occurs. On the other hand, it may even be that the victim *prefers* the accident to occur. If the court overcompensates the victim, such as by punishing the injurer and awarding excessive damages, the victim is made better off after the accident occurs.

Whatever the case may be, there is one unambiguous fact—the strict liability rule does not provide the victim with the incentive to take due care. Even if it is unrealistic to think of the victim as being made whole, it is certainly the case that the victim does not bear his full damages when strict liability is being used. Whether this encourages the victim to take less than due care or no care at all, his incentive to behave efficiently is dampened by the rule. Furthermore, strict liability may no longer create the incentive for the injurer to behave efficiently—she may take *more* than due care.

Consider the following scenario. You are strictly liable for any automobile accident you have with pedestrians, regardless of how the pedestrians are behaving. If they are taking due care when crossing streets, you will optimize on the margin for your care level *given* that they are taking due care. But with strict liability and full compensation for damages, pedestrians will not have the incentive to take due care—they will take less (or no) care. How does this influence your behavior?

Imagine now that you are driving in an area where pedestrians are being careless—crossing in the middle of the street, or against red lights, or without looking both ways, and so on. If you maintain the same care level you did when pedestrians were also taking due care, the probability of your being in an accident must increase after they become more careless. Because you are still strictly liable, you respond to the more dangerous situation by increasing your care level. You still optimize on the margin, but now it is a *different* margin. Thus, if you were taking due care before, you will take more than due care afterward. In general, strict liability provides an incentive for the injurer to take more than due care when victims are taking less than due care.

It may seem that if the injurer takes more than due care, and the victim takes less than due care, strict liability may still be an efficient rule because the two effects balance out. But this is not the case. To minimize the social loss of the accident in a bilateral setting, both parties must simultaneously take due care. *Any* other combination of care levels must necessarily increase the social loss. Simply put, strict liability is not an efficient liability rule in a bilateral accident setting. But what about the negligence rule?

In a bilateral accident setting, the negligence rule provides the incentives for *both* the injurer and the victim to behave efficiently. The injurer will take due care to completely avoid liability, and this will leave the victim *always* liable for his damages. How will the victim behave? He will optimize on the margin, meaning it will be in his best interest to keep spending one dollar on care to lower expected damages by more than one dollar. Eventually, when he reaches the due care level, the next dollar spent will lower expected damages by less than one dollar, so he will not have an incentive to exceed due care. In a sense, the victim is "strictly liable" only when the injurer is taking due care. This gives the victim the incentive to optimize on the *correct* margin. The fact that the negligence rule is an efficient liability rule in a bilateral accident setting provides a strong argument in its favor over strict liability.

Activity Levels

In addition to how much care an injurer (or victim) takes, there is the issue of *how often* she engages in whatever activity is being considered. While greater care reduces the probability of an accident, a higher activity level typically increases it. For example, each time you drive your car, there are numerous dimensions of care to consider: how fast are you driving, whether your headlights are on, whether you are obeying the traffic lights and stop signs, whether you are sober, whether you are texting, and so on. Let's assume that you take due care across every dimension, but there is still always a possibility that you will be involved in an accident with a pedestrian. The more often you drive your car, even if always taking due care, the more likely it is that you will be involved in an accident. If it is important to control your activity level, how can liability rules do so?

First consider the negligence rule. If you take less than due care, in any dimension, you will be liable for the victim's damages. But if you take due care, you will always avoid liability. We know that the negligence rule gives you the incentive to take due care, which means you will never be liable *regardless* of how often you drive your car. The negligence rule, then, does not control your activity level. Under strict liability, however, your activity level will be controlled. Because you are always liable, you not only need to optimize on the margin in terms of care level, you need to optimize on *every* margin. When considering how often to drive your car, strict liability will have you consider all the costs and benefits of that activity, including the possibility of tort liability if you are in an accident.

In general, an injurer's activity level can be better controlled by strict liability than by negligence, so when her activity level is an important aspect of the tort setting, that can be a useful factor in choosing one rule over the other. But not only does the injurer's activity level matter, so can the victim's. The icy sidewalk example provides a good illustration. As far as the injurer is concerned, how often the sidewalk gets icy is completely out of her control—it depends on weather conditions. How often the victim walks along the icy sidewalk, however, is within his control. If the injurer's activity level plays no role in this setting, but the victim's is important, this is an argument in favor of the negligence rule over strict liability. The injurer will take due care to avoid liability, and the victim will need to optimize on every margin, including his activity level. On the other hand, with strict liability, the victim is never liable and will not have to control his activity level. So now we have a result that is opposite to the one above: if the victim's activity level is important to control, the negligence rule is favored over strict liability.

It should be noted that, in determining liability, the courts are rarely interested in addressing the following question: *should* you have been undertaking the activity at the time of the accident? For example, if you drive to the office every day even though you live just a short walk away, and you are involved in an accident, the court is not going to hold you liable because you shouldn't have been driving such a short distance. Trying to determine an "optimal" activity level is extremely difficult to do. Instead, liability rules can be used to *indirectly* control activity. Strict liability controls the injurer's, and negligence controls the victim's, but neither rule can simultaneously control both.

Victim's Fault

One thing that both strict liability and negligence have in common is that in their implementation, neither rule addresses the behavior of the victim. Strict liability is a no-fault rule, and so it doesn't address the behavior of either party. While negligence is a fault rule, it addresses the behavior of the injurer, and *only* the injurer. If, for example, both the injurer and the victim take due care, the injurer avoids liability independent of the victim's also behaving efficiently. Likewise, if both take less than due care, the injurer is liable independent of the victim's also behaving inefficiently. Some legal analysts favor a liability rule that explicitly considers the fault of the victim in determining injurer liability. One such rule is known as *contributory negligence.*

There are a few rules that use a contributory negligence component, but the one we will discuss here is exactly the opposite of the negligence rule (it is known as *strict liability plus contributory negligence*, but we will refer to it simply as *contributory negligence*): if the victim takes due care, he avoids liability; if the victim takes less than due care, he is liable for damages. Contributory negligence, then, does not consider the care level of the injurer—her liability depends only on the actions of the victim.

Contributory negligence is often praised for improving on strict liability's weaknesses as a liability rule. We have seen that, in a bilateral accident setting, strict liability is an inefficient rule in that it does not give the victim the incentive to take due care, and this may cause the injurer to take more than due care. By adding contributory negligence, the victim now has a strong incentive to take due care—he will avoid liability if he does. By taking due care, the victim shifts liability to the injurer, and she now has the incentive to optimize on the margin and also take due care. Furthermore, the injurer will be optimizing on the *correct* margin, as she will be strictly liable while the victim is taking due care. Thus, unlike strict liability, contributory negligence is an efficient liability rule that minimizes the social loss of accidents.

How does contributory negligence compare to strict liability in terms of claims costs? To the extent that the victim takes due care (which he has the incentive to do), there will be many claims. But in situations when, for whatever reasons, the victim takes less than due care, he will not have a successful claim. In short, we should expect to see no more, and possibly fewer, claims with contributory negligence when compared to strict liability.

In terms of information costs, however, contributory negligence performs poorly relative to strict liability. As a fault rule, contributory negligence faces the same implementation problems found with the negligence rule. To apply the rule, the court has to determine the victim's due care level and actual care level. As argued above with negligence, this may be very difficult to do, and is likely to involve inaccuracies. Strict liability, as a no-fault rule, has low implementation costs.

So how do the contributory negligence and strict liability rules ultimately compare? When applying a fault rule to the victim, the benefit in terms of minimizing social loss is offset by the substantial increase in implementation costs. But this exact trade-off can be identified when comparing the negligence rule to strict liability—when applying a fault rule to the *injurer*, the benefit in terms of minimizing social loss is offset by the substantial increase in implementation costs. Because strict liability and contributory negligence have high claims costs, and negligence generally has low claims costs, an important question needs to be addressed: if the efficiency gain of using a fault rule over a no-fault rule is worth the implementation costs, why ever use a high-claims-cost fault rule over a low-claims-cost fault rule? In other words, why ever bother using contributory negligence over negligence?

While much of the scholarly literature debates the use of fault rules versus no-fault rules, it is also interesting to compare and contrast different fault rules. We already know that contributory negligence has higher claims costs compared to negligence, so what advantages does it offer? One clear distinction involves activity levels. Because both rules are efficient, both the injurer and the victim have the incentive to take due care. When this occurs, negligence places liability on the victim and controls his activity level, and contributory negligence places liability on the injurer and controls her activity level. If it is important to control one specific party's activity level, this can be a factor in choosing one rule over the other.

Another way to distinguish between the two fault rules is to consider their implementation costs. Both rules are costly to implement, but the key question is, what are their *relative* costs? The negligence rule requires information about due care and actual care levels of the injurer. Contributory negligence requires similar information, but for the victim. If, in a particular tort setting, the court has more information about the injurer, this suggests an advantage in using the negligence rule; more information about the victim favors using contributory negligence.

Finally, although not of primary importance to most economists, many legal scholars argue in favor of strict liability because it provides *compensation* to the victim. After all, in our simple, unilateral accident setting, it is the injurer who causes the accident and the victim who suffers the damages. Regardless of the efficiency of the negligence rule, isn't it "fair" for the injurer to compensate the victim? If victim compensation is an objective in choosing between liability rules, strict liability has an advantage over negligence. In a bilateral accident setting, however, strict liability does not provide the victim with the proper incentive to take due care. In that situation, contributory negligence can have an advantage over negligence. By adding contributory negligence to strict liability, the victim not only has an incentive to take due care to avoid liability, but also will be compensated even when the injurer takes due care. The issue of victim compensation will be further discussed when considering product liability in the next chapter.

The above analysis can be succinctly summarized with an understanding of one general principle —*every* liability rule has some advantage (and disadvantage) over the other rules. In *Indiana Harbor*, which we now return to, the court considers the key issue to involve the injurer's activity level. If the injurer's activity level is important to control, this strengthens the argument for using strict liability; if it isn't important to control, this weakens the argument.

Court's Decision

Indiana Harbor presented two claims against Cyanamid: (1) Cyanamid should be held liable for damages because it was negligent in maintaining the leased tank car, and (2) Cyanamid should be held strictly liable for damages because it was involved in the highly dangerous activity of transporting a toxic chemical through the Chicago metropolitan area. Presenting more than one claim is a reasonably common litigation strategy—try to win through as many avenues as possible. But in an earlier appeals decision, the federal court would not consider the two claims as anything more than separate theories involving the same facts. So the issue the court addressed was to decide on using one rule *or* the other. Thus, it boiled down to the "great debate" in tort law—which rule should be used, strict liability or negligence?

In his opinion, Judge Posner clearly explains one of the major advantages of strict liability over the negligence rule—strict liability controls the injurer's activity level:

> The baseline common law regime of tort liability is negligence. When it is a workable regime, because the hazards of an activity can be avoided by being careful (which is to say, nonnegligent), there is no need to switch to strict liability. Sometimes, however, a particular type of accident cannot be prevented by taking care but can be avoided, or its consequences minimized, by shifting the activity in which the accident occurs to another locale, where the risk of harm of an accident will be less, or by reducing the scale of the activity in order to minimize the number of accidents caused by it. By making the actor strictly liable—by denying him in other words an excuse based on his inability to avoid accidents by being more careful—we give him an incentive, missing in a negligence regime, to experiment with methods of preventing accidents that involve not great exertions of care, assumed to be futile, but instead relocating, changing, or reducing (perhaps to the vanishing point) the activity giving rise to the accident.

Is this case one in which the injurer's activity level needed to be controlled with strict liability? The court did not think so.

In reaching its decision, the court referred to section 520 of the *Restatement (Second) of Torts*, an influential treatise on American tort law issued by the American Law Institute for the purpose of informing judges and lawyers about common law principles:

> In determining whether an activity is abnormally dangerous, the following factors are to be considered:
>   (a) existence of a high degree of risk of some harm to the person, land or chattels of others;

(b) likelihood that the harm that results from it will be great;

(c) inability to eliminate the risk by the exercise of reasonable care;

(d) extent to which the activity is not a matter of common usage;

(e) inappropriateness of the activity to the place where it is carried on; and

(f) extent to which its value to the community is outweighed by its dangerous attributes. (quoted in Sykes 2007, 1913)

The court then applied some of these factors to the facts in the case.

The court did not find that the leak in this case was caused by any corrosive properties inherent in acrylonitrile. Instead, it was believed that the railroad car used to ship the chemical had not been carefully maintained or inspected. *Had* the railroad car been properly maintained, the likelihood of a chemical spill was found to be negligible. What about concern over the fact that the spill occurred in a densely populated area? While true, the problem with this concern is that it ignores the technological aspects of railway shipping. The railroad system operates with hubs and spokes, and hubs typically are in large metropolitan areas. The shipping of hazardous chemicals by rail inevitably involves routes that go through metropolitan areas, and to avoid these areas (if feasible) would likely require a substantial increase in shipping costs. Because of these findings, the court concluded that strict liability was not the appropriate rule to apply. The case was remanded back to the lower court for consideration of Indiana Harbor's claim under the negligence rule.

Two legal scholars, Sykes (2007) and Rosenberg (2007), publishing in highly prestigious law journals, argue for a reconsideration of the approach taken in Judge Posner's opinion. Both commentators are not overly concerned with Posner's analysis *given* his reliance on the Restatement in considering the role of strict liability in this case. Instead, they question why he relied on the Restatement at all. They both see the Restatement's criteria as the wrong way to approach the facts in this case, and believe that Judge Posner overlooked a simpler way to resolve Indiana Harbor's claim against Cyanamid.

For example, one of the advantages of strict liability discussed above is that it involves low information costs to implement. In using the Restatement's factors, however, Judge Posner had to work through a fairly complicated and speculative cost-benefit analysis, thus undermining one of the strengths of the strict liability rule. As one commentator observes, "Testing the efficacy of strict liability by determining whether the defendant had reasonable options for reducing its activity level—in *Indiana*

Harbor Belt, for example, rerouting chemical-laden tank cars—involves precisely the negligence-style cost-benefit analysis of activity level that generally proves too expensive and complex for courts to perform effectively and that justifies turning to strict liability in the first place" (Rosenberg 2007, 1215). It should be noted, however, that Judge Posner believed that the issue of applying strict liability to the facts of *Indiana Harbor* was novel to Illinois case law. It is possible, then, that whatever information costs were incurred in this case to *rule out* strict liability, these costs would not have to be incurred in similar future cases.

Another issue has to do with the Restatement's factor (e), which Judge Posner is mostly concerned with. This factor may have little to do with the injurer's activity level. Activity level issues are primarily concerned with "how often" questions. In this case, factor (e) is more concerned with *where* the activity takes place, as opposed to how often it takes place. If Judge Posner can apply a cost-benefit analysis to conclude that the hub-spoke system of railway transportation through metropolitan areas is in itself due care in shipping hazardous chemicals, why is that analysis being used to determine if strict liability should apply in this case? If the court lacks the ability to determine what is due care in shipping routes, *that fact* may be an argument in favor of strict liability, as that rule forces the injurer to optimize on all margins. This leads one commentator to suggest that "Judge Posner might have done more to debunk the Restatement (Second)'s reliance on this factor" (Sykes 2007, 1926).

Finally, both commentators suggest that considering this case as involving tort liability was perhaps misplaced. All the potential parties involved in this case—Indiana Harbor, Cyanamid, Missouri Pacific, and Conrail—were part of a contractual network. Indiana Harbor was clearly experienced in handling railway cars carrying hazardous chemicals. Had it assumed the risk of damages when compensated for accepting the Cyanamid car at its switching line? If Indiana Harbor did not want to assume the risk of damages, could its contracts have specified who would bear the damages in case of an accidental spill?

But as we have seen in chapter 5, contractual negotiations can be costly, and postbreach damage remedies can be difficult to anticipate and may further enhance the prebreach negotiation costs. Also, contractual breach cases are costly to litigate and resolve. Thus, there may be strong reasons for using tort law instead of contract law to address the issues in this case. Many commentators, however, tend to favor contractual solutions over tort ones when the tort setting involves parties involved in a preexisting contractual relationship, arguing that the administrative costs of using tort law tend to grossly outweigh the administrative costs of using contract law. This debate among some of the top legal scholars further illustrates that not only is it difficult to choose between tort liability rules, it is also difficult to choose between completely different systems of law when resolving these types of disputes.

Discussion Questions

1. Consider the following (hypothetical) liability rule. The injurer will be held strictly liable for any damages that the victim suffers, but the payment will not be transferred to the victim. Instead, the payment will be collected by the state. In other words, tort liability will be treated as a fine paid to the state, as opposed to restitution paid to the victim. Thoroughly evaluate this liability rule, especially when compared to the traditional strict liability rule discussed throughout this chapter.

2. Another fault rule that is commonly used in several tort settings is known as *comparative negligence*. This rule is very similar to the negligence rule: if the injurer takes due care, she avoids liability regardless of what the victim is doing; if the injurer takes less than due care and the victim takes due care, the injurer is liable for damages. But here is where the rules differ: under negligence, if the injurer and victim both take less than due care, the injurer is liable; under comparative negligence, when both parties take less than due care, the damages will be *shared* between them, and the share will depend on the court's assessment of each party's responsibility. For example, if the court concludes that the injurer was 80 percent at fault, the injurer will pay 80 percent of the damages, and the victim will bear the remaining 20 percent. Provide a thorough evaluation of this rule, especially when compared to other fault rules such as negligence and contributory negligence.

3. Consider this description of the doctrine of *last clear chance*:

   A rule of law in determining responsibility for damages caused by negligence, which provides that if the plaintiff (the party suing for damages) is negligent, that will not matter if the defendant (the party being sued for damages caused by his/her negligence) could still have avoided the accident by reasonable care in the final moments (no matter how slight) before the accident. The theory is that although the plaintiff may have been negligent, his/her negligence no longer was the cause of the accident because the defendant could have prevented the accident. Most commonly applied to auto accidents, a typical case of last clear chance would be when one driver drifts over the center line, and this action was noted by an oncoming driver who proceeds without taking simple evasive action, crashed into the first driver and is thus liable for the injuries to the first driver who was over the line. In the few states which apply the strict "contributory negligence" rule which keeps a negligent plaintiff from recovering damages from a negligent defendant, "last clear chance" can save the plaintiff's lawsuit. (from *law.com*)

Evaluate the doctrine of last clear chance, especially in relation to other liability rules discussed in this chapter.

References

Rosenberg, D. 2007. "The Judicial Posner on Negligence versus Strict Liability: *Indiana Harbor Belt Railroad Co. v. American Cyanamid Co." Harvard Law Review* 120:1210–22.

Sykes, A. O. 2007. "Strict Liability versus Negligence in Indiana Harbor." *University of Chicago Law Review* 74:1911–31.

CHAPTER EIGHT

Should Firms Be Held Liable for Product Defects?

Voss v. Black and Decker *(1983) and the Economics of Product Liability*

Facts

Carlton Voss was using a circular power saw to cut two-by-four boards. The saw is designed with a housing that covers all but the lower portion of the circular blade, and there is a guard on that lower portion that is designed to move back as the blade makes contact with the wood. The purpose of the guard is to protect the operator, but for the saw to operate properly, part of the blade must always be exposed to facilitate initial contact with wood, even when the guard is in closed position.

While Voss was using the saw to make a cut, he hit a knot in the wood and this caused the saw to project upward. The guard properly closed, but the very lowest portion of the blade was still exposed, and Voss suffered a serious laceration to his hand and had part of his thumb severed. It was taken as fact that the saw and the guard were working properly, so at issue in this case is whether there was a *design defect* in the manufacture of the saw. That is, could the saw have been designed differently such that the current design would be deemed defective?

Court's Decision

The appeals court decision in this case did not decide on liability. Instead, it questioned the lower court judge's instructions to the jury. The judge did not allow the jury to consider strict liability when assessing the plaintiff's claim against the firm; the jury could only consider whether the firm was negligent in its design of the circular saw. The jury found that there was no negligence, and Voss would have to bear the burden of his damages. The upper court, however, decided the jury could be instructed to consider strict liability, so they returned the case to the lower court for a new trial to take place. (No further public record of this case can be found; therefore, it is likely that it was finally settled out of court.)

The difficult aspect of any design defect case is to determine if the product's design is actually defective. The court addressed this issue:

We have held that a defectively designed product is one which, at the time it leaves the seller's hands, is in a condition not reasonably contemplated by the ultimate consumer and is unreasonably dangerous for its intended use; that is one whose utility does not outweigh the danger inherent in its introduction into the stream of commerce.

Then the court continued in distinguishing between strict liability and the negligence rule:

Strict products liability for design defect thus differs from a cause of action for a negligently designed product in that the plaintiff is not required to prove that the manufacturer acted unreasonably in designing the product. The focus shifts from the conduct of the manufacturer to whether the product, as designed, was not reasonably safe. A manufacturer is held liable regardless of his lack of actual knowledge of the condition of the product because he is in the superior position to discover any design defects and alter the design before making the product available to the public. Liability attaches when the product, as designed, presents an unreasonable risk of harm to the user.

Because of the court's distinction between the negligence rule and strict liability in determining the existence of a design defect, it believed that a jury could legitimately deny a claim when applying the negligence standard and support the same claim when applying the court's interpretation of a strict liability rule. But as we will see in this chapter, an important point that has been raised in the product liability scholarly literature is that there may be little distinction between the two liability rules in design defect cases.

Economic Analysis

Product liability is a branch of tort law that has received a substantial amount of scholarly attention. This is not surprising given that manufactured products affect nearly every aspect of our daily lives, and the risk of product-related injuries is ever present. The typical debate follows the discussion of the previous chapter: should a strict liability rule or a negligence rule govern product-related accidents? But in addition, as we will discuss later in this chapter, some scholars believe that a no-liability rule is a perfectly viable rule in a product-related setting. These scholars argue for a substantial downsizing of the tort system with respect to product defects.

When examining the efficiency of liability rules in a product defect case, it is crucial to distinguish between two types of defects—a manufacturing defect and a design defect. The Voss case, as mentioned above, involves a design defect. The circular saw was performing just as designed. In contrast, a manufacturing defect exists when a product is not as designed. For example, suppose that in *Voss* the guard on the circular saw did not properly close when the saw jumped up after hitting a knot in the wood. This would be a manufacturing defect because the guard was designed to close in just such a situation. But determining how much of the lower part of the blade must always be exposed when the guard is properly closed is a design issue. To keep the distinctions between these two types of defects clear, it is useful to analyze each separately.

Manufacturing Defects

In any manufacturing process, there is always a chance that some of the units produced will be defective, meaning that they will not be as designed. For example, a somewhat common manufacturing defect involves the finding of a foreign object in food. While a can of vegetables is certainly not designed to have a dead cockroach in it, there is always a chance that such a can will end up on a store shelf and be purchased by someone. Using this scenario, let's consider a hypothetical numerical example to help illustrate some key points about the economics of manufacturing defects and product liability law. (Some of these points will be similar to those made in the previous chapter concerning more general tort settings, so in these instances we can be fairly brief.)

Assume that a firm produces one million units of canned vegetables using a manufacturing process that allows for a two-in-a-million chance of a dead cockroach ending up in a can. Thus, *on average*, we expect two units of the canned vegetables to have a cockroach in them. If a consumer does purchase such a can, let's further assume that the damage caused by the defect will be $100. The firm is aware of this potential defect, and has the ability to alter its manufacturing process to lower the defect rate, but it will have to incur a cost to do so: it will cost $75 to lower the defect rate to one in a million, and it will cost *an additional* $150 to lower it to zero. (Also note that this is a *unilateral* accident setting, since the victim's behavior does not affect the probability of the accident's occurring.) With three potential defect rates—two in a million, one in a million, and zero—which rate is the efficient one from a social perspective?

To determine the socially efficient outcome, we must consider both the costs and the benefits of lowering the defect rate. If the firm spends $75 to lower the rate to one in a million, one incidence of damages equal to $100 will be saved. This creates a *net savings* of $25, and this will reduce the social loss of the accident. If the firm spends an additional $150 to lower the defect rate to zero, another incidence of damages equal to $100 will be saved. This creates a *net loss* of $50, and this will increase the social loss of the accident. Of the three defect rates, then, the efficient rate is one in a million as it leads to the lowest social loss of the three rates.

For many manufacturing processes, it may be infeasible to eliminate *all* defective units simply due to technological constraints. But when it is feasible to do so, as in this example, it may be tempting to argue that it would be in society's best interest for the firm to produce no defective units. After all, isn't it just common sense to prefer safer products over defective ones? The sense of this statement depends on the social objective. If, for example, the policy goal is to eliminate all defective units, then the optimal solution is to have a zero defect rate. But this solution comes at a cost—reducing the rate from one in a million to zero is not a good deal. It doesn't mean that the objective of eliminating all risk is wrong; it just means that it is not an objective that most economists would be comfortable pursuing.

If we stick with the objective of achieving the efficient defect rate of one in a million, both the strict liability rule and the negligence rule will be efficient. A firm that is strictly liable has to optimize on the margin. Consider the $75 cost of reducing the defect rate from two in a million to one in a million. If the firm doesn't do that, it will face two defective units and have to pay damages of $200. If the firm does reduce the rate, it will spend $75 to save $100 in damages. That is a good deal for the firm. Now consider spending an additional $150 to reduce the rate from one in a million to zero. This will cost $150 but save only $100 in damages. This is not a good deal, so the firm *prefers* to be liable with a one-in-a-million rate than to completely avoid damages with a zero rate. Thus, the strict liability rule provides the firm with the incentive to behave precisely how society wants it to behave.

Under a negligence rule, the firm is held liable for damages if it fails to lower the defect rate to one in a million—the *due care* rate in this example. We already know that the firm has an incentive to lower the defect rate to one in a million because it only costs $75 to save the $100 in damages, but now the firm also saves the damages from the one-in-a-million units that will still be defective. Once at the due care level, the firm avoids liability for any defective units that remain. So once again, the negligence rule provides the incentive for the firm to behave precisely how society wants it to behave.

While both liability rules lead to the efficient defect rate, it is the information costs of applying each rule that lead to a strong argument against the negligence rule. It is important to note that with a manufacturing defect, the existence of a defect in and of itself does not imply that the firm is negligent (unless the optimal defect rate is zero). So, observing a manufacturing defect is where the analysis begins, not ends. To apply the negligence rule, the court has to determine not only the efficient defect rate, but also the actual defect rate that the firm was achieving. Let's make the court's job easier and (unrealistically) assume that the court can determine the actual defect rate and correctly conclude that one-in-a-million units will be defective. How, then, is the court to determine whether that defect rate is the efficient one? A typical manufacturing process is likely to involve numerous technological considerations, many of which will be well beyond the scope of a judge or jury to completely understand, even with the aid of expert witnesses. Under strict liability, on the other hand, no determination of the actual or efficient defect rate needs to be made. The court only needs to determine if an accident was caused by the product.

A related argument in favor of strict liability is that it provides an incentive for the firm to continually adopt new safety efforts as technological advances in the manufacturing process change over time. Whenever the firm determines the cost of a new safety effort is more than offset by the reduction in expected liability, the effort will be worth taking. But with the negligence rule, it is the court that must continually update its estimate of due care, and this can be a difficult and slow process. If the court has due care lagging behind what technology offers, the firm may have less reason to continually modify its manufacturing process. We would expect that a firm actually involved in the production process would be in the better position, relative to the court, to determine the value of technological advances. Strict liability takes advantage of this idea.

There is still at least one serious drawback to strict liability: it is a liability rule that is expected to lead to a tremendous amount of litigation. In effect, *every* manufacturing defect can lead to a claim against the firm. On the other hand, under the negligence rule a *successful* claim can only be made against a firm that was taking less than due care, and the rule itself does not give the firm an incentive to maintain an inefficient defect rate. Nevertheless, there is still the potential for claims as firms may at times be negligent, or as victims rely on the possibility of the negligence rule being misapplied by the courts.

Design Defects

In a manufacturing defect case, the existence of a defect is often obvious: a dead cockroach does not belong in a can of vegetables. While determining an optimal manufacturing defect rate can be very challenging to do, it is often not difficult to determine that a defect exists (either before or after an accident occurs). In design defect cases, however, the issue of determining if a defect exists is far more complex. *Every* product has a design. The key question, then, is—what is the optimal design for each product? We argued above that the advantage of a strict liability rule for manufacturing defects is that it places the burden on the firm to control its defect rate. Does this same advantage hold true for design defects?

In the excerpt from the court's opinion above, strict liability requires a determination that a product must be designed to be not reasonably safe to be considered defective. But what exactly is meant by *not reasonably safe*? Consider a compact car. It is well known that small cars are not as crashworthy as large cars. Compact cars may have an advantage in terms of price or gas mileage, but not in terms of avoiding injury in case of an accident. Does the design of a compact car, in and of itself, suggest that all such cars are defective? Are compact cars not reasonably safe? What about motorcycles? They are inherently risky products. Indeed, that is part of their appeal. Are all motorcycles not reasonably safe?

Obviously, every product that offers even the slightest risk of injury (and every other product as well) must have a final design before it can be sold to consumers. Just as obviously, the courts are not willing to consider all products that have some risk of injury associated with them as being defectively designed. So just how is a defective design established under a strict liability rule? Furthermore, and maybe even more important, is there truly a difference between strict liability and the negligence rule in a design defect case?

The modern analysis of strict liability for design defects is usually traced back to the work of legal scholar John Wade (1973), who proposed a *risk-utility test* that included seven factors:

1. The usefulness and desirability of the product—its utility to the user and to the public as a whole.
2. The safety aspects of the product—the likelihood that it will cause injury, and the probable seriousness of the injury.
3. The availability of a substitute product that would meet the same need and not be as unsafe.
4. The manufacturer's ability to eliminate the unsafe character of the product without impairing its usefulness or making it too expensive to maintain its utility.
5. The user's ability to avoid danger by the exercise of care in the use of the product.
6. The user's anticipated awareness of the dangers inherent in the product and their avoidability, because of the general public knowledge of the obvious condition of the product, or of the existence of suitable warnings or instructions.
7. The feasibility, on the part of the manufacturer, of spreading the loss by setting the price of the product or carrying liability insurance.

Economists are usually strong supporters of using cost-benefit analyses in evaluating social policy. The risk-utility test fits into that approach. It considers many of the factors that would be of prime importance to an economic analysis: the value of the product to consumers; the probability of an accident occurring; the extent of the damages; the cost of increased care; the consumer's ability to avoid the damages; the perception of risk, and so on. Yet one criticism of Wade's approach is that while risk-utility has the appearance of applying a cost-benefit analysis to product design, the seven-part test lacks a coherent and workable economic framework.

There have been several attempts to refine Wade's approach, perhaps the most economically sound by economist Kip Viscusi (1990, 614), who advances the following argument:

Dean Wade's original article enunciated the original basis for risk-utility analysis and outlined many of the considerations that enter, but it did not organize these considerations in any systematic manner. For instance, its benefits and

THE ECONOMICS OF PRODUCT LIABILITY

costs concerns are intermingled with specification of alternative types of tests to be undertaken. Subsequent legal scholarship has done little to improve upon this situation, as authors have occasionally suggested other sets of factors to be considered, but did not bring to bear any systematic conceptual framework for approaching the risk-utility judgment in a sound manner.

Viscusi, while embracing the spirit of Wade's approach, reconfigures risk-utility analysis into a three-step test.

The first step considers a *consumer's* risk-utility test. Would the consumer reap gains from trade from the suggested product design? Not all possible safety features would be of interest to consumers. For example, it certainly is technically feasible to design a car that can go no faster than thirty miles an hour. While this car may be safer in terms of fewer, and less dangerous, accidents, not many consumers would place a high value on such a car. If the consumer test does not pass, the suggested design is not considered optimal and should not be manufactured. If this test does pass, the second step is considered.

Step two builds on step one by considering the *producer's* profit. Would the producer reap gains from trade from the suggested product design? Some safety features, for example, may involve large up-front costs, such as reconfiguring an assembly line to produce a newly designed product. Consumers may be willing to pay the incremental cost of some specific safety feature, but the producer may not be able to easily recover its up-front investment (just as we saw in chapter 4 for the case of copyright protection). A product design that passes test one but does not pass test two should not be marketed. If both steps are passed, the final step is considered.

Step three considers a *social* risk-utility test. This involves the "big picture" of product design. Are there parties other than the consumers and producers who may also be affected by the product design? For example, an inherently risky product that nevertheless passes the first two tests may impose costs on others in private or social health insurance pools. If more accidents lead to higher medical costs, everyone in these pools will bear part of these costs. In theory, a social test tries to identify absolutely everyone who is affected by product design, and then considers the magnitude of the costs and benefits to these individuals. But this step only comes into play if the first two tests are passed. If that is the case, and the social test is not passed, the product should not be marketed.

While there are various degrees of praise and criticism of risk-utility tests in the academic literature, there is one thing that is not debated — these tests involve a tremendous amount of information costs to apply.

Viscusi explicitly identifies his risk-utility test as a form of the negligence liability rule, so the application of his three-step approach involves the usual complications associated with that rule. Ironically, while the title of Wade's original article refers to his risk-utility test as involving "strict tort liability," he later in his article admits that this really isn't the case. In Wade's (1973, 841) own words, when considering risk-utility analysis for design defects, "there is little difference here between the negligence action and the action for strict liability."

The difficulties involved in applying risk-utility tests have led many critics to strongly argue against their use. For one example, consider this eloquent argument put forth by Richard Epstein (1987, 469):

> My basic thesis is that rules should be preferred to balancing tests, both for basic liability and for defenses. To be sure, this opposition between rules and balancing is not ironclad. Every system has to have a little "give" in the joints to take care of the complex or unanticipated cases that do not fall neatly into the available paradigms. Bright line rules are not etched with laser sharpness. . . . The advantage of well-crafted rules is that they can account for the routine case in a predictable and sensible fashion, while reserving the give in the system for the few atypical cases that remain.

So all that's left for the critics of risk-utility to address is, what are its alternatives?

In terms of hard-and-fast rules, one that we are familiar with is strict liability. Certainly, it is feasible to adopt a rule of strict liability for design defect cases, but consider its main implication: *every* product-related injury will be susceptible to a liability claim. In contrast, strict liability for manufacturing defects only leads to claims for those units found to be not as designed, which can still be an overwhelming number of claims. Perhaps a contributory negligence defense for consumer product misuse can alleviate a number of claims, but will that be enough to keep claims costs manageable? Recall that contributory negligence gives the victim the incentive to take due care, which suggests that there still will be many claims. Furthermore, contributory negligence can involve high information costs when victims pursue liability claims in spite of the possibility of not being successful.

Yet strict liability for design defects does have one strong advantage. As we saw with manufacturing defects, strict liability will keep producers on their toes when considering how to design their products. By constantly facing liability from product-related accidents, producers will have the incentive to incorporate safety features that lower their expected liability by a greater amount than the costs they incur for increased safety. Still, with strict liability, short of not producing at all, producers will undoubtedly have to face an overwhelming number of claims.

There is another hard-and-fast rule that can replace a risk-utility test— have no product liability law at all (or at least greatly reduce its scope). This radical idea is well formulated by prominent law and economics scholars Mitchell Polinsky and Steven Shavell (2010a). They begin their critique of product liability law by offering an examination of the benefits of the law. There are three main benefits that they identify: (1) the law provides incentives for firms to produce safer products, (2) the law leads to an efficient increase in prices of risky products, and (3) the law provides compensation to injured consumers. The authors argue that these factors, while providing benefits, need to be seriously reevaluated to determine if they provide the level of benefits commonly believed to exist.

Product Liability and Safer Products

We know that liability rules can provide an incentive for firms to produce safer products. There is no doubt that, in isolation, this is a tremendous benefit of product liability law. But product liability law does not exist in isolation, and this leads to an important question: if there are other forces that provide an incentive for firms to produce safer products, is product liability law necessary? Two such other forces are markets and government regulation.

To some, there is a belief that a world without product liability law would allow firms to do whatever they wanted to do, including producing overly risky products. This would make some people uncomfortable. But economists know that market forces on their own can provide strong incentives for firms to produce safer products. Firms that gain a reputation for producing unsafe products are unlikely to survive in the market for very long. Even firms that suffer a random one-time unfortunate product defect incident may find themselves facing a long-term decline in sales. Furthermore, firms that aggressively pursue product safety improvements can often gain market share at the expense of their rivals that lag behind. And just as customer demand provides incentives for firms to produce products in the first place, the demand for safety provides incentives for firms to produce *safer* products.

Market forces are likely to be at their strongest when consumers are well informed about product risks. Consider the case where this isn't true, and a consumer is poorly informed instead. If a consumer is choosing between two products that are similar in function, but cannot determine which one is safer, the less safe one may be less expensive and, therefore, more likely to be purchased. To be willing to pay for safety features, a consumer must appreciate that these features exist and that they reduce product risk.

The question, then, is, how well informed are consumers about product risks? There is certainly no lack of available information sources: magazines, newspapers, television, various government agencies, and especially the Internet, are all excellent sources. Firms that produce unsafe products can be assured of having that information published *somewhere*. And let's not forget about word-of-mouth communications or consumer product reviews. How many of us read the one-star reviews on Amazon before we read the five-star ones? But even with a wealth of information sources, for market forces to work well consumers must actually access these sources and properly interpret the information that is available.

Market forces are likely to be at their strongest when we consider firms that widely sell many units, and firms that are diversified in their product line. Large national (or regional) firms may have much to lose with a poor reputation, and diversified firms that suffer a product defect in one line may be punished by the market across *all* their lines. Certainly, small (local) firms that try for a short-term gain without concern about their future reputation are less likely to be swayed by market forces to provide safer products. While market forces are not always going to provide incentives for firms to produce safer products, any firm that hopes to survive in the marketplace for a significant length of time must be concerned about its reputation, regardless of the potential threat of product liability litigation.

Government regulation is another force that induces firms to produce safer products. There are numerous government agencies that oversee safety standards for a wide variety of products: the National Highway Traffic Safety Administration (automobiles), the Food and Drug Administration (pharmaceuticals), the Federal Aviation Administration (aircraft), the Consumer Product Safety Commission (various consumer goods), and so on. These agencies determine and enforce safety standards, and punish (usually with fines) firms that do not adopt the required standards.

Critics often argue that because market forces can promote safety, the enforcement costs that regulatory agencies must incur can be wasteful. A common justification for government regulation, however, is that it is required precisely when market forces, for various reasons, are not sufficient to promote safety. The point here is not to weigh the costs and benefits of government regulation, but to compare the role of product liability law in a system that also allows for such regulation. And if the product liability system was suddenly to be disbanded, we would not immediately be thrust into a world in which there was no government oversight in promoting product safety.

It is not being argued here that product liability law has no value in promoting safety. Instead, its ability to promote safety must be evaluated within the proper context. How do market forces, government regulation, and product liability law all fit together? To what extent are these forces substitutes for each other? To what extent are they complements to each other? Can a product safety regime be identified that allows these forces to efficiently coexist? These are the key questions to address when arguing for or against the safety benefits of product liability law.

Product Liability and Efficient Prices

When consumers buy a product, in addition to the explicit monetary price they must pay, an implicit (nonmonetary) *risk premium* may also exist. In the absence of product liability, if consumers privately bear their own losses when a defect causes an accident, the product, in a sense, is more expensive for them to purchase. Thus, the *full price* consumers pay for a product includes monetary and nonmonetary components. From an efficiency standpoint, gains from trade exist when consumers value the product more than its full price. The optimal amount of units are sold when all consumers who value the product more than the full price buy it, and all consumers who value the product less than the full price do not buy it.

While this seems like a straightforward application of the concept of gains from trade, a complication arises when consumers are not perfectly informed about the product risks they face. Consider consumers who *underestimate* the product risk. How will this affect their purchasing decision? The *perceived* full price they have to pay is less than the true full price, meaning that the product appears less expensive to them. These consumers will purchase too many units of the product. Conversely, consumers who *overestimate* the product risk have a perceived full price that is greater than the true full price, and so they will purchase too few units of the product.

When consumers misperceive the true product risk, they no longer purchase the optimal amount of the product. This is where product liability can have a beneficial impact. If firms are strictly liable for product-related damages, they will incur not only an incremental production cost in selling their product, but also an expected liability cost. This additional cost raises the price of the product, but in an efficient way. The implicit risk-premium component of the price is now converted into an explicit monetary component. If consumers no longer bear their own risks due to product liability law, the monetary price they must pay is now equal to the true full price. In other words, it no longer matters what perception of risk consumers have — they will only buy the good if their value exceeds the monetary price, which is now equivalent to the socially efficient full price.

Even when consumers have perfect information about the product risks they face, this advantage of product liability can still hold. If consumers (as is quite common) have insurance policies that cover losses due to accidents, they don't actually bear the full risk of any product-related accidents — their insurance companies bear part of the loss. Without the efficient price adjustment brought about by product liability, then, consumers may purchase too many units of the product. So, product liability can correctly control the number of units purchased when consumers misperceive risk or whenever they do not bear the full losses they suffer through product-related accidents. It is possible, however, for product liability to have an inefficient impact on product prices, as we will discuss below when considering the costs of the tort system.

Product Liability and Victims' Compensation

By definition, victims of a product-related accident suffer losses. These losses typically involve monetary components, such as medical bills and lost wages, and nonmonetary components, including pain and suffering. Although compensation in and of itself tends to be more of an equity (distribution of wealth) issue than an efficiency issue, there are many who feel that victim compensation is the main goal of product liability law. As mentioned in chapter 7, if a product causes an injury, isn't it simply fair for the victim to be compensated by the producing firm? While the importance of this goal can certainly be debated, for now we will consider compensation as a legitimate concern and evaluate how well the product liability system achieves this goal.

There are a few problems with the notion of product liability providing adequate compensation to victims. The first is that a substantial number of people have some form of insurance coverage — health, property, life, disability — through private insurance markets or public insurance systems.

It is common for insurance contracts to include what is known as a *subrogation* clause. With subrogation, the insurance company is given the right to sue the firm in place of the victim. The victim, once compensated through the insurance company, cannot "double dip" and be compensated again through product liability. There are various arrangements that can be made based on how much compensation the victim receives through insurance, and what the actual tort award is, but the bottom line is that subrogation reduces the amount of compensation available to the victim *through* product liability.

The second problem is that the majority of product liability cases involve lawyer contingency fees, meaning that lawyers are paid only if they win a settlement for their clients. Although this allows many victims access to legal representation, these fees are routinely as much as one-third of the settlement award, thus significantly reducing the amount of compensation available to the victim. Finally, tort awards may take years to actually end up in the hands of the victims, and this delay also reduces the compensation value of product-related losses.

Taken together, these three benefits of product liability law do not present as strong a case for the law as is often believed, according to Polinsky and Shavell (2010a). Furthermore, regardless of how strong these benefits are, they are only part of the story—we must also consider the costs of the law. There are two main costs the authors identify, and not only can these costs be substantial, they are also far less subject to debate.

The first and most obvious costs are the administrative costs of maintaining the product liability legal system. It is not uncommon for studies to find that for every dollar spent by defendant firms in these cases, no more (and sometimes quite a bit less) than fifty cents of each dollar ends up in the hands of victims. In other words, for every dollar of compensation received by victims, at least one dollar of tort administrative costs is incurred. And these studies often do not consider other costs of the tort system, such as time costs to the litigants and judicial operating costs. Thus, it is an inescapable conclusion that the product liability system is an expensive one to maintain.

The second cost of the product liability system is related to the second benefit discussed above—how does liability affect product price? When liability efficiently affects product price, consumers must actually pay the true full price to purchase the good. This leads to the optimal number of units being purchased. But liability can affect product price in other ways, leading to an inefficiently high price and too few units being purchased.

The authors identify two sources of price distortions—litigation expenses and liability for nonmonetary losses. Firms facing product liability lawsuits obviously incur legal expenses. So, in addition to the expected liability raising the product price, the expected legal expenses further raise the price. This additional increase in price, however, does not correct for any consumers' misperception of risk, so it acts more like a tax on production and distorts the true full price of the product, leading to an inefficient reduction in consumption.

A similar (but more complicated) argument exists for having product liability hold firms liable for victims' monetary *and* nonmonetary damages. Briefly, it can be shown that in many situations, when individuals purchase health insurance, for example, they prefer to cover monetary losses such as medical bills but not nonmonetary losses such as pain and suffering. While pain and suffering are real damages, they often have no effect on the victims' value for money. In other words, being compensated with money for pain and suffering may not greatly improve a person's well-being (such as may be the case with financial compensation for the loss of a child). If this is true, there will be no gains from trade to purchase insurance for nonmonetary losses. Yet it is routinely the case that firms are held liable for nonmonetary damages in product liability cases, affecting the product price, and having consumers pay more for insurance through the product price than they would pay if they purchased insurance directly.

In all, Polinsky and Shavell offer the following conclusion:

> If our assessment of product liability is accepted, it implies that serious consideration should be given to curtailing such liability. This could be accomplished through application of legal doctrines that make the imposition of product liability depend on several factors suggested by our analysis. One is whether consumers are likely to know about a product's risk. Another is whether the product is subject to significant regulation. We expect the appropriate consideration of these two factors would, for reasons that we have explained, disfavor liability for harms caused by many widely sold products. A third factor is the likelihood that the plaintiff has insurance coverage sufficient to compensate for the monetary losses sustained. Use of these factors would encourage the courts to reduce the scope of product liability when such liability would be unlikely to significantly promote product safety or compensation, but still allow for the imposition of product liability when it would be advantageous. (2010a, 1491–92)

The real problem, however, is that their assessment of product liability is *not* always accepted.

Consider this counterargument to the Polinsky and Shavell article, written by legal scholars John Goldberg and Benjamin Zipursky (also see Polinsky and Shavell's [2010b] rejoinder):

> What shall we say, then, about the justifiability of products liability law—conceived as a modernized amalgam of negligence, misrepresentation, and warranty that, through the concept of a defective product, permits certain injury victims to hold manufacturers (and retailers) accountable? We should say that the case for products liability law, so conceived, is *easy*. It holds manufacturers accountable to persons victimized by their wrongful conduct. It empowers certain injury victims to invoke the law and apparatus of government to vindicate important interests of theirs. It instantiates notions of equality before the law and articulates and reinforces norms of responsibility. And in doing all these things, it contributes in direct and indirect ways to deterrence and provides welfare-enhancing compensation. For all these reasons and others, it is extremely valuable that courts, at the behest of victims, have the authority to order commercial sellers of defective products that cause injury to compensate their victims. (2010, 1948)

Yet even for those who have no doubt that product liability law is valuable, that still leaves the key question, which is very difficult to resolve: are the law's benefits worth its costs? And if yes, there still remains the issue of how product liability law should best be implemented.

Discussion Questions

1. In addition to a manufacturing defect and a design defect, there is also a *warning defect* that that can be considered in determining if a firm should be held liable for damages in a product-related accident. Simply put, a warning defect exists if the firm failed to warn of a product-related risk. Less simply put, there are several factors that the courts typically consider in such cases: did the product pose certain risks that the firm knew or could reasonably have known about; did the potential risks present a substantial danger to users of the product; would an ordinary consumer recognize the risks without a warning; did the firm fail to adequately warn about the risks; did the plaintiff use or misuse the product in a way that the firm could reasonably have foreseen; was a lack of warning a substantial factor in why the plaintiff was injured?

    How would you evaluate the role of warning defects in product liability cases, especially when considering their coexistence with manufacturing defects and design defects? For example, if a warning defect does not exist, should that protect the firm from liability regardless of the existence of a manufacturing or design defect? Conversely, if there are no manufacturing or design defects, should the existence of a warning defect nevertheless hold the firm liable for damages?

2. The *collateral source rule* does not allow evidence of third-party payments (such as from an insurance company) to bar the extent of a firm's liability for damages in a product liability case. One common tort reform is to allow for *collateral source offsets*: if a victim receives payments from a third party, the amount received reduces the amount of damages that can be assigned to the injurer; thus, the victim cannot "double collect" from two sources. How do you believe this reform will affect the behavior of firms and consumers in a product liability setting?

3. One alternative to tort law for product-related accidents is to rely on contract law instead. Under a rule of no liability, for example, if consumers still value some implicit liability rule, firms can offer legally binding warranties. Evaluate the use of warranties in promoting product safety.

References

Epstein, R. A. 1987. "The Risks of Risk-Utility." *Ohio State Law Journal* 48:469–77.

Goldberg, J. C. P., and B. C. Zipursky. 2010. "The Easy Case for Products Liability Law: A Response to Professors Polinsky and Shavell." *Harvard Law Review* 123:1919–48.

Polinsky, A. M., and S. Shavell. 2010a. "The Uneasy Case for Product Liability." *Harvard Law Review* 123:1437–92.

———. 2010b. "A Skeptical Attitude about Product Liability *Is* Justified: A Reply to Professors Goldberg and Zipursky." *Harvard Law Review* 123:1949–68.

Viscusi, W. K. 1990. "Wading Through the Muddle of Risk-Utility Analysis." *American University Law Review* 39:573–614.

Wade, J. W. 1973. "On the Nature of Strict Tort Liability for Products." *Mississippi Law Journal* 44:825–51.

CHAPTER NINE

Does Malpractice Liability Induce Physicians to Provide *Too Much* Health Care?

Helling v. Carey *(1974) and the Economics of Medical Malpractice Law*

Facts

In 1959, Barbara Helling, a twenty-three-year-old woman, first consulted doctors Thomas Carey and Robert Laughlin, partners in an ophthalmology practice. Her complaint was about nearsightedness, and she was fitted with contact lenses. She returned to the ophthalmologists several times over the next decade, including three visits in 1967 and five visits in 1968. While the doctors continued to be convinced that her complaints stemmed from her discomfort with her contact lenses, in October 1968, they finally pursued a different track. They gave Helling (then thirty-two years old) a pressure test to determine if she suffered from glaucoma. The test was positive, but by this time she had suffered substantial and permanent damage to her eyes. Helling sued the doctors for being negligent in not administering the pressure test to detect glaucoma at an earlier date.

Court Decision

After a jury verdict and an appeals court dismissed the complaint against the doctors, the Supreme Court of Washington sent a shock wave through the medical profession by finding for the patient. It wasn't just that the higher court held the doctors liable for Helling's damages that concerned the medical profession, but precisely *why* the court held the doctors liable. It had to do with implementing the negligence rule, and it is one of the problems with this rule that we addressed in chapter 7.

The court needed to determine two things: how much care did the doctors actually take, and how much care should they have taken (that is, the due care level). The first issue was simple—the doctors did not perform the pressure test. The second issue was far more complicated—*should* the doctors have performed the pressure test? How is a court supposed to determine what is due care in terms of a medical procedure? Here's one way to do it: ask the doctors.

At that time, the medical standards in the ophthalmology profession were *not* to routinely administer the pressure test to anyone under the age of forty. There simply wasn't a high enough incidence of the disease in younger people to warrant routinely giving the test. The due care standard at the time in medical malpractice cases was to consider the customary standards of the medical profession, what was generally referred to as "good medical practice." The court in this case, however, boldly rejected this notion of due care, and instead imposed its own interpretation of what reasonable medical care would consist of:

> Under the facts of this case reasonable prudence required the timely giving of the pressure test to this plaintiff. The precaution of giving this test to detect the incidence of glaucoma to patients under 40 years of age is so imperative that irrespective of its disregard by the standards of the ophthalmology profession, it is the duty of the courts to say what is required to protect patients under 40 from the damaging results of glaucoma.

> We therefore hold, as a matter of law, that the reasonable standard test that should have been followed under the undisputed facts of this case was the timely giving of this simple, harmless pressure test to this plaintiff and that, in failing to do so, the defendants were negligent, which proximately resulted in the blindness sustained by the plaintiff for which the defendants are liable.

The courts were now in the business of determining "good medical practices." It is no wonder that the medical profession was in an uproar over this decision.

Economic Analysis

Immediately after this case was decided, the medical profession challenged the sense of the decision. For example, the court considered the pressure test to be "simple and harmless," and while this is basically correct, it is far from perfectly correct. In the opinion of one ophthalmologist who commented on the case: "Agreed, the test is generally simple to perform and usually innocuous. There are, however, instances when it is not easy to get accurate results and the times when the test itself can be traumatic and injurious. Tonometer-induced injuries to the cornea are well known" (Charfoos 1975, 697). Furthermore, even if each test has only a modest cost (but note, that modest cost may still exceed the expected benefit, especially for a young person), the court could impose a substantial *aggregate* cost on society: "If nationally followed, *Helling* could result in 100,000,000 citizens receiving tonometer tests on some regular basis every second or third year. The increased medical costs would be extraordinary" (Charfoos 1975, 701).

While it certainly is important and legitimate to criticize this decision based on the sense of allowing the courts to determine medical standards, another interesting approach is to accept this decision and consider its impact on physician behavior. If it is the courts that determine due care in medical malpractice cases, and not the medical profession, how will this affect the *actual* care levels doctors will take?

Let's say due care in this case is not to perform the pressure test. What this explicitly means, then, is that the cost of performing the test exceeds its expected benefit. With the negligence rule and with due care set correctly, the doctors would not be compelled to perform the test to avoid liability. But what if the courts sometimes, either purposely (as in *Helling*) or mistakenly (as is more common), hold the doctors liable if the test isn't performed? In that case, the doctors can spend a little more on care and save a lot more in liability. In other words, by incurring a *marginal* cost, they can avoid the *total* cost of liability.

There is a general principle underlying this thinking. If there is uncertainty in the application of the negligence rule and the courts do not correctly hold the injurer to due care (because they misidentify either the due care level or the actual care level), the injurer is likely to take more than due care to avoid liability. In a sense, the negligence rule encourages doctors to subscribe to the old saying that it's better to err on the side of safety. From a medical decision standpoint, then, the negligence rule can provide doctors the incentive to take greater care when treating their patients. While this seems like a benefit of the rule, from a social welfare perspective greater care may also mean less efficient care. If the increased care has costs that exceed its expected benefits, too much care is being provided.

There is one other important point that should be noted. Just because ophthalmologists perform the pressure test, this does not necessarily shield them from liability under a negligence standard. There are two dimensions of negligence that are in play in this case: the doctor may be negligent by not performing the test, and the doctor may be negligent *when* performing the test. For example, what if the doctor negligently scratches the eye when performing the pressure test? What is most interesting about this scenario is that increased medical malpractice pressure has two opposing tensions: one tension leads to more care in the form of more testing, and the other tension leads to less care in the form of avoiding risky procedures (when they are possible to avoid). So, while it is often the case that the negligence rule leads to more medical care, it is not always the case.

These potential opposing effects of malpractice liability are well understood by policy makers. When doctors make medical decisions to avoid liability, this is known as practicing *defensive medicine*, as defined by the US Congress Office of Technology Assessment (1994, 13): "Defensive medicine occurs when doctors order tests, procedures, or visits, or avoid high-risk patients or procedures, primarily (but not necessarily solely) to reduce their exposure to malpractice liability. When physicians do extra tests or procedures primarily to reduce malpractice liability, they are practicing positive defensive medicine. When they avoid certain patients or procedures, they are practicing negative defensive medicine." Defensive medicine is an important issue that has led to much debate about medical malpractice reform. But at the heart of this issue is one crucial question: is there empirical evidence demonstrating that doctors actually practice defensive medicine?

Here we will primarily focus on *positive* defensive medicine, as it is the more commonly analyzed behavior. Determining if doctors take too much care *because* they are faced with malpractice liability can be a very difficult thing to do. Doctors can have many valid reasons for providing what may seem to be excessive care that have nothing to do with malpractice liability. There are legitimate differences in treatment philosophies among doctors. Furthermore, diagnosing illness and recommending treatment may often be as much art as it is science. Who's to determine precisely what due care is in any given situation? The key to identifying positive defensive medicine, then, is to abstract away from confounding factors that affect care decisions and focus specifically on the impact of malpractice liability.

Many economic studies focus on the field of obstetrics to provide empirical evidence of positive defensive medicine. An example of positive defensive medicine in this field is when doctors overuse a surgical procedure, such as a cesarean section (C-section), not for sound medical reasons but to reduce the probability of facing malpractice liability in the event of an adverse birth outcome to the baby during a nonsurgical delivery. In the opinion of one medical scholar, "The answer to the question 'How safe is c-section?' depends on who is answering. If a c-section is done, the woman and her baby take the risks while if a c-section is not done, the doctor takes the risk. This helps to explain why documented risks to the woman and her baby are not widely discussed and often not presented by doctors" (Wagner 2000, 1677). The key medical benefit of a C-section is when the baby has a problem that requires emergency surgical intervention. This is always a sound justification for performing a C-section. But if a C-section is performed not to protect the safety of the baby but instead to protect the doctor from malpractice liability, what are the risks to the mother and her baby?

First, consider the relative risks of a C-section compared to a natural birth for the mother: increased chance of death, increased chance of injury through surgical accident, increased chance of postoperative infection, and so on. Next, the increased risks for the baby: laceration from the surgeon's knife, respiratory distress syndrome in preterm infants (but this risk is greatly reduced if the C-section is performed after the mother goes into labor), and so on. In all, a C-section is far from a benign procedure, but these risks can be well worth bearing in emergency situations. Interestingly, the mother (as opposed to the doctor) may feel these risks are worth bearing in a nonemergency sense for several reasons (such as less pain and the convenience in scheduling delivery) that have led many medical scholars and journals to champion a woman's right to choose a C-section. (See Wagner 2000 for a fascinating discussion of these issues.)

It may seem ironic that even with the increased risks associated with C-sections, positive defensive medicine predicts doctors will perform *more*

C-sections. This is exactly the issue discussed above about the different tensions doctors face. From a liability perspective, doctors may face more dimensions in which negligence can be found when C-sections are used, but they also may be more likely to bear liability when C-sections are *not* used. The key issue, then, is, do doctors perform more C-sections when faced with increased medical malpractice liability pressure?

One study (Dubay, Kaestner, and Waidmann 1999) nicely illustrates how malpractice liability may affect the C-section rate for nonmedical reasons. The study presents some descriptive evidence that obstetricians, relative to other physicians, face a high threat of malpractice suits. In a 1990 survey, more than 75 percent of obstetricians had been sued for malpractice at least once, and their average malpractice insurance premium was more than twice that of the average physician. Thus, obstetricians are likely to be well aware of the constant risk of facing a malpractice suit.

The study's first concern is to determine how malpractice liability affects the C-section rate, while attempting to isolate away from several other factors that also affect that rate, such as clinical indications, hospital and physician characteristics, insurance coverage, and demographic characteristics of mothers. As a measure of malpractice risk, the study uses malpractice insurance premiums. An insurance premium is made up of basically two components: the frequency of claims against the doctor, and the severity of the damages that must be paid (the premium must also cover the costs of providing insurance coverage, and some profit to the insurance company, but these are not that important for this discussion). In other words, the insurance premium represents the *expected loss* associated with medical malpractice incidents. The prediction is that the greater the expected loss, the greater the risk confronting the doctor, and the more likely defensive medicine will be practiced. This provides the testable link between malpractice risk and the C-section rate, and the study finds that the risk of malpractice liability does increase the C-section rate.

The study's second concern is to try to assess the social value of an increased C-section rate. Even if malpractice liability risk is leading to more C-sections, and these procedures involve risks to the mother and baby, there may still be benefits to the C-sections if they are associated with improved health outcomes for the baby. To examine this, the study examines the link between malpractice liability and the health of the newborn. If the increased C-section rate is not associated with improved health outcomes, the positive defensive medicine identified in this study is socially wasteful.

To measure health outcomes of the baby, the study relies on the widely used five-minute *Apgar score*, devised by anesthesiologist Virginia Apgar in 1952. The Apgar test is performed one minute after birth, and then again five minutes after birth. The first test is to measure how well the baby tolerated birth, and the second test measures how well the baby is doing outside the womb. The test consists of evaluating the baby on five criteria—breathing effort, heart rate, muscle tone, reflexes, and skin color—assigning a value of 0, 1, or 2 for each criterion. Thus, the maximum score is 10, and the minimum score is 0, with 7 and above being normal, 4 to 6 being fairly low, and below 4 being critically low. Using the Apgar score, the study does not find that increased malpractice liability affects the health outcome of the baby.

The study concludes that increased risk of medical malpractice liability does lead to positive defensive medicine in the field of obstetrics, specifically concerning the practice of increasing the use of C-sections for delivering babies. Although the study does not find any increased benefits from the excessive use of C-sections in terms of improved health outcomes of the baby, it does find that, in the aggregate, the costs (in the United States) of this form of defensive medicine are very small relative to the total costs of obstetrics care.

Two studies (Yang et al. 2009 and 2012) provide a confirmation and updating of the above results. The 2009 study confirms the results that malpractice liability premiums increase the cesarean rate and that the impact is not large. It is the 2012 study, however, that provides a more thorough updating of the impact of liability on the health outcome of the baby. The study uses four measures of an adverse health outcome: low Apgar score, low birth weight, preterm birth (that is, before thirty-seven completed weeks), and birth injury. In measuring malpractice liability, in addition to using insurance premiums, the study examines various tort reforms and how they affect health outcomes.

There are several types of tort reforms (often relating to limiting damages that injurers have to pay when liable), and they are often considered sound social policy to reduce the burden of malpractice liability on doctors. In states where tort reforms are strong, it is predicted that obstetricians have less incentive to practice defensive medicine. If C-sections improve the health outcome of babies, and if doctors perform fewer C-sections due to the relaxed liability regime, the prediction is that tort reforms negatively affect the health outcome of the baby. (Conversely, in states with weak tort reform, the prediction is that there will be more C-sections and better health outcomes). If tort reforms have no impact on health outcomes, this suggests that malpractice liability is leading to socially wasteful defensive medicine.

The main finding of the study is that increased medical malpractice risk does not affect the health outcomes of babies, whether that risk is measured with insurance premiums or tort reforms. But if this increased pressure is leading to more C-sections, yet again we have an empirical verification of socially costly positive defensive medicine. The study offers this conclusion: "These findings are dispiriting. They suggest that the high cost of the medical liability system (the overhead costs of which are over 50 percent) are not justified by the system's benefits, at least as measured in health outcomes. Some may find a silver lining in the reasonable inference that if liability pressure does not improve health outcomes, then limiting liability will not worsen them" (Yang et al. 2012, 240).

Another study (Dranove and Watanabe 2010) considers the impact of malpractice liability on the C-section rate but takes a completely different approach from the ones above. Instead of looking at the threat of liability as measured by insurance premiums or tort reforms, this study considers how the C-section rate is affected by how obstetricians respond to malpractice suits that are filed against themselves or their colleagues: "A physician who has been sued may believe that the probability of malpractice litigation is high and exercise greater caution. If the physician's colleagues learn about the suit, they may also believe that the probability of litigation is high. They may pressure the physician who was sued to take greater care and may exercise greater caution themselves. A hospital that is sued might do the same; for example, by implementing treatment protocols that influence how physicians practice" (70).

The study argues that when examining the impact of insurance premiums or tort reforms on C-section rates, it is not surprising that only modest results are found. Malpractice insurance premiums are typically rated by community, not by specific physician. This means that in a given community, doctors with varying likelihoods of committing malpractice will face the same premiums. This allows a more "careless" doctor to not face an above-average, but individually rated, premium. Similarly, tort reforms are enacted statewide and not focused on specific doctors or hospitals. Thus, these "macro" measures of liability risk are not expected to have a strong impact on the behavior of doctors.

On the other hand, a "micro" measure of liability risk, such as a doctor's directly being sued, is expected to have a stronger behavioral impact than the macro measures. There is, however, a potential flaw in this thinking. One can argue that doctors, especially obstetricians, are *always* aware of the threat of a medical malpractice suit. Thus, actually being sued, or seeing colleagues being sued, shouldn't have much of an impact on behavior because the risk is anticipated. But this potential problem can be addressed.

It is possible that whatever the doctor believes the risk of being sued is to begin with, actually being sued leads to a higher future assessment of the risk. This can influence the doctor's behavior and lead to defensive medicine. Related to this, some doctors may be susceptible to a concept known as *optimism bias*. Let's say you were to survey a group of obstetricians and ask each of them the following question: Out of one hundred of your colleagues, how many of them do you believe will be sued for malpractice in the next year? Assume the average response is twenty. Now ask the same obstetricians the following question: What do you believe is your own probability of being sued for malpractice in the next year? The answer to this question may be 5 percent.

Optimism bias deals with the way we perceive risks to others compared to how we perceive risks to ourselves. The optimistic bias is that we place a higher likelihood of adverse outcomes happening to others (20 percent of being sued) than we do on ourselves (5 percent of being sued). This may well be occurring with the typical obstetrician. Other obstetricians (you don't personally know) being sued may not affect your risk assessment, but you or close colleagues being sued may be the "slap in the face" that has you reassess your risk of being sued in the future. This may influence your behavior and lead to defensive medicine.

The study finds two results suggesting that obstetricians practice defensive medicine. First, when the hospital receives a request for medical records due to the initiation of a claim against one of the doctors on staff, the *hospital-wide* C-section rate slightly increases. This likely occurs because when confronted with a lawsuit, the hospital initiates an immediate "be more careful" policy among its obstetricians as it begins to sort out the extent and legitimacy of the claim. The increased C-section rate is short lived, lasting only about three months.

The second result confirms defensive medicine at the physician level, specifically for the physician who is named in the claim. This increase in the C-section rate is larger than the hospital-wide impact, but it has a completely different timing—it occurs approximately nine months after the initial request for records. After initially being contacted about a malpractice suit, an obstetrician is likely to have a strong reaction to the claim, and may start counseling new patients about the benefits of C-sections over natural births. If this is the case, it is not until many months later that the study observes an increase in C-sections. But this increased C-section rate is also short lived (again, lasting about three months).

Although these results confirm the practice of defensive medicine, both impacts are extremely short lived and the study does not consider litigation risk as offering much explanatory power in affecting the C-section rate. It is likely that after the initial shock wears off, an obstetrician may quickly realize that a typical malpractice claim won't lead to substantial litigation costs or loss of reputation. Physicians rarely end up making payments to the plaintiffs, as the vast majority of medical malpractice suits resolve favorably for doctors.

These few studies on the impact of malpractice liability on the C-section rate commonly find no more than modest evidence of obstetricians practicing defensive medicine. There are other studies on C-section rates that find similar results, with some interesting exceptions. One study (Currie and MacLeod 2008) finds that the C-section rate may actually *decrease* with increased malpractice liability risk. The reason why this occurs relates to the dual tensions of malpractice liability discussed above.

Let's say that in addition to (or instead of) liability risk, obstetricians increase the C-section rate because there are financial incentives to do so. C-section fees are significantly larger than natural birth fees, and C-sections typically take much less time to perform. A higher fee per delivery coupled with more deliveries can be an attractive lure for obstetricians to perform more C-sections. However, if there is the potential for medical errors to be made during C-section surgeries, the greater the malpractice liability risk the stronger incentive there is to perform *fewer* C-sections, especially if the initially high C-section rate is primarily due to factors *not* relating to malpractice risk.

Thus, in theory, how increased malpractice liability risk affects the C-section rate is ambiguous. Defensive medicine can lead to more C-sections if this is believed to reduce liability risk, or defensive medicine can lead to fewer C-sections if obstetricians are trying to avoid risky procedures to reduce liability risk. This study finds evidence that tort reforms that reduce liability risk can lead to more C-sections. This is the same thing as saying that increased liability risk leads to fewer C-sections, a result that runs counter to the studies discussed above.

Another exception to the studies above is that increased liability risk may have no impact on the C-section rate, one way or the other. One study (Frakes 2012) finds that reduced malpractice liability through various tort reforms does not impact the C-section rate, but does find other evidence of defensive medicine. The study looks at two other obstetric practices—episiotomies and postdelivery hospital bed days. An episiotomy is a surgical incision of the perineum to enlarge the vaginal opening for obstetrical purposes during the birth process. The length of the hospital stay is another decision that obstetricians must consider in caring for their patients. Both of these practices certainly serve legitimate medical purposes in many scenarios, but they also both have the potential to be used solely to reduce the risk of malpractice liability. The study indeed finds that increased liability pressure does lead to the practice of positive defensive medicine in both episiotomies and length of postdelivery bed days.

There are many additional studies of defensive medicine that relate to other fields of medicine, and, as with the C-section studies, the results vary. In putting all these results into some policy context, perhaps the conclusion of Daniel Kessler (2011, 105–6), a leading scholar in the field of medical malpractice law and economics, can offer some guidance: "Empirical research into the effects of the malpractice system and potential reform suggest two main findings. First, doctors do practice defensive medicine. Studies of the effects of malpractice pressure on positive defensive medicine find that decreases in malpractice pressure lead to decreases in the supply of care having minimal medical benefit—that is, to decreases in healthcare costs, with essentially no adverse consequences for health outcomes. Second, tort reforms reduce the prevalence and cost of defensive medicine." Although the aggregate cost of defensive medicine is much debated, Kessler claims that even at 2 or 3 percent of total health care spending, expenditures on defensive medicine would exceed $50 billion a year.

While Kessler's conclusion suggests that tort reform in this environment may be worth its costs, it must be noted that there are numerous studies that do not find defensive medicine to be a pressing health care problem. For the purposes of this discussion, however, the important point that economic analysis stresses is that doctors may not be making medical decisions *solely* based on what is in their patients' best interests. Doctors may be taking too much care, or too little care when avoiding risky procedures, at least partially because of the medical malpractice liability regimes that govern their actions.

Discussion Questions

1. Tort reforms have often been motivated by the supposed "crisis" in medical malpractice liability law. The typical justification for a reform is that physicians are facing too severe of a liability risk, and this affects their behavior in socially costly ways. Here are two examples of tort reforms that have been debated and, in some states, enacted:

   Punitive damages cap. Damage awards that are meant to punish bad behavior (as opposed to payments meant to compensate the victim) are capped at a statutory dollar amount.

   Noneconomic damages cap. Damage awards to compensate the victim for nonmonetary costs, such as pain and suffering costs, are capped at a statutory dollar amount. Nonmonetary costs are distinguished from monetary costs, such as medical costs and lost wages from missed work.

   How would you use economic reasoning to evaluate each of these tort reforms?

2. The above tort reforms work *within* the negligence rule, as opposed to reforms that *change* the liability rule. In dealing with medical malpractice, how would you evaluate the pros and cons of adopting strict liability in place of the negligence rule? How would you evaluate a rule of no liability?

3. If (at least part of) the goal of tort reform for medical malpractice is to discourage doctors from practicing defensive medicine and taking too much care, how well do you think the same argument can be applied to tort reform for product liability? Should we discourage firms from making products *too safe*?

References

Charfoos, L. S. 1975. "*Helling*: The Law of Medical Malpractice Rewritten." *Ohio Northern University Law Review* 1975:692–703.

Currie, J., and W. B. MacLeod. 2008. "First Do No Harm? Tort Reform and Birth Outcomes." *Quarterly Journal of Economics* 123:795–830.

Dranove, D., and Y. Watanabe. 2010. "Influence and Deterrence: How Obstetricians Respond to Litigation against Themselves and their Colleagues." *American Law and Economics Review* 12:69–94.

Dubay, L., R. Kaestner, and T. Waidmann. 1999. "The Impact of Malpractice Fears on Cesarean Section Rates." *Journal of Health Economics* 18:491–522.

Frakes, M. 2012. "Defensive Medicine and Obstetrics Practices." *Journal of Empirical Legal Studies* 9:457–81.

Kessler, D. P. 2011. "Evaluating the Medical Malpractice System and Options for Reform." *Journal of Economic Perspectives* 25:93–110.

US Congress. Office of Technology Assessment. 1994. *Defensive Medicine and Medical Malpractice.* OTA-H-602. Washington, DC: Government Printing Office.

Wagner, M. 2000. "Choosing Caesarean Section." *Lancet* 356:1677–80.

Yang, Y. T., M. M. Mello, S. V. Subramanian, and D. M. Studdert. 2009. "Relationship between Malpractice Litigation Pressure and Rates of Cesarean Section and Vaginal Birth after Cesarean Section." *Medical Care* 47:234–42.

Yang, Y. T., D. M. Studdert, S. V. Subramanian, and M. M. Mello. 2012. "Does Tort Law Improve the Health of Newborns, or Miscarry? A Longitudinal Analysis of the Effect of Liability Pressure on Birth Outcomes." *Journal of Empirical Legal Studies* 9:217–45.

PART IV

Crime and Punishment

CHAPTER TEN

Are Criminals Rational?

*Gary Becker and the Dawn of Rational
Crime Analysis (1968)*

Background

In 1968, one of the most prestigious economic journals, the *Journal of
Political Economy*, published an article by Nobel Laureate Gary Becker
titled, "Crime and Punishment: An Economic Approach." This seminal
article singlehandedly led to the development of what is now a substantial
field in economics—the economics of crime. In the article, Becker clearly
expresses his purpose of approaching crime and punishment from an economic perspective:

> How many resources *should* be used to enforce different kinds of legislation?
> Put equivalently, although more strangely, how many offenses *should* be per-
> mitted and how many offenders *should* go unpunished? The method used for-
> mulates a measure of the social loss from offenses and finds those expenditures
> of resources and punishments that minimize this loss.

> The optimal amount of enforcement is shown to depend on, among other things,
> the cost of catching and convicting offenders, the nature of punishments—for
> example, whether they are fines or prison terms—and the responses of offend-
> ers to changes in enforcement. (170; emphasis in original)

In other words, *rational* criminals will determine how much crime to commit based on the enforcement strategies of the authorities, and this is an
important factor to consider when designing such strategies.

Imagine a criminal planning on committing a crime, such as stealing a car. What factors will enter into his personal cost-benefit analysis to determine if he should commit the crime? Let's keep the benefits side of the story simple. He will have an assessment of the resale value of the stolen car and be able to calculate his ultimate monetary reward. On the costs side, he will surely recognize that he has some chance of being apprehended by the authorities, possibly tried and convicted, and then punished. But will he have an *accurate* assessment of these factors? What is the actual probability that he will be apprehended? And if apprehended, what is the actual probability that he will be tried and convicted? And if convicted, what will his ultimate punishment be?

It may be the case that we are dealing with an experienced car thief who has observed the criminal justice system for many years. He may have a reasonably accurate understanding of his chances of being caught and punished. That is, he may be fairly rational. But still, with even slight misperceptions, he will not be perfectly rational. So, is "fairly" rational the best we can hope for? And how does this thinking apply to a wide variety of criminals, from litterers and traffic violators, to petty thieves and burglars, to child molesters, rapists, and murderers? Do we need to distinguish between juvenile and adult criminals, or between sane and mentally impaired criminals? Is it absurd to consider *any* criminal behavior as perfectly rational? It very well may be, and yet that still won't matter from an economic perspective. What does matter is precisely what Becker points out—*the responses of offenders to changes in enforcement.*

The idea behind rational crime analysis is not that the criminals sit with pen and paper and explicitly calculate the costs and benefits of their actions. There may even be a very large number of criminals who barely pay any attention to the future ramifications of their current behavior. All that is needed to motivate rational crime analysis is that *some* criminals respond to changes in crime enforcement strategies. We can then ask whether crime rates will fall when more resources are devoted to apprehension and conviction, or when punishments are made more severe. Fundamental economic reasoning predicts that this is exactly what we should observe, because as the costs of committing crimes increase, fewer crimes should be committed.

Thus, we have the first premise of rational crime analysis—the benefit of devoting resources to combating crime is that criminals will commit fewer crimes. This is known as the *deterrent effect*. Yet as elegant as this seems from a theoretical perspective, it is not clear that the deterrent effect even exists. Perhaps most criminals are in no sense rational, and manipulating the costs of their criminal behavior will not affect the crime rate. If this is the case, not only is it reasonable to question how effective are resources in combating crime, from a social policy perspective it is *necessary* to do so. It boils down, then, to an empirical question—is there evidence to support the existence of the deterrent effect?

The second premise of rational crime analysis is far less ambiguous—fighting crime requires the use of costly resources. This absolutely must be true. Costs must be incurred to maintain police forces, courts, prisons, and other aspects of a vast criminal justice system. This allows us to ask if fighting crime is a good bang for the buck, and if there are some crimes that are worth fighting but others that are not. But even if some crimes are not worth fighting from a financial cost-benefit perspective, should they be fought from some other social perspective? For example, the so-called war on drugs is often criticized as requiring a tremendous amount of resources yet offering little in return in terms of reduced drug production and drug use. But drugs are often thought of as being a repugnant scourge on society, and even small gains in fighting this disease may be worth an enormous investment in resource costs.

What, then, is the social objective in fighting crime? Becker's economic model of crime and punishment provides the starting point for addressing this and other questions. As is typical of *all* economic models, his is necessarily abstract and hypothetical and should not be thought of as a precise real-world accounting of criminal behavior. It simply presents a theoretical framework that allows economists to examine the costs and benefits of the criminal justice system and to develop some unique, interesting, and controversial results for one of society's most serious public policy issues. All of the economics of crime research that will be discussed in this section, if not directly drawn from Becker's article, is almost certainly inspired by it.

Economic Analysis

Perhaps the best starting point for introducing the economics of crime and punishment is to consider precisely what is meant by the term *punishment*. The usual meaning involves the final sanction a convicted criminal faces, from the most common ones, such as community service, probation, fines, and prison sentences, to more severe ones, such as solitary confinement, hard labor, torture, and the death penalty. But these consider the *severity* of punishment, which is only half the story. The other half includes the *certainty* of punishment.

There are three main components to the economic concept of punishment: the probability of apprehension, the probability of conviction (given apprehension), and the sanction. The first two probabilities multiplied together make up the certainty of punishment, and the sanction makes up the severity. When the certainty is multiplied by the severity, we have the *expected punishment.* A hypothetical example can illustrate what all this means.

Suppose that you are the manager of a convenience store, and if you (or your employees) are caught selling cigarettes to minors, you will be fined $20,000. This may seem like a very severe punishment, and on its own it is, but we know nothing yet about the likelihood that you would face such a fine. The probability of being caught selling cigarettes to minors is likely to be small. Let's say it happens in only 1 out of every 100 incidents, but if you are caught, the probability of conviction (that is, the probability of the fine being enforced) is quite high, say 90 percent. Putting all this together, we find the expected punishment to be (.01 × .90) × $20,000 = $180. This number conveys a different sense of "punishment" than does the original $20,000, when the severity of the fine was thought of without regard to its certainty.

Explicitly identifying the separate components of punishment allows for an intricate analysis of how the authorities can choose to expend resources when considering how to punish different criminal behavior. For example, if the authorities want to maintain the expected punishment at $180 in this example but feel that they are devoting too many resources to apprehension, they can easily make the following changes: cut the probability of apprehension in half to 1 in 200, and double the fine to $40,000. Or, maybe the authorities feel that a punishment of $20,000 is too severe, so they double the original probability of apprehension to 2 in 100, and cut the fine in half to $10,000. All three combinations, as well as many others, lead to an identical expected punishment of $180.

So how, then, are the authorities to choose which of these combinations to use? Becker's model addresses this question directly. For any level of expected punishment that the authorities wish to maintain, the efficient combination of certainty and severity of punishment requires the use of as few resources as possible. To this end, Becker suggests two things: use the sanction of fines as often as possible, and combine a low level of certainty with a high level of severity.

Why use fines over other forms of sanctions? Let's compare fines to prison sentences, two of the most common forms of sanctions. It is well known that maintaining a prison system is very costly to do, not even considering the up-front costs of building prisons in the first place. As for fines, once a monetary penalty is determined, all that's left is for the guilty defendant to pay that amount. There certainly will be administration costs and enforcement costs of maintaining a system of fines, but these costs are likely to be very modest compared to the costs involved in maintaining prisons.

In addition, once a system of fines is in place, adjusting the severity of the punishment is virtually costless. Consider the example above. How many additional resources would be required to double the original fine of $20,000 to the new fine of $40,000? Not many, as basically what needs to be done is to establish a new monetary amount. But how many additional resources would be needed to double a prison sentence? Whatever incremental resource costs must be incurred to incarcerate a prisoner, those costs would now double. And let's not forget that to whatever extent fines are actually paid by convicted criminals, these payments go to the authorities, perhaps more than offsetting the costs of maintaining the system.

So let's take it as fact that as far as severity goes, fines are the most efficient form of punishment. The next step is for the authorities to determine the efficient trade-off between the severity of punishment and its certainty. To increase the probabilities of apprehending and convicting criminals, additional resources must be devoted to enhance police and prosecutorial efforts. To increase a fine, as already mentioned, a larger dollar amount needs to be stated. Thus, not only are fines an efficient form of punishment compared to other sanctions, they allow severity of punishment to be more efficient than certainty. If resources are expended to increase certainty, but not to increase severity, the efficient expected punishment should involve a very low certainty, but a very high severity. In the numerical example above, then, of the three combinations listed, the one with a 1 in 200 chance of apprehension coupled with a $40,000 fine uses the fewest resources.

So far, one social goal of the criminal justice system is to achieve the desired expected punishment using the fewest resources possible. That goal may be achieved, at least in certain scenarios, by maintaining a low certainty of punishment and a high monetary severity of punishment. But what hasn't been discussed yet is, how do we determine the socially desirable expected punishment? What factors need to be considered in such a calculation?

Let's start with an extreme goal—the elimination of *all* crime, that is, 100 percent crime deterrence. The first problem with achieving this goal is that it is not likely to be technically feasible. Even if society devoted a phenomenal amount of resources to crime deterrence, undoubtedly some crimes would still be committed. The second problem is related to Becker's model. Even if it were technically feasible to eliminate all crime, economists ask what, to some, might be an unusual question: would it be *desirable* to do so? For example, would we be better off living in a society in which no murders occurred? You might think that the obvious answer to that question is yes, but an economist is likely to argue just the opposite.

Think about how difficult it would be to cut the murder rate in half, let alone to eliminate it. How many resources would society have to devote to such an enormous task? We would have to draw resources away from many other social programs—health care, education, infrastructure, and so on—to spend more on apprehending, convicting, and punishing murderers. In fact, it is possible that we would have to *eliminate* many other social programs. Simply put, under these circumstances it is unlikely that it would be desirable, even if feasible, to reduce the murder rate by 50 percent. In other words, the "optimal" amount of crime is likely to be positive. It is worth spending an additional dollar on crime prevention only if the benefit of reduced crime exceeds that dollar. If not, reducing crime, on the margin, is not a good bang for the buck.

From an economic perspective, determining how many resources to devote to reducing crime requires a fairly complicated consideration of not only how many resources to devote to fighting crime but also how to allocate those resources between the certainty of punishment and the severity of punishment. Becker's model predicts that devoting few resources to certainty and using fines for severity will provide the optimal solution to combating crime. But how well does Becker's prediction hold up to real-world scrutiny?

The Problems with Fines

Why do we not observe high fines applied with low certainties of punishment for a wide variety of crimes, especially violent crimes? We don't even observe large fines for crimes that are usually just punished through fines. For example, consider the crime of driving at a speed exceeding the speed limit. Tickets for speeding are typically set in the hundreds-of-dollars range.

But why not in the thousands-of-dollars range instead? We wouldn't need to put more state troopers on the road, yet speeding incidents would be reduced, possibly by a large amount, with such severe fines. This would easily satisfy Becker's idea of not using costlier resources to enhance the certainty of punishment, but greatly enhancing the severity of punishment at a low resource cost.

This obvious lack of real-world relevance of Becker's approach to optimal punishment often has critics doubt the value of applying economic reasoning to crime deterrence policies. Yet Becker's model can be thought of not as a blueprint for pragmatic policy advice, but as a starting point to consider when his principles may be best applied, and when they are likely to fail. There have been many refinements to Becker's original model in an attempt to take its basic theoretical principles and offer more practical policy advice. Reconsidering the nature of fines is a common starting point for such refinements.

The most obvious problem with large fines, one Becker recognizes himself, is that many criminals would simply not be able to afford to pay such fines. Imagine a criminal who could not afford a $10,000 fine. If we keep the certainty of punishment constant, and increase the severity with a larger and larger fine, the expected punishment would increase, yet it would have no additional deterrence impact on this criminal—if she can't afford $10,000, she can't afford any amount greater than that. The only way, then, to add deterrence impact on this criminal's behavior is to increase the certainty of punishment or to use a higher-resource-cost punishment such as prison.

This shortcoming of fines, however, doesn't greatly change Becker's approach to designing optimal punishment levels. It simply requires a slight change in language. Instead of using very large fines to increase the severity of punishment with as few resources as possible, the authorities should use fines *as best they can*, and then augment the punishment with a higher-resource-cost severity of punishment (or a higher-resource-cost certainty of punishment). In other words, the basic idea of using as few resources as possible to maintain a specific expected punishment still holds, but "as few resources as possible" may nevertheless entail a large cost.

This leads us down another difficult path. Exactly how should authorities use fines? It is possible to peg fines to the wealth of the criminal, setting them as high as possible in each individual case, before (if necessary) augmenting the punishment with a prison sentence. But what would be the implication of bankrupting criminals? If they were completely stripped of their wealth, would this not further enhance their likelihood of committing future crimes? And if the wealthy were punished differently from the poor, regardless of the efficiencies associated with this differentiation, there would no doubt be a vast public outcry accusing the criminal justice system of being unfair to the poor. This would be true especially if fines were used to punish violent crimes. Can you imagine the public outcry over a wealthy murderer's being punished *solely* with a fine, even if the amount was in the millions of dollars?

Even if a reasonable system of fines can be maintained by the authorities, there are at least two other potential problems that work against Becker's idea of efficient punishment. The first involves the nature of fines as a revenue stream for the authorities to enjoy. If the police, for example, are profiting from collecting money from fines, this may give them the incentive to use a high monetary sanction coupled with a *high* certainty of punishment. In addition, the police may devote fewer resources to apprehending other criminals who would be punished with nonmonetary sanctions. In other words, crimes that are punished with fines will be over-deterred while other crimes will be underdeterred. While this can be a problem for an honest police department who only focuses its attention on apprehending the guilty, it can be a serious problem if the lure of financial gain corrupts the police into apprehending the innocent as well.

The other potential problem of maintaining an efficient system of fines is that criminals may not only be concerned with the level of expected punishment, but with the magnitudes of its various components. Consider the following two ways of maintaining an expected punishment of $900: a 20 percent chance of being apprehended and then fined $4,500, and a 90 percent chance of being apprehended and then fined $1,000. If the level of expected punishment is all that matters to criminals, these two combinations create an equal deterrent effect. But if criminals care about being apprehended to a greater degree than they care about being fined, it is possible that a 90 percent chance of a smaller sanction creates *more* of a deterrent effect than a 20 percent chance of the larger sanction.

Apprehension is the first step in a chain of criminal justice events that can take months, and even years, to resolve. This may be one reason why criminals are more concerned about apprehension over severity, or even apprehension over conviction. And apprehension has a punitive component that can be quite stigmatizing in and of itself. An accountant who is arrested for embezzlement, for example, can face substantial repercussions in terms of current and future employment opportunities, even if eventually exonerated from any wrongdoing. The immediacy of apprehension, then, can be quite severe all on its own.

If the separate components of expected punishment affect criminal behavior in different ways, resources used to enhance the probability of apprehension may yield high benefits in terms of crime deterrence, even if the sanction does not involve the use of costly resources. And if, unlike with fines, the severity of punishment does take the form of a high-resource-cost sanction such as prison, then it is additionally important to determine how criminals respond to the different components of expected punishment. In addressing these issues, a large body of empirical research has developed that attempts to test the rational crime model in various ways. A few of these studies relating to apprehension, conviction, and capital punishment will be discussed throughout the rest of this chapter. The impact of prison sentences in deterring crime, a hugely important topic, will be discussed separately in the next chapter.

Police as a Crime Deterrent

One of the most basic beliefs about deterring crime is that the hiring of more police officers will reduce the crime rate. After all, not only is it the police who are largely responsible for apprehending criminals who have already committed crimes, the physical presence of patrolling police officers should act as a crime deterrent. The economic prediction is usually succinctly stated as: *more police, less crime*. It isn't uncommon, however, for empirical crime research to find that the size of the police force is *positively* correlated with the crime rate. This unusual result is attributed to a phenomenon known as *reverse causation*.

In considering the link between the police and crime, we must take into account that the crime rate itself may play a large role in determining the size of the police force. In cities where crime rates are high, there are likely to be larger police forces. And as crime rates rise, one public policy response is to increase the size of the police force. So now we have another economic prediction that can be succinctly stated as: *more crime, more police*. This positive relationship can hold simultaneously with the negative relationship predicted above, and so empirically finding a police deterrent effect requires a careful consideration of reverse causation.

One important study (Levitt 1997) offers a clever way to break the reverse causation. This is done by finding a variable that affects the size of the police force but does not affect the crime rate. This allows for the relationship between police and crime to move in only one direction. The variable used in this study is mayoral or gubernatorial election years.

In these election years, it is common for incumbent candidates to adopt "tough on crime" positions. After all, one big advantage that incumbents have over challengers is that they can actually enact public policy while in office. If in these years, incumbents hire more police officers as part of their campaign strategies, the increased number of police is *not* motivated by changing crime rates. This allows for a clear link between the size of the police force having an effect on the crime rate, as opposed to the other way around.

The study looks at police hiring in fifty-nine cities with populations of 250,000 or more between the years 1970 and 1992. The data show that the size of police forces remains constant in nonelection years, but increases by about 2 percent during election years, presumably attributed to political forces. The results of the study find that the hiring of more police does reduce the crime rate, but the magnitude of the effect is small. The reliability of this result, however, was questioned in another study (Mc-Crary 2002) that pointed to a methodological flaw in the previous study. Whatever the case, the importance of the original study lies not in its specific empirical result but in its approach to breaking the reverse causation problem.

The empirical strategy of breaking reverse causation can be seen in other studies. For example, one study (Lin 2009) uses state sales tax rates for fifty-one US states for the years 1970 to 2000. The idea is the following: changes in state sales tax rates leads to changes in state revenue, which in turn leads to changes in tax revenue shared with local government, which in turn can lead to changes in the hiring of local police officers, which in turn can lead to changes in the crime rate. Furthermore, the sales tax rates used are lagged by one year. This eliminates the potential for current crime rates to affect current sales tax rates, thus ultimately leading to more police hired *because* of the change in crime rates. By creating a link between police and crime that runs only one way, the study finds that there is a deterrent effect—the hiring of local police has a significant impact on reducing both property and violent crimes.

Another interesting way to break the reverse causation link is to examine an extreme event that is not affected by crime rates but can lead to a sudden increase in police presence. A terrorist attack represents such an event. When a terrorist attack occurs, the authorities usually respond by immediately increasing police presence in the vicinity of the attack, a move that is highly unlikely to have anything to do with local crime rates. This enhanced policing effort is maintained for an amount of time that depends on the specifics of the situation, but during this time we expect to see less crime, at least in these specific areas. Several related economic studies put this expectation to the test.

The first study (Di Tella and Schargrodsky 2004) examines a terrorist attack on the main Jewish center in Argentina in 1994. Eighty-five people were killed when a bomb exploded, and many more were injured. One week later, the federal government assigned police protection to every Jewish building in the country and, to prevent retaliatory attacks, to every Muslim building as well. The study examines three neighborhoods (a total of 876 blocks) in Buenos Aires and compares the number of car thefts for approximately three months before the attack, to car thefts five months after the enhanced protection was in place, for each block. The main result is that car thefts fell by nearly 75 percent, a substantial impact. The impact was extremely localized, however: areas one or two blocks away from those studied did not see a drop in car thefts.

One important issue that needs to be addressed with enhanced police protection is whether this strategy deters crime or simply *displaces* it. That is, do car thieves simply move from a well-protected block to one that is less protected? The above study briefly considers displacement, arguing that while it does not seem to be relevant for blocks adjacent to the ones protected, it may very well be important for blocks farther away. The study, however, offers no evidence to confirm or refute this hypothesis. Another study (Donohue, Ho, and Leahy 2014) reexamines the attack in Argentina and considers not only the displacement issue but two other factors that may cast doubt on the original study's finding of a police deterrent effect.

First, if some blocks are being given additional police resources, it is likely that some of this increase is coming from other areas of the city. If this is true, the reduced police presence in other areas can lead to increases in crime rates there, even if the increases are not caused by displaced criminals from the protected areas. Second, the number of parked cars found in the protected areas may have changed due to police restrictions on parking. Fewer cars in these areas may also be reducing the car theft rate. This study does find evidence of displacement, but it admits that its findings are not strong. Importantly, though, it concludes that the original study's findings are also not strong and do not rule out displacement. Nevertheless, both studies point to the importance of considering extreme events like terrorist attacks in order to examine the link between enhanced police presence and a reduced crime rate.

One other similar study (Draca, Machin, and Witt 2011) finds strong evidence of a police deterrent effect on crime rates *without* any corresponding displacement effect. This study examines the terrorist bombing attacks (some successful and some unsuccessful) in central London in July 2005. These attacks led to a precise six-week enhanced police presence, and the study finds immediate impacts on crime rates—first falling, then rising—that correspond closely with the start and end dates of this deployment. The study finds that the enhanced police presence, mostly foot and mobile patrols around transportation system hubs (where the bombings occurred), reduced the types of crimes you'd expect to see reduced, like street-level thefts and violent crimes. Furthermore, the study does not find evidence of two types of crime displacement—spatial and temporal. Crime rates did not appear to rise in other areas of London, and crime rates did not return to an excessively high level after the deployment ended. In other words, criminals didn't seem to "hold off" on crimes in central London simply to commit them there when the deployment ended.

The Probability of Conviction and Deterrence

Although there isn't a large economic literature examining how changes in the probability of conviction affect crime rates, one interesting study (Atkins and Rubin 2003) provides an instructive illustration. In *Mapp v. Ohio* (1961), the Supreme Court ruled that any evidence obtained by the police illegally, that is, in violation of the Fourth Amendment, was to be excluded from consideration at trial. This is known as the *exclusionary rule*. To the extent that the exclusionary rule makes it more difficult for prosecutors to convict criminals, criminals may face a lower expected punishment and, therefore, commit more crimes.

The study takes advantage of the fact that prior to the Court's ruling in *Mapp*, exactly half of the forty-eight continental states had already adopted some form of the exclusionary rule, while the other half had not. States that already had an exclusionary rule should not have been affected by the Court's decision since it did not apply to them. But for the other states that now faced the exclusionary rule, the change in the probability of conviction could have led to higher crime rates. By comparing the differential crime rates between the two categories of states, the study finds that the exclusionary rule did lead to higher crime rates. For an example of a quantitative result, the study finds that in suburban areas of states now subject to the exclusionary rule, violent crimes increased by 27 percent and property crimes increased by 20 percent (relative to the other states).

Deterrence and the Death Penalty

Perhaps there is no greater challenge in accepting the rational crime model than trying to determine if it can be applied to murderers. Are murderers rational? Or, to rephrase the question in a more pragmatic way: can the authorities reduce the murder rate by manipulating the expected punishment? One prominent, and highly controversial, social policy debate involves the use of the death penalty as a punishment for committing murder. The debate among economists, and scholars from many other disciplines, largely is concerned with one main issue: does the death penalty deter murder? This is a question that economists have been trying to answer for nearly forty years, and to many it is still a question left unanswered. Why is that?

Economists are generally in wide agreement over how the death penalty is predicted to deter murder. If the death penalty is considered to be a harsher punishment than its next alternative—say, life imprisonment without parole—the enhanced punishment imposes higher costs on criminals who are considering committing murder. Higher costs of committing crimes are expected to lead to less criminal activity. Thus, the death penalty deters murder. While this theoretical prediction is not particularly controversial among economists, the empirical verification of this prediction offers nothing but controversy.

Consider the conclusions of the following economists who have published empirical research on the death penalty:

Recent empirical studies by economists have shown, without exception, that capital punishment deters crime. Using large data sets that combine information from all fifty states over many years, the studies show that, on average, an additional execution deters many murders. (Shepherd 2005, 204)

The U.S. data simply do not speak clearly about whether the death penalty has a deterrent or anti-deterrent effect. The only clear conclusion is that execution policy drives little of the year-to-year variation in homicide rates. As to

whether executions raise or lower the homicide rate, we remain profoundly
uncertain. (Donahue and Wolfers 2005, 843)

Inconsistent empirical results, which often paint economics in a bad light,
have little to do with the way economists think about social issues. As we
have seen several times in previous chapters, it is simply the nature of empirical work, especially in the social sciences, that leads not only to a wide
variety of results for whatever issue is at hand, but to the realization that
a definitive answer may never be found.

One study (Dezhbakhsh, Rubin, and Shepherd 2003) provides a nice
representative example of how economists typically depict the deterrent
effect of the death penalty. The study estimates what is known as a *life-
life trade-off*, that is, the number of lives saved (or murders deterred) for
each convicted murderer who is actually executed. Using data from 1977
to 1996, the study finds the life-life trade-off to be, on average, eighteen
(with a margin of error of plus or minus ten). This and other studies (not
discussed here) conclude that there is empirical verification of the deterrent effect of the death penalty.

These studies, however, have been subjected to serious critical review.
One study (Donohue and Wolfers 2005) has access to much data that have
been used in previous studies, and checks to see if the deterrent effect stands
up well to *robustness* tests; that is, do the results of these studies stand up
to small changes in the empirical specifications? The study strongly concludes that these approaches do not stand up well to robustness tests, and
casts doubt on the confidence that can be placed on the empirical verification of the deterrent effect of the death penalty (but see Dezhbakhsh and
Rubin 2011 for a scathing reply to this conclusion).

So why is there substantial disagreement over the empirical verification
of the deterrent effect of capital punishment? One well-understood problem in this literature is that the available data on capital punishment are
quite "thin." In the United States between the years 1930 and 2005, there
were only 4,863 executions. Between the years 1968 and 1976, due to a national moratorium on the death penalty, there were none. After the moratorium was lifted, there were only 1,004 executions between the years
1977 and 2005, but there were more than a half million homicides (see US
Bureau of Justice Statistics 2005). Thus, death sentences have not often
been handed down in homicide cases, and even when handed down, they
are not strongly enforced. According to Levitt (2004), the probability that
a convicted murderer will be executed is approximately 1 in 200.

It is important to note that the fact that the death penalty has not been used often does not, in and of itself, cast doubt on the *possibility* of there being a deterrent effect. Perhaps it is precisely because the death penalty is rarely used that it is difficult to verify its deterrent effect. In other words, it is an *implementation* problem, not a deterrence problem, that leads to weak empirical results. If the death penalty were carried out more quickly or used more often, the deterrent effect might be more confidently verified. Along these lines, two related studies (Shepherd 2004 and 2005) find that if the time on death row is shortened, or if states have a certain threshold number of executions, a statistically significant deterrent effect can be found.

Another study (Hjalmarsson 2009) attempts to circumvent the problem of having thin aggregate data in death penalty studies by taking an extremely localized view of the potential deterrent effect. The study disaggregates the data across two dimensions—geographic and temporal. Geographically, the study looks at *city-level* data, specifically for three Texas cities—Dallas, Houston, and San Antonio. Temporally, the study uses *daily* data on homicide and execution rates. The advantage of using highly disaggregated data is that it is likely that aggregate data will not pick up slight variations in murder and execution rates. For example, maybe an execution deters murders in the very short run or in a specific city, but this impact is lost when murder rate and execution rate data are compiled annually and statewide.

The study uses Texas data because the application of the death penalty in Texas is far more common than it is nationally. For example, compared to the national average, in Texas there are nearly twice as many death sentences handed down per 1,000 homicides. Furthermore, the percentage of death row inmates who are executed each year in Texas is more than seven times larger than the national average. Thus, the Texas data may be as good as it gets for death penalty studies.

For the death penalty to have a deterrent effect, potential criminals must have some idea of the likelihood of being executed. Rational crime analysis does not require that a criminal have perfect information but, instead, that he adjust his *perceived* probability of being executed in the face of an event, such as another offender's execution that is actually carried out. If the media publicize such an event, and potential criminals are exposed to the coverage, this may be a channel through which the deterrent effect exists. This study hypothesizes that if there is evidence of a deterrent effect of the death penalty, it should be seen in the days immediately surrounding an execution, should be larger for executions with the most media coverage, and should have a more pronounced local effect.

For the sample period used in the study, 1999 to 2004, there were a total of 172 executions in Texas. The main daily newspaper in each of the three cities of interest provided coverage of some of the executions. The *Dallas Morning News* covered 65 percent of the total executions, but 83 percent of those for offenders sentenced in, or native to, Dallas. The corresponding numbers (total and local for the specific city) for the *Houston Chronicle* are 35 percent and 76 percent, and for the *San Antonio Express* they are 30 percent and 100 percent. Thus, each newspaper provided greater coverage of executions with a local component compared to coverage of statewide executions.

Using a seven-day window—three days before, the day of, and three days after an execution—the study examines the deterrent effect of executions on local homicides, using the number of homicides on a given day in a given city as the main variable of interest. The main result is that very little evidence of a deterrent effect is found, since the total number of Texas executions has no effect on local city homicide rates. One problem with this result, however, is that the variable the study uses includes *all* homicides, even those that are not eligible for the death penalty and, therefore, not expected to affect murder rates.

The study does have data on capital murder cases for Houston, and that is where a slight deterrent effect is found—there are fewer murders in Houston during the seven-day window surrounding a Texas execution. But this result is problematic, because the study does not find that local executions (as opposed to statewide executions) affect local murder rates. This inconsistency in results casts doubt on the reliability of the slight deterrent effect that is found.

The study also finds no evidence that local media coverage has an impact on the number of homicides. For the media coverage hypothesis to make sense, however, offenders must be exposed to the coverage. What if the newspaper coverage is a poor proxy for how the execution stories are disseminated to potential criminals? The study also has data on local television coverage of executions for Dallas, but again no deterrent effect is found relating to this coverage. One last test involves a management change at the *Dallas Morning News* that occurred in June 2001. Prior to the change, the *Morning News* covered 98 percent of the executions, but after the change the coverage was only 34 percent. This suggests that if media coverage of executions has an impact on the number of homicides, there should be more of a deterrent effect before the change. No such deterrent effect was found before or after the change.

Other than the small deterrent effect found for Houston capital cases, statewide executions, local executions, and media coverage of executions are all found not to have an impact on the number of local homicides. While this study concludes that the death penalty does not have a deterrent effect on murder, it would be interesting to further pursue the problem of only having data that do not allow capital cases to be separated from noncapital cases. The small spark of a result of a deterrent effect for Houston capital cases can be dismissed as a statistical anomaly, or it can be the stepping-stone to further research. This study yet again demonstrates the difficulties associated with death penalty studies. Not only are there conflicting results *across* studies, there can be conflicting results *within* a study.

So, in general, what can we conclude about the empirical analysis of the deterrent effect of the death penalty? While there have been studies that have found evidence supporting the deterrent effect, these studies have faced serious scrutiny that has cast doubt on their results. Can we point to even a loose consensus? Perhaps, but (arguably) the result that most consistently shows up is forcefully captured in a National Research Council Report (2012, 2) that offers the following conclusion:

> The committee concludes that research to date on the effect of capital punishment on homicide is not informative about whether capital punishment decreases, increases, or has no effect on homicide rates. Therefore, the committee recommends that these studies not be used to inform deliberations requiring judgments about the effect of the death penalty on homicide. Consequently, claims that research demonstrates that capital punishment decreases or increases the homicide rate by a specified amount or has no effect on the homicide rate should not influence policy judgments about capital punishment.

Notice that this is not the same thing as saying that there is *no* deterrent effect. What is being said is that, based on the scholarly papers that contributed to the report's conclusion (see the special edition of the *Journal of Quantitative Criminology* [vol. 29, no. 1, 2013] for these papers), the committee agrees with Donohue and Wolfers's (2005) conclusion quoted above: "As to whether executions raise or lower the homicide rate, we remain profoundly uncertain."

In all, many of the studies discussed in this chapter (and the next) do provide support for Becker's rational criminal model. That is, we can point to a body of evidence demonstrating that crime may be deterred by the threat of punishment. While this evidence does not go unchallenged, and even at its strongest it is very far from definitive, it does suggest that resources under the control of the authorities may have some ability to influence the behavior of criminals. At a minimum, these studies underline the importance of continuing this avenue of research to inform public policy, especially considering the phenomenal amount of resources that society devotes to fighting crime.

Discussion Questions

1. In August 2010, a man was caught in Switzerland driving his $215,000 Mercedes-Benz more than 100 mph *over* the speed limit. The Swiss use two criteria to determine the fine for speeding: the extent to which the offender exceeded the speed limit, and the income of the offender. Using these criteria, the fine for this incident of speeding was the largest in history—just over $1 million (crushing the previous world record of $290,000, also in Switzerland). Evaluate this approach to deterring speeding.

2. Sexual molestation is typically thought of as a particularly heinous crime. When sexual offenders are released from prison, they are still subject to restrictions imposed on them by the criminal justice system. These restrictions vary by state, but they generally take two forms: registration and notification. A released sexual offender is required to register with the local authorities. Furthermore, the local authorities may notify local residents that a released sexual offender will be living in their neighborhood. Evaluate the costs and benefits of sexual offender registration and notification laws.

3. While there is a substantial debate as to whether the death penalty actually provides a crime deterrence benefit, there is little debate about one of its most serious costs—wrongful conviction/execution. Provide a thorough analysis of this potential cost of capital punishment.

References

Atkins, R. A., and P. H. Rubin. 2003. "Effects of Criminal Procedure on Crime Rates: Mapping out the Consequences of the Exclusionary Rule." *Journal of Law and Economics* 46:157–79.

Becker, G. S. 1968. "Crime and Punishment: An Economic Approach." *Journal of Political Economy* 76:169–217.

Dezhbakhsh, H., P. H. Rubin, and J. M. Shepherd. 2003. "Does Capital Punishment Have a Deterrent Effect? New Evidence from Postmoratorium Panel Data." *American Law and Economics Review* 5:344–76.

———. 2011. "From the 'Econometrics of Capital Punishment' to the 'Capital Punishment' of Econometrics: On the Use and Abuse of Sensitivity Analysis." *Applied Economics* 43:3655–70.

Di Tella, R., and E. Schargrodsky. 2004. "Do Police Reduce Crime? Estimates Using the Allocation of Police Forces after a Terrorist Attack." *American Economic Review* 94:115–33.

Donohue, J. J., D. E. Ho, and P. Leahy. 2014. "Do Police Reduce Crime? A Reexamination of a Natural Experiment." *Empirical Legal Analysis: Assessing the Performance of Legal Institutions*, edited by Y. Chang, 125–43. London: Routledge.

Donohue, J. J., III, and J. Wolfers. 2005. "Uses and Abuses of Empirical Evidence in the Death Penalty Debate." *Stanford Law Review* 58:791–846.

Draca, M., S. Machin, and R. Witt. 2011. "Panic on the Streets of London: Police, Crime, and the July 2005 Terror Attacks." *American Economic Review* 101: 2157–81.

Hjalmarsson, R. 2009. "Does Capital Punishment Have a 'Local' Deterrent Effect on Homicides?" *American Law and Economics Review* 11:310–34.

Levitt, S. D. 1997. "Using Electoral Cycles in Police Hiring to Estimate the Effect of Police on Crime." *American Economic Review* 87:270–90.

———. 2004. "Understanding Why Crime Fell in the 1990s: Four Factors that Explain the Decline and Six that Do Not." *Journal of Economic Perspectives* 18:163–90.

Lin, M. 2009. "More Police, Less Crime: Evidence from US State Data." *International Review of Law and Economics* 29:73–80.

McCrary, J. 2002. "Using Electoral Cycles in Police Hiring to Estimate the Effect of Police on Crime: Comment." *American Economic Review* 92:1236–43.

National Research Council Report. 2012. *Deterrence and the Death Penalty*. Edited by D. S. Nagin and J. V. Pepper.

Shepherd, J. M. 2004. "Murders of Passion, Execution Delays, and the Deterrence of Capital Punishment." *Journal of Legal Studies* 33:283–321.

———. 2005. "Deterrence versus Brutalization: Capital Punishment's Differing Impacts among States." *Michigan Law Review* 104:203–55.

US Bureau of Justice Statistics. 2005. *Capital Punishment, 2005: Homicide Trends in the United States*.

CHAPTER ELEVEN

Does Prison Reduce Crime through Deterrence or Incapacitation?

Ewing v. California (2003) and the Economics of the Three-Strikes Law

Facts

In March 2000, Gary Ewing walked into the pro shop of the El Segundo Golf Course in El Segundo, California, and stuffed three golf clubs down his pants leg. With great difficulty, Ewing limped his way toward the exit, arousing the suspicion of a pro shop employee, who immediately called the police. Before Ewing got out of the parking lot, he was arrested for stealing three golf clubs worth $399 each. This seemingly unremarkable crime gained notoriety and massive media attention when Ewing was found guilty and sentenced to a remarkable twenty-five years to life imprisonment. Why was Ewing given such a severe sentence for such a minor crime? He had the misfortune of being subjected to California's *three-strikes law*.

The California three-strikes law took effect in March 1994. The idea behind the law was to impose a very severe punishment on habitual criminals. To earn a first strike, a serious crime must be committed, such as murder, rape, robbery, drug sales to minors, or one of several other offenses. Importantly, not all first crimes are labeled as strikes. But once a criminal earns a first strike, any following felony can be considered a second strike (even if it would not have been considered a first strike). The punishment for a second strike is twice the current offense term. For a third strike, a prison term of twenty-five years to life is imposed.

When Ewing stole the golf clubs, he was on parole from a nine-year prison sentence for one count of robbery and three counts of residential burglary committed in 1993. With four serious crimes (and several minor ones) in his past criminal history, the current crime of stealing the golf clubs was eligible to be considered a third strike. While prosecutors and trial judges have discretion in classifying minor third crimes as misdemeanors instead of third-strike felonies, Ewing's minor crime was classified as a third strike and he was sentenced accordingly.

Court's Decision

Ewing was ultimately decided by the US Supreme Court. The main issue the Court had to address was whether the three-strikes law in this case yielded a punishment that was "cruel and unusual," thus in violation of the Eighth Amendment of the US Constitution. Justice Sandra Day O'Connor wrote the majority opinion (in a 5–4 vote) and offered the following conclusion:

> Ewing's sentence is justified by the State's public-safety interest in incapacitating and deterring recidivist felons, and amply supported by his own long, serious criminal record. . . . To be sure, Ewing's sentence is a long one. But it reflects a rational legislative judgment, entitled to deference, that offenders who have committed serious or violent felonies and who continue to commit felonies must be incapacitated. The State of California was entitled to place upon Ewing the onus of one who is simply unable to bring his conduct within the social norms prescribed by the criminal law of the State. Ewing's is not the rare case in which a threshold comparison of the crime committed and the sentence imposed leads to an inference of gross disproportionality.

Thus, the Court upheld the State of California's severe three-strikes punishment of Ewing.

Economic Analysis

A typical criticism that followed the Supreme Court's ruling questioned the sense of using such a harsh prison sentence to punish a minor crime, third strike or not. For example, in November 2007, the JFA Institute, a nonprofit organization concerned with criminal justice policies, released a well-publicized and controversial report titled, *Unlocking America: Why and How to Reduce America's Prison Population*. The report expressed a growing concern over the expanding prison population, the racial inequities involved in sentencing, and the use of prison as an effective way to reduce crime. The report called for extensive prison reforms. In doing so, the report presented what it considered to be three *myths* about crime and prison:

1. Tougher penalties are needed to protect the public from "dangerous" criminals.
2. Tougher penalties will deter criminals.
3. There are "career criminals" we can identify and whose imprisonment will reduce crime.

The first myth concerns the *incapacitation effect* of prison. Put simply, if a criminal is behind bars, he cannot commit any more crimes, at least not in public. The second myth concerns the *deterrent effect* of prison, a concept well explained in chapter 10. In this context, it is the *threat* of imprisonment that reduces the crime rate, not the actual imprisonment of criminals. The final myth deals with *recidivism*, the problem of habitual criminals who, upon release from prison, return to committing crimes. The three-strikes law is specifically designed to deal harshly with this type of criminal.

It is an obvious fact that prisons are extremely costly to build and maintain. From a public policy perspective, then, it is important to understand the role of prisons in combating crime. If these "myths" truly are myths, then the commonly perceived benefits of prison are not actually being realized, strengthening the case for comprehensive prison reform. There have been a vast number of empirical economic studies that address whether and how prison can reduce crime. But before reviewing some of these studies, it is important to clearly distinguish between the two main ways prison, at least in theory, can reduce crime—through the incapacitation effect and through the deterrent effect.

It may seem that because prison obviously incapacitates criminals, any additional crime reduction through deterrence is just a bonus. But this is not the case. The optimal length of a prison sentence will depend on whether the role of prison is to incapacitate or deter (see Shavell 1987). To illustrate this point, assume for the time being that prison lacks the ability to deter crime. That is, the only way prison can affect the crime rate is by keeping criminals locked up. If this is true, how are optimal prison sentences to be determined? The basic premise here is a simple economic one: keep the criminal locked up as long as the benefits of imprisonment (in terms of reduced crime) exceed the costs. How do we implement this premise?

If prison only works through incapacitation, the length of a sentence is determined by when it is the right time to release a prisoner. But this can have some unusual consequences. For example, consider a man who gets drunk for the first time and winds up killing someone while he is highly intoxicated. How long should he be imprisoned? *If* it can be demonstrated that this was a one-time incident, and that the man will never get drunk again and pose no harm to society, he shouldn't be imprisoned for very long at all. If we expect no more criminal activity from this man, we have no reason to incur any costs to keep him locked up. Now consider a woman who steals cars. If it can be determined that she will always steal cars if she is not imprisoned, and the costs of her crimes exceed the costs of imprisonment, she should be kept locked up for a long time. Stealing cars is not as severe a crime as murder, but in this case the car thief should face a longer prison sentence than the murderer.

From an incapacitation perspective, then, the severity of the punishment may not be linked to the severity of the crime. Furthermore, another unusual aspect of the incapacitation effect is that the severity of the punishment may no longer be traded off against the certainty of the punishment. While the authorities must still decide on a level of certainty of punishment, the length of the prison sentence primarily depends on the potential harm a released criminal will inflict on society and the cost of continued imprisonment.

The difficult question, of course, is, how do we determine when a criminal should be released from prison? Similar to the idea of parole, there may be some general principles that can be applied. For example, older or sickly prisoners may be less likely to return to criminal activities post-release. If prisoners further their education while incapacitated, or develop certain job skills, they too may be less likely to return to criminal activities. Predicting recidivism will always be a difficult thing to do, but that is precisely what needs to be done if the only role of prison is to incapacitate.

For deterrence, however, prison sentences must be determined in a different way. Consider the murderer again. If we want to deter murder, the *threat* of a harsh sentence is necessary. If a murderer expects to be quickly released, it's not likely that the threat of prison will deter the crime. In addition, let's say it is widely known that once a prisoner turns forty years old, he is very likely to be released. If a thirty-year-old faces an optimal deterrent sentence length of twenty years in prison for committing a certain crime, the actual sentence will only effectively be ten years, and this lowers the deterrence value of prison. The deterrent effect of prison requires not only the threat of a prison sentence but a *credible* threat. Thus, any prison sentence that is optimal for deterrence purposes may not be optimal from an incapacitation standpoint.

Due to the different policy implications of the deterrent and incapacitation effects, it is important to separate out the two when examining the impact of prison on reducing crime rates. To determine if a deterrent effect does exist, researchers must find something in the data that explicitly allows for that effect to be identified. There have been several studies that have done just that.

One study (Kessler and Levitt 1999) uses the California sentence enhancement laws, enacted in 1982, to distinguish the deterrent effect from the incapacitation effect. Sentence enhancements create a sudden change in the length of a prison sentence associated with a certain crime. With an immediate change in the severity of punishment, it is likely that in the short run, the deterrent effect will have more of an impact on reducing crime than will the incapacitation effect. Consider a criminal who today faces a ten-year sentence for a crime but tomorrow faces a fifteen-year sentence for the same crime due to a sentence enhancement. How does this increase affect the incapacitation effect? For the first ten years, it doesn't. If imprisoned, the criminal will be incapacitated for the first ten years under both sentences. Only after the ten years have passed will the enhanced sentence have an increased incapacitation effect. The deterrent effect, however, can have an immediate impact. In considering committing the crime, the one-day difference can have an impact on the criminal's likelihood to go through with it.

The California sentence enhancements were quite severe: five years for each prior conviction for a serious felony *or* one year for each prior prison term served for any offense, whichever was greater. In addition, the law eliminated the statute of limitations that previously allowed the courts to consider a criminal's past record for only ten years, prohibited judges from allowing the enhancements to be served concurrently with the base sentence, and required the enhancements themselves to be served consecutively.

To control for other factors that may affect crime rates and isolate the impact of sentence enhancements, the study compares crime rates for crimes that were eligible for the enhancements (murder, rape, robbery, aggravated assault with a firearm, and burglary of a residence) with crimes that were not eligible (aggravated assault without a firearm, burglary of a nonresidence, motor vehicle theft, and larceny). Crime rates for the eligible crimes were found to have dropped in the first year after the enhancements relative to the crime rates for the ineligible crimes. This short-term effect can be attributed to the deterrent effect of prison.

In a similar vein, another study (Levitt 1998) looks for a deterrent effect by taking advantage of how prison sentences abruptly change when a criminal is just at the age of being classified as an adult offender instead of as a juvenile offender. While the definition of the age of majority differs across states, all states have some form of sentence enhancement when that age is reached. Some states, however, have relatively harsh enhancements for that crossover age, compared to other states with less severe enhancements. Comparing across these two types of states, the study finds that there is a drop in crime rates for criminals who have reached the age of majority in the past year. As with the previous study, this abrupt change in the severity of prison sentences provides evidence of a deterrent effect.

One other study (Katz, Levitt, and Shustorovich 2003) presents a nice verification of the deterrent effect of prison without considering sentence enhancements. This study considers the *harshness* of a prison sentence as opposed to its length. Two sentences of identical length will have identical incapacitation effects. If you are in prison for five years, regardless of the environment, you cannot commit crimes in public for five years. But two identical sentences lengthwise can offer different deterrent effects if the sentences are served in different prison environments—the harsher the environment, the greater the deterrent effect.

The study uses the death rate among prisoners as a proxy for the quality of prison life. It is argued that the higher the death rate, the harsher the prison environment. The prison death rate is not a perfect measure of prison harshness since prisoners may die from reasons that have little to do with the prison environment, such as old age or other natural causes. The important point is that the prison death is considered to be correlated with prison harshness, and this is likely to be true. The study finds that the prison death rate does reduce the crime rate, both for violent crimes and property crimes. Thus, for identical prison sentences, a deterrent effect is still found to exist.

One other study (Drago, Galbiati and Vertova 2009) demonstrates the deterrent effect of prison by using data from a significant prison-policy reform law in Italy. In July 2006, the Italian parliament passed the Collective Clemency Bill to alleviate the serious overcrowding of Italian prisons. Current inmates who had committed a crime before May 2006 received a sentence reduction of three years. This led to an immediate release on August 1, 2006, of more than 20,000 inmates (nearly 40 percent of the Italian prison population). While certain serious crimes were excluded from the bill (organized crime, terrorism, kidnapping, felony sex crimes, and some others), the release of such a substantial number of prisoners allows the study to draw on a unique data set in which to address some interesting questions about the deterrent effect of prison.

The study takes advantage of a built-in variation in sentencing for released criminals who commit new crimes. The bill states that if a former inmate commits a crime within five years after his release from prison, to whatever sentence he receives for that crime will be added the remaining time left on the previous sentence he was serving. For example, consider a criminal who had eighteen months left to serve when he was released. If he commits a new crime and is sentenced to thirty months, he will have to serve a total of forty-eight months. What is extremely useful about this particular policy feature is that it allows for natural variation in the sentences offenders will face even if committing the same crime.

Consider a second released prisoner who commits the exact same new crime as the previous criminal. He too will be sentenced to thirty months in prison for the new crime. However, when he was released due to the bill, he only had three months left to serve, making the total of the new sentence thirty-three months as opposed to the other criminal's forty-eight-month sentence. When considering many criminals committing the same new crime, each will face a sentence enhancement of anywhere from one to thirty-six months (since only criminals with three years or less left on their original sentences were released). With all these similar criminals facing different sentences, the study has the variation needed to examine the deterrent effect of prison.

The main result is that an increase in the prison sentence does affect the propensity of these former inmates to commit new crimes. Quantitatively, the study finds that a one-month increase in the prison sentence for a new crime reduces the probability of committing that crime by approximately 1.3 percent. Although this seems like a small number, 1.3 percent is actually a fairly large effect for just a one-month enhancement. Thus, once again, the study finds empirical support for the deterrent effect of prison.

While much effort has gone into verifying the deterrent effect of prison, the incapacitation effect is usually thought of as being obvious. After all, as long as prisoners are not escaping each night to commit crimes in public, incapacitation *must* reduce crime. Enforcing prison sentences, however, requires the use of costly resources, so an important public policy question concerning incapacitation is, how many crimes would imprisoned criminals have committed *had they not been imprisoned*? This counterfactual question can be tricky to answer.

Consider a sentence enhancement that affects one group of criminals but not another, such that the first group stays in prison one year longer than the second group. If the behavior of criminals in the second group is followed for one year after their release, it can help predict how much crime criminals in the first group would have committed had they too been released. Unfortunately, this would not work well because sentence enhancements are usually imposed on the worst offenders who have the highest rates of recidivism. Thus, the postrelease criminal behavior of those with the shorter sentences is not a good predictor of what would have been the criminal behavior of those who received the enhanced sentence.

Instead, an ideal study would (hypothetically) randomly assign criminals to short or long prison sentences. The random assignment acts as a control because the criminals aren't being distinguished by their criminal history. Then, if you look at the postrelease criminal behavior of the "lucky" criminals who receive the shorter sentence, you can use this to guess at the criminal behavior that would have existed for the "unlucky" criminals who received the longer sentence. This guess at the criminal behavior provides a measure of the incapacitation effect of prison. Of course, the conditions necessary to perform this ideal study do not exist, but one economic study (Owens 2009) offers a clever way to mimic the ideal scenario.

The state of Maryland uses sentencing guidelines to determine how a convicted offender will be sentenced based on his criminal history and the crime for which he is convicted. An offender score is calculated to determine the seriousness of the offense, with four elements considered: prior adult criminal history, juvenile criminal history, parole violations history, and current relationship to the criminal justice system (incarcerated, on probation, and so on). On July 1, 2001, Maryland changed the guidelines in a significant way. Prior to that date, an offender's juvenile record was excluded from his history when the offender reached the age of twenty-six. After that date, the juvenile record was excluded at the younger age of twenty-three. In other words, the guidelines change acts as a sentence *dis*enhancement. For criminals between the age of twenty-three and twenty-six, their offender score would now be lower because of the weakening of one of the four elements.

172   CHAPTER ELEVEN

This sentencing change has some nice features that allows it to be used to measure the incapacitation effect of prison. The motivation for the change was a belief that Maryland's sentencing guidelines were unfair relative to other states' guidelines. Thus, the sentencing change was *not* in response to a change in crime rates. This allows the study to focus on the impact of the sentencing change on crime rates, and not the other way around, breaking the reverse causation problem discussed in chapter 10. Also, the sentencing change is not expected to have a significant deterrent effect because it was not well publicized. For example, between 1998 (when the reforms were first being considered) and 2004, there was no mention of the change in major and local Maryland newspapers. This allows the study to distinguish between the incapacitation and deterrent effects of prison.

The study then proceeds to consider certain criminals who were "lucky" to be sentenced after July 1, 2001. For criminals aged twenty-three, twenty-four, and twenty-five, after the guidelines change they were lucky to face a shorter prison sentence than they would have faced before the change. The study is then able to calculate the sentences these criminals would have received had they been "unlucky" instead, and sentenced under the old guidelines. So, any crimes the lucky criminals commit when they are released would not have been committed had they been unlucky instead and still imprisoned. In effect, the sentencing guidelines change had a random impact on criminals of a certain age, and this allows the study to compare a lucky group of criminals to a similar unlucky group to see how the crime rate was affected.

Quantitatively, the study finds that the lucky criminals were arrested at an average rate of 2.8 times per year and were involved in approximately 1.5 serious crimes per year while they would have otherwise been incapacitated. Thus, the incapacitation effect is found to reduce crime (or, more precisely for this study, the lack of incapacitation is found to increase crime). Then, comparing the *marginal* cost of incarcerating a prisoner for one additional year (as opposed to the *average* cost which includes upfront costs that are not affected by incarcerating one more prisoner), the study finds that the marginal benefit in terms of crime prevention slightly outweighs the marginal cost of incarceration. In short, the incapacitation effect of prison is, at least according to this single study, just barely a good bang for the buck.

With a good understanding of the deterrent and incapacitation effects, we can now examine the three-strikes law. As far as incapacitation is concerned, it may not be efficient to devote a tremendous amount of resources to imprison a criminal whose future crimes impose only a modest cost on society. On the other hand, if the three-strikes law is designed to deal with habitual criminals, will it be more efficient to lock up such a criminal once for twenty-five years or to continually deal with (what is believed to be the inevitable) many episodes of arrest, conviction, and imprisonment over a twenty-five-year period?

As for the deterrent effect, while it may seem like overkill to sentence someone who steals three golf clubs to a twenty-five-year prison sentence, the key question to ask is this: how many crimes, both minor and major ones, are *not* being committed because of the three-strikes law? Undoubtedly, there is likely to be far less criticism of harsh sentences imposed on violent third-strike crimes. Furthermore, for habitual criminals, perhaps a severe second- and third-strike sentence is needed to deter their behavior. Whatever the case, even without an explicit three-strikes law, most punishments are at least somewhat enhanced for criminals who have a criminal history. The three-strikes law is just a more explicit, formally designed version of sentence enhancements. Still, as in all cases, the three-strikes law has benefits and costs, and some economic studies have attempted to sort through these trade-offs.

One study (Iyengar 2008) finds a very clever way to isolate the impact of the three-strikes law on criminal behavior. Consider two criminals, Bob and Joe, each of whom has committed two crimes—a theft and a burglary. A key difference between them, however, is the ordering of the crimes. Bob first committed a theft, then a burglary. Joe first committed a burglary, then a theft.

Before the enactment of the three-strikes law, both criminals would face similar sentencing eligibility if they committed an identical third crime. After the three-strikes law, their sentencing eligibility would differ for that crime. In Bob's case, the theft was not considered a first strike, but the burglary was. This makes Bob's third crime only a second strike. In Joe's case, the burglary was the first strike, making the theft a second strike, making his third crime a third strike. Thus, even though Bob and Joe have similar criminal histories, because of the orderings of their crimes they would face different sentence eligibility for an identical third crime—Joe would face the harsher punishment. The study then compares pairs of individuals with the same criminal history but different ordering of crimes, before and after the enactment of the California three-strikes law, to determine the effect of the sentence enhancements on criminal behavior.

The study finds that the three-strikes law does reduce participation in criminal activity in California, by 20 percent for second strike-eligible offenders and by 28 percent for third strike-eligible offenders. But because of the enhanced sentencing for third strikes, eligible offenders were more likely to commit violent crimes as opposed to nonviolent ones. Simply put, if you face the risk of being imprisoned for a very long time regardless of the crime you commit, you may as well be more aggressive. Thus, while the three-strikes law reduces crime, the crimes that are committed tend to be, on average, more severe. The study also performs a fairly concise cost-benefit analysis of the California three-strikes law. Without going into detail, the bottom line is that the law is estimated to save approximately $200 million in crime costs annually due to the reduction in nonviolent and violent crimes (this includes netting out the effect of the increase in violent crimes) yet costs approximately $500 million annually in prison operating costs.

Another study (Helland and Tabarrok 2007) confirms this cost-benefit result with some calculations of their own. This study too finds a deterrent effect of the three-strikes law, with approximately 31,000 crimes deterred annually in California. The increase in prison time because of the law is approximately 16.6 years per prisoner, for a total cost per prisoner of $583,000. With nearly 8,000 more prisoners due to the law, the total prison cost is nearly $4.6 billion, or $148,000 per crime avoided. However, the cost per crime (that is, the savings due to deterrence) is estimated to be approximately $34,000, and this falls well short of the prison cost per crime avoided.

Both of these studies conclude that while there are crime-reduction benefits to the three-strikes law, these benefits come at a pretty steep cost. One other study (Marvell and Moody 2001) paints a much bleaker picture. This study does not find evidence of a deterrent effect, but does find that the three-strikes law increases the homicide rate due to the possibility of enhanced violence when committing a third-strike crime. Perhaps criminals anticipating severe punishment are more likely to murder potential witnesses if they feel this will lower their chances of apprehension and conviction.

Comparing homicide rates in the mid-1990s for twenty-four states that had three-strikes laws to the other twenty-six states that did not, the study concludes that the laws are associated with a 23–29 percent increase in the long-run homicide rate. Quantitatively, the study finds this long-run rate to translate into an additional 3,300 homicides each year. Using a value-of-life estimate of $3.2 million, it concludes that the long-run social cost of the three-strikes laws is approximately $11 billion per year. The study offers a blunt final conclusion: "Given their unintended consequences in terms of human lives, we see no justification for the three-strikes laws"

(Marvell and Moody 2001, 106). Taken together, all three studies discussed here do not provide compelling evidence that the crime-reducing impact of the three-strikes laws are worth their costs.

Let's return to the JFA Institute's report, which concludes by claiming to have demonstrated that the three myths truly are myths, and emphasizes the need to reduce the size of the prison population. It argues that this reduction can bring a considerable savings to taxpayers without affecting crime rates. This kind of argument typically does not sit well with economists. It is one thing to say that prison reform may have benefits that exceed its costs, but another thing to say that it will *only* have benefits. Sure, taxpayers will save money if fewer criminals are imprisoned or if sentence lengths are reduced, but it is highly unlikely that this will have *no* impact on crime rates. And regardless of how difficult it is to accurately measure the impact prison has on crime rates, any sensible policy reform should at least consider the elusive deterrent effect and the more obvious incapacitation effect.

Discussion Questions

1. Evaluate a policy designed to make prison conditions harsher in an attempt to enhance the deterrent effect of prison.
2. One criticism of California's three-strikes law is that it leads to criminal migration to bordering states with less severe penalty structures. For example, a third strike-eligible criminal in California may decide to commit her next crime in Nevada or Arizona, where the sentencing structures are less severe. How does this migration of crime from one state to others affect your evaluation of California's three-strikes law?
3. Roughly 9 percent of all prisoners in the United States are imprisoned in *private* prisons. Discuss the advantages and disadvantages of allowing private corporations to operate prisons.

References

Drago, F., R. Galbiati, and P. Vertova. 2009. "The Deterrent Effects of Prison: Evidence from a Natural Experiment." *Journal of Political Economy* 117:257–80.

Helland, E., and A. Tabarrok. 2007. "Does Three Strikes Deter? A Nonparametric Estimation." *Journal of Human Resources* 42:309–30.

Iyengar, R. 2008. "I'd Rather Be Hanged for a Sheep Than a Lamb: The Unintended Consequences of the Three-Strikes Law." NBER Working Paper 13784.

Katz, L., S. D. Levitt, and E. Shustorovich. 2003. "Prison Conditions, Capital Punishment, and Deterrence." *American Law and Economics Review* 5:318–43.

Kessler, D., and S. D. Levitt. 1999. "Using Sentence Enhancements to Distinguish between Deterrence and Incapacitation." *Journal of Law and Economics*
42:256–76.

Levitt, S. D. 1998. "Juvenile Crime and Punishment." *Journal of Political Economy* 106:1156–85.

Marvell, T. B., and C. E. Moody. 2001. "The Lethal Effects of the Three-Strikes
Laws." *Journal of Legal Studies* 30:89–106.

Owens, E. G. 2009. "More Time, Less Crime? Estimating the Incapacitative Effect
of Sentence Enhancements." *Journal of Law and Economics* 52:551–79.

Shavell, S. 1987. "A Model of Optimal Incapacitation." *American Economic Review: Papers and Proceedings* 77:107–10.

Is Racial Profiling a Nondiscriminatory Policing Strategy?

Anderson v. Cornejo *(2004) and the Economics of Police Search Procedures*

Facts

Sharon Anderson and eighty-nine other plaintiffs contended that they were discriminated against at Chicago's O'Hare Airport between March 1996 and August 1999. All ninety plaintiffs were black women who were chosen for nonroutine searches after returning to the United States from foreign travel. They claimed that Customs officials subjected them to pat-downs, strip searches, X-ray inspections, or body-cavity searches because of racial and sexual bias and not due to any reasonable suspicion that they were violating the law. None of the searches yielded illegal contraband.

To support their claim of discrimination, the plaintiffs referred to data collected by the General Accounting Office (GAO). Using a national sample of airline passengers, the report presented evidence that black women were far more likely to be subjected to X-ray searches than were other groups. Black women had a 6.4 percent chance of being X-rayed, compared to .73 percent for white women, .53 percent for white men, and 4.6 percent for black men. Thus, black women were eight times more likely than white women, twelve times more likely than white men, and 40 percent more likely than black men to be X-rayed. According to the plaintiffs, these numbers appear to leave little doubt that black women were being discriminated against.

Court's Decision

The main issue the court had to deal with is whether the managers at the airport should be liable for the actions of their inspectors. The court ultimately reached the following conclusion: "There may well have been race or sex discrimination at O'Hare Airport, but the managerial defendants are not liable on account of discrimination practiced by the line inspectors." While this decision is of great importance to the litigants, it is not very interesting from an economic perspective. What is interesting, however, is that the court, while not relying on the GAO data for its decision, nevertheless pointed to another group of statistics that the women thought supported their case but that the court viewed otherwise.

In addition to the X-ray search rates listed above, the court's opinion referred to the GAO report's strip-search *hit rates*, meaning the percentage of searches that successfully yielded contraband. The hit rate for black women was 27.6 percent, compared to 19.5 percent for white women, 25.1 percent for white men, and 61.6 percent for black men. Thus, concluded the plaintiffs, significantly higher search rates were not coupled with significantly higher success rates in terms of finding contraband, further supporting the claim of discrimination against black women.

The court, however, viewed the hit-rate data in a different light:

> Data from the GAO's report do not imply that Customs officials are searching black women (or any other group) but not similarly-situated passengers in other groups. The report's outcome-by-group tables—we gave one example above, concerning the success rate of strip searches—show that Customs officials search black women with (on average) the same degree of suspicion that leads them to search white women or white men. A 27.6% success rate for a particular kind of border search is not to be sneezed at. It may imply that the Customs officials are conducting too few searches, not too many.

In interpreting the hit-rate data, the court explicitly referred to (at that time) state-of-the-art economic research which concluded that different search rates for different groups does not necessarily imply discrimination. Instead, it is different hit rates that suggest discriminatory practices on the part of the authorities, and the discrimination is found against the group with the *lowest* hit rate. Thus, using the strip-search hit-rate numbers from the GAO report, it is white women who are most discriminated against, black women and white men are treated similarly, and black men who are least discriminated against. These seemingly unusual results require far more explanation.

Economic Analysis

The court in *Anderson* argued that a distinction must be made between search rates and hit rates. To understand this distinction in a model of police search, let's begin with a fairly simple conceptual example that for the time being does not involve the controversial issue of race. Consider two groups of people—the old and the young. The first important assumption is that these two groups are fairly easy to distinguish just by looking at them. Perhaps by "old" we mean over the age of fifty, and by "young" we mean under the age of twenty-five (but not a teenager). The second assumption is that these two groups have different propensities to commit crime. Let's say the young are more likely to sell illicit drugs than the old. Assume 35 percent of the young sell drugs but only 15 percent of the old do.

Next, consider the motives of the police officers who are conducting the searches. These searches will involve motor vehicle stops, a very common form of police search. The police position themselves in a way that allows them to easily distinguish the age of the driver or passengers. Assume for the time being that these police officers are *completely unbiased*. In other words, they have no interest in searching either group due to any biases against that group. The goal of the police is to maximize the probability that a search will find contraband. The police want to fight crime, and that is all they want to do. By putting all of these assumptions together, how should the police proceed with motor vehicle stops?

Let's begin with the police treating each group equally by stopping one in every ten vehicles with a young driver, and one in every ten vehicles with an old driver. This leads to an equal search rate of 10 percent for each group. While this has the appearance of being "fair," it is not efficient from the perspective of maximizing the probability of finding contraband. To demonstrate this point, let's think about the next (or marginal) search only.

If the police know that the young are more likely to be carrying drugs than the old, the next search will yield a 35 percent chance of finding contraband if the police search the young but only a 15 percent chance if they search the old (these are the hit rates). To maximize the probability of finding contraband, then, the police need to focus their next search on the young. In a model of rational criminal behavior, as the police change the intensity of search, the criminals are predicted to change their propensity to commit crimes. As the police increase the search rate of the young, the young will now be less likely to carry contraband because they will be more likely to be caught. Likewise, as the police reduce the search rate of the old, the old will now be more likely to carry contraband because they will be less likely to be caught. Numerically, let's say the hit rate among the young drops from 35 percent to 30 percent but rises among the old from 15 percent to 20 percent. While these rates are now closer, they are not yet equal. It is still more likely for the marginal search to find contraband on the young than on the old.

Along the same lines, the police should further continue to increase their search rate of the young and reduce their search rate of the old. Only when the propensity to carry contraband is the same across both groups should the police stop adjusting their search rates. Notice, however, that because the police began with a 10 percent search rate of each group, and then increased the rate for the young and reduced the rate for the old, the final (or efficient) search rates can no longer be identical: *the young will be searched at a higher rate than the old.* What will be identical are the hit rates, that is, the probability of finding contraband in either group. Perhaps, in the end, the search rate will be 15 percent for the young and 5 percent for the old, and the hit rate will be 25 percent for each group.

One of the key implications of this model is that efficient police searches may require different groups to be searched at different rates. This result may be thought of as condoning police discriminatory practices, but that would be a *gross* misunderstanding. Instead, this model is designed to *identify* discrimination, not encourage it. The model demonstrates that different search rates do not mean that the police are biased. Remember, in our example above, the police are explicitly assumed to be unbiased. Discrimination is identified by different hit rates. More specifically, it is the group with the *lower* hit rate that is being discriminated against. Why is this so?

As the police intensify their search of one group, that group will have a lower propensity to commit crime. If the police are biased against the young, for example, they may want to stop young drivers specifically because they don't like the young and want to impose costs upon them. So, the hit rate for the young will fall below 25 percent because the decision to search is not based solely on the objective of finding contraband. The more intensely a group is searched, the less likely contraband will be found on them, and the more they are biased against. Thus, the model leads to a simple test to identify the existence of police bias: if discrimination exists, different groups will have different hit rates. Thus, the existence of discrimination cannot *solely* be inferred from differences in search rates.

This model of optimal police search is applicable in a wide range of settings, but much of the economic research focuses on identifying one particular type of police bias—racial bias. There is a large, long-standing, and widely varied body of research across many academic disciplines on racism in the criminal justice system. Numerous studies have identified racial bias from all agents (police officers, prosecutors, juries, and judges) of the criminal justice system. The argument that the criminal justice system discriminates against blacks often begins with one striking fact—while blacks make up only 12 percent of the total population in the United States, they make up 40 percent of the prison population. That is, the black population in prison grossly overrepresents the black population in the whole country.

But what are we to make of this fact? Consider another striking fact— while men make up only 50 percent of the total population in the United States, they make up nearly 90 percent of the prison population. That is, the male population in prison grossly overrepresents the male population in the whole country. Does this suggest that men are discriminated against in the criminal justice system, or is there a simpler explanation, such as men are more likely than women to commit crimes? In terms of race, the succinct question becomes: does race predict criminal behavior? If so, race can be used as an easily observable characteristic that aids the police in performing efficient searches.

This thinking still leads to a difficult question: if the crime rate is higher among blacks than it is among whites, why is this so? The most likely explanation is not that race in and of itself predicts criminal behavior, but that other characteristics that are correlated with race do, such as income, education, employment, and so on. These other factors may be difficult for police officers to observe when considering whom to search, so race acts as an observable proxy.

And there is no shortage of theories (well beyond the scope of this book) among criminologists and other social scientists that try to account for racial differences in crime rates, with the common objective of recommending social reforms to help combat crime at its root causes. Nevertheless, while it may be extremely important to understand why different groups have different propensities to commit crime, an efficient police search strategy needs to consider these differences *regardless* of why they exist.

The seminal economic study (Knowles, Persico, and Todd 2001) on police searches and racial bias begins with a striking fact of its own: between January 1995 and January 1999, blacks made up 63 percent of motorists searched for illegal drugs or other contraband on Interstate 95 by Maryland state police, but blacks made up only 18 percent of motorists on the road. But without examining the hit rates of these searches, little can be said at this point about whether the police in Maryland are using racial profiling because they are biased against blacks. The study makes it clear that it is not *differences* in the way blacks and whites are treated by the police that identifies racism, but in determining the *reasons* for the differences. In this case, one reason may be that race is a predictor of crime. Another reason may be that the police are racially biased. The study tries to distinguish between these two competing explanations (which the authors state more formally as distinguishing between *statistical* discrimination and *racial* discrimination).

The study uses data on all motor vehicle searches (a total of 1,590) on a stretch of Interstate 95 for the time period stated above. First, the study assumes that the objective of the police is to maximize the number of successful searches, or hits. While the search rate is 63 percent for blacks and only 29 percent for whites, the study finds that the hit rates are almost identical (34 percent for blacks and 32 percent for whites). This finding does not support the belief that the differential search rates for blacks and whites are discriminatory. However, the study finds slight evidence of discrimination (that is, relatively low hit rates) against Hispanics and white women, but because those groups each make up a small percentage of the total searches, the results are weak.

The study also considers a slightly different objective for the police— maximizing the number of hits that involve a "large" amount of drugs, or "hard" drugs. For example, when searching for drugs that constitute a felony charge under Maryland's laws, the study finds the hit rate for blacks to be 13 percent and for whites to be 3 percent. This result implies that it is whites who face discrimination, as their lower hit rate suggests that they are being searched too intensely relative to the nondiscriminatory rate of search.

In all, the study does not find evidence that the differential search rates indicate a racial bias against blacks. A follow-up study (Sanga 2009), however, expands on the former study in two ways: it extends the sample period from 1995 to 2006; and it includes all police searches of motor vehicles in Maryland (a total of 19,000), not just those along Interstate 95. With this larger data set, the new study finds that hit rates are 38 percent for whites, 28 percent for blacks, and 8 percent for Hispanics. This suggests racial bias against blacks, and especially against Hispanics, as the lower hit rates for these groups (relative to whites) can be explained by the police searching them too intensely.

Another way to empirically investigate the existence of bias associated with racial profiling is to distinguish *police officers* by race, as opposed to just distinguishing the victims of search by race. If the police are not racially biased when they search individuals, black and white police officers should approach racial profiling in similar ways. If there is an efficient unequal search rate for two groups of individuals, any police officer with a nonbiased objective, regardless of race, should be applying the same technique. But if the race of a police officer affects the rate of search, this is an indication of possible racial bias.

One study (Antonovics and Knight 2009), using data from the Boston Police Department from 2001 to 2003, finds that the race of the police officer does have an effect on search rates. If the race of the officer is different from the race of the motorist, there is a higher probability that the motorist will be searched. This holds for white officers searching black motorists, and for black officers searching white motorists.

Another study (Sanga 2014) takes a different approach to testing how police behavior is affected by the race of the officer. Instead of using search rates and hit rates, this study looks at differences in police officers' *stop rates*. Stopping a suspect is only the first step in a series of potential actions a police officer can undertake. Once stopped, will a suspect quickly be released? Will the suspect be cited for one or more violations, and if so, which ones? Will the suspect and the vehicle be searched, and if so, how intensely? Will the suspect be arrested? Thus, officer discretion plays a large role in the decision on how to proceed once a stop occurs. Furthermore, how a researcher interprets data from the complete stop process depends largely on how the police officer reports what is done, and this report is unlikely to accurately reflect the officer's motives for all actions taken and, perhaps even more important, all actions *not taken*. For these reasons, empirical studies that use differential hit rates to identify police bias are unlikely to be capturing all the potential ways for police bias to surface: "Such discretion should make us wary to base inferences of racial discrimination on stop outcomes like citation or arrest codes or even the results of a search, especially since there are legal ways for officers to manipulate these both for and against the suspect" (Sanga 2014, 408).

On the other hand, when focusing *solely* on the initial decision to stop a suspect, there is far less police discretion to be concerned about. Of course there will be some discretion, as the officer will have to decide when to stop a suspect. This decision can depend on many factors, some that depend on the behavior of the suspect and some possibly relating to officer bias. In addition, the officer is required by law not only to report the stop but to report it accurately. Thus, whatever information a stop yields to the researcher should be fairly precise, not only because the law requires accuracy but because there isn't much information for an officer to manipulate. And this is one of the downsides of using stop-rate data—they really don't yield much information. The study overcomes this deficiency, however, by finding a clever way to use stop rates to determine if the race of the police officer has an impact on stop behavior.

To determine if officer race matters, it would be ideal to examine the stop behavior of two different police officers—one white and one black—who are placed in *identical* policing situations. Let's say this scenario can be realized, and it is observed that the white police officer stops more black suspects and fewer white suspects than does the black officer. We can conclude from this fact that the white officer discriminates against black suspects *relative* to the black officer. The stop-rate data can be used to identify relative discrimination in this scenario because we are explicitly assuming that the policing situations are identical. Therefore, any differences in officer behavior must be due to some type of bias. What the stop rates don't tell us, however, is precisely what *type* of bias.

For example, assume that both officers are completely racially unbiased. What can account for their different stop behavior? Perhaps the white officer has a sincere, but mistaken belief that blacks have a higher propensity to commit crime relative to whites. In his mind, then, efficient policing would require him to devote more resources to stopping blacks than whites. If the black officer doesn't have this mistaken belief, the white officer's behavior will look like discrimination relative to the black officer's behavior. In this particular example (which is only one of many possibilities), the white officer uses different information than the black officer does but, by assumption, is not racially biased. This doesn't mean that another example can't be discussed in which it is racial bias that leads to different stop rates; it just means that there is no obvious explanation as to why the rates are different.

To replicate the ideal of identical policing situations as best as possible using real-world data, the study attempts to control for the area an officer patrols. Using data from Oakland, California, from 2005 to 2010, the study can track the neighborhood, day, and time an officer is on patrol. For example, a white police officer is assigned to patrol a specific neighborhood on Thursday at 6 p.m., and then a black police officer is assigned to patrol the same neighborhood the next Thursday at 6 p.m. This allows, at least somewhat, for stop-rate data to be compared across similar policing situations to determine if one officer discriminates relative to the other.

When examining officer behavior specifically *within* neighborhoods, the stop-rate test suggests that relative discrimination does occur and that the race of the officer matters. But there is a peculiarity in the results. In minority neighborhoods, the study finds that black officers discriminate in favor of minorities and against whites relative to white officers. In white neighborhoods, however, black officers discriminate in favor of whites and against minorities relative to white officers. In other words, the *same officers* discriminate in favor of their own race in some neighborhoods but against their own race in others. This leads the study to conclude that *where* a suspect is stopped may be more important than by whom a suspect is stopped. Whatever is causing officer race to matter in explaining differential stop rates, the lack of a consistent bias directed toward a specific race makes it difficult for the study to accept that these differences are motivated by racial bias.

Rather than examining differential search rates, hit rates, or stop rates, a completely different approach to detecting racial bias in the criminal justice system is the focus of another study (Tomic and Hakes 2008). When detaining a suspect to perform a search, police officers are attempting to gather information to determine if an arrest should be made. Therefore, a low level of evidentiary standard, such as an officer's intuition or suspicion, must be met to justify the search. When actually arresting a suspect, however, a greater degree of evidentiary standard must be met since there must be a sufficient amount of information to justify the arrest. Thus, if racial bias is factoring into an officer's decision to arrest a suspect, compared to arrests that are not motivated by bias, there may be a greater chance of future dismissal of the charges due to the higher evidentiary standard that must ultimately be met.

The study examines different categories of crimes that involve differences in the discretion an arresting officer can use at the time of arrest. For example, a fully developed murder investigation that eventually leads to the arrest of a suspect is likely to involve a very low level of officer discretion, if any, in making the arrest. In contrast, when an officer feels compelled to make an "on-scene" arrest, such as with a drug or weapons offense, a high level of officer discretion is used. If racial bias is present, it is predicted to be observed more often in the arrests that involve a high level of officer discretion. Indeed, this is precisely what the study finds.

Using data from approximately 58,000 felony cases in the United States from 1990 to 1998, the study finds that blacks face a higher dismissal rate compared to whites for arrests that involve a high level of officer discretion, but the dismissal rates are not different for arrests that do not involve a high level of discretion. Thus, police officers' arrest discretion is found to be racially motivated. At first blush, it may seem comforting that whatever bias is present at the time of arrest, it is corrected further down the line in the criminal justice system. But unlike a racially motivated vehicle stop for a traffic violation, which causes short-term annoyance and minor costs, an actual arrest involves a fair amount of administrative costs, in addition to whatever social stigma costs are incurred by the defendant.

While these various studies try to disentangle the reasons for differential search rates across racial groups, what is by far the most likely case is that racial profiling *simultaneously* involves efficient policing and racial bias. Policy makers, then, face the difficult task of determining if the benefits of racial profiling as an effective policing technique outweigh the costs associated with racially biased police behavior. Complicating this task, policy makers have to confront a strong public outcry against racial profiling. This has led to several jurisdictions enacting reforms in an attempt to reduce or eliminate the practice. And this leads to an interesting question: what is the impact on crime rates when the police are no longer allowed to use racial profiling?

In an attempt to answer this question, one study (Heaton 2010) takes advantage of a high-profile, controversial policing incident in New Jersey in the late 1990s that led to immediate reforms. The study examines whether these reforms had an unintended impact on criminal behavior. More specifically, did these reforms reduce the arrest rates of minorities, thus leading to an increase in minority crime rates?

In April 1998, two white New Jersey state troopers shot at four men, three blacks and one Hispanic, who were driving in a van on the New Jersey Turnpike. The troopers pulled the van over for speeding, and as one of them approached the van on foot, it began to slowly roll backward. When the van did not come to a complete stop, the troopers fired eleven rounds into it, wounding three of the occupants. The driver of the van claimed that the van rolled backward because he did not properly place it into park. Furthermore, he claimed that he was not exceeding the speed limit in the first place. The troopers claimed that the van was speeding, although they did not have a radar detector with them to accurately measure the extent of the speeding. None of the occupants of the van were armed, and no drugs were found. The troopers claimed that they were threatened when the van continued to roll backward and that their actions were justified to protect themselves and to prevent the van from fleeing.

This particular incident led to public outrage over the practice of racial profiling by the New Jersey state police, as well as among police officers in general. Not only was a civil suit filed against the state of New Jersey, the two troopers involved in the shooting were indicted on attempted murder and assault charges. Although the criminal charges were ultimately dismissed, the state paid nearly $13 million to settle the lawsuit. Most significant, however, from a public policy perspective, the incident directly led to an explicit change in state police policy concerning racial profiling and vehicle stops.

In response to the incident, the governor of New Jersey ordered the state Attorney General's Office to write a detailed report documenting the state police's racial profiling practices and to offer a number of reforms to greatly reduce the incidence of such practices. Among the many reforms offered, these two provide a good representation of the report's objectives:

> [The report] recommends that the State Police enhance and modify their training programs to make certain that the policies regarding racial profiling and the disparate treatment of minorities proposed in this Interim report are understood by all State Troopers who are assigned to patrol, their supervisors, and dispatchers.

> [The report] recommends the development of a legislative initiative to create new official misconduct offenses to deal specifically with the use of police authority to knowingly or purposely violate a citizen's civil rights.

In short, the shooting incident led to concrete policy changes governing the behavior of the New Jersey state police.

Racial profiling became, and continued to be, an extremely well-publicized issue in New Jersey in the aftermath of the turnpike shooting. Other incidents relating to the shooting (controversial public statements by public officials, charges brought against the troopers, officials being fired) kept the local, regional, and national media busy. Thus, the public was made well aware of the reforms that would now guide police behavior. In addition to the heightened public scrutiny, the reforms themselves could directly affect the behavior of state troopers since they would now face disciplinary measures if racial bias was believed to be present in the performance of their duties.

Examining this anticipated change in police behavior, the study finds that the reforms did lead to a fairly substantial reduction in the number of arrests (between 16 percent and 33 percent) of blacks relative to whites for motor vehicle thefts, a crime that is often detected through vehicle stops. The study also finds that minorities respond to changes in police procedures in a similar fashion to the general population—higher arrest rates lead to less crime, and lower arrest rates lead to more crime—and so the lower arrest rates led to higher rates of motor vehicle theft in minority areas. Because the New Jersey policing scandal led to substantial policy changes that were enacted reasonably quickly, the study attributes the change in arrest and crime rates largely to the sudden changes in police procedures concerning racial profiling. In short, the reduction in racial profiling as a policing technique led to an increase in the minority crime rate (in this case, motor vehicle thefts).

In all, there is nearly universal acceptance of the fact that racial profiling exists. Individuals of different races (as well as other demographic characteristics) face very different search rates by the authorities. The key contribution of economic reasoning, however, is to emphasize that different search rates, even substantially different search rates, are not *necessarily* an indication of racial bias. Some studies conclude that racial profiling is an efficient policing technique involving statistical discrimination that takes advantage of the fact that different races have different propensities to commit crime. Other studies conclude that racial profiling involves racial discrimination: either police officers (in general) are biased against specific races, or the race of a particular police officer determines the direction of the bias for that officer. As with other empirical debates we have discussed, there is no easy way to identify and evaluate the advantages and disadvantages of such a controversial policing technique. One thing is certain: even if racial profiling involves efficient statistical discrimination, any policing procedure that relies on a demographic such as race is bound to lead to a substantial public outcry, making the public policy implications of using such a procedure all the more difficult to assess.

Discussion Questions

1. Social welfare analysis begins with the identification of the social costs and social benefits of whatever issue is at hand. What are the social costs of racial discrimination in the criminal justice system? Can you identify any social benefits?

2. If it is the case that racial profiling simultaneously involves efficient policing and racial bias, how would you design public policy to deal with the problem? Would you apply a consistent policy across other demographic characteristics such as gender, age, ethnicity, and citizenship?

3. Many states have laws prohibiting employers from using criminal background checks when considering hiring prospective employees. The main benefit of these laws is that they help released offenders find legitimate employment opportunities to discourage future criminal behavior. But one of the main costs of these laws that economists have identified is that they may encourage racial discrimination. Why might that be? How would you evaluate the costs and benefits of these laws?

References

Antonovics, K., and B. G. Knight. 2009. "A New Look at Racial Profiling: Evidence from the Boston Police Department." *Review of Economics and Statistics* 91:163–77.

Heaton, P. 2010. "Understanding the Effects of Antiprofiling Policies." *Journal of Law and Economics* 53:29–64.

Knowles, J., N. Persico, and P. Todd. 2001. "Racial Bias in Motor Vehicle Searches: Theory and Evidence." *Journal of Political Economy* 109:203–29.

Sanga, S. 2009. "Reconsidering Racial Bias in Motor Vehicle Searches: Theory and Evidence." *Journal of Political Economy* 117:1155–59.

———. 2014. "Does Officer Race Matter?" *American Law and Economics Review* 16:403–32.

Tomic, A., and J. K. Hakes. 2008. "Case Dismissed: Police Discretion and Racial Differences in Dismissals of Felony Charges." *American Law and Economics Review* 10:110–41.

CHAPTER THIRTEEN

Do Judges Discriminate When Sentencing?

The Sentencing Reform Act and Federal Sentencing Guidelines (1984)

Background

In 1984, the Sentencing Reform Act established the United States Sentencing Commission, an independent commission of the judicial branch of government:

> The commission is responsible for developing guidelines that prescribe a range of sentences for federal judges to use in criminal cases. According to the statute, the guidelines are intended to establish fairness in sentencing, to prevent disparities in the sentencing of similar defendants, and to reflect "advancement in knowledge of human behavior as it relates to the criminal justice process." The act also indicated that the guidelines should reflect the seriousness of the crime, deter other criminal activity, and protect public security. (Federal Judicial Center website)

Using the guidelines to derive the sentence recommendation for a specific case involves several steps. Consider this example for a federal drug case ("Understanding a Basic Federal Drug Case Sentencing," Families against Mandatory Minimums' website, July 16, 2013). The defendant is convicted for conspiracy to possess with intent to distribute at least 500 grams of cocaine. The sentence, however, can be based on a different amount of drugs due to the *relevant conduct* rules. In short, these rules allow the court to hold the defendant accountable for drugs sold, manufactured, or imported by other people involved in the conspiracy, even if the defendant was never convicted of possessing more than 500 grams. Let's say this brings the total drug possession to 550 grams. This makes the base offense level 26. If the defendant possessed a gun during the drug offense, this would add 2 to the base level. If the defendant played only a minor role in the offense, that would reduce the level by 2, bringing it back down to 26. If the defendant accepted responsibility and pleaded guilty, that would reduce the level by another 3. This leaves the final offense level at 23.

Once the offense level is determined, the criminal history category must be calculated. If the defendant had one prior felony drug conviction and served fourteen months in prison, had no other prior criminal history, was not on parole or probation at the time of the recent offense, this would be worth 3 points and represent criminal history category II. With an offense level of 23 points and criminal history category II, the guideline sentence range is fifty-one to sixty-three months. But it does not end here.

There may be a mandatory minimum attached to the statute applied to the defendant. Let's say in this example that minimum is five years. If this minimum applies, it effectively raises the low end of the sentence range from fifty-one months to sixty months. Yet even if a minimum does apply, the defendant may qualify for a "safety valve" that allows the mandatory minimum to be circumvented. The safety valve depends on several factors relating to the defendant's criminal history and behavior during the commission of the crime. But even if the safety valve does not apply in this case, the defendant may still circumvent the mandatory minimum if "substantial assistance" is provided to the prosecution. It is also possible for the sentence to exceed the maximum of sixty-three months, however, if the court finds that substantial aggravating factors warrant an increase in the sentence.

Even though the main objective of the guidelines is to constrain judges and reduce the potential for judicial bias, this example demonstrates that there is plenty of wiggle room in using the guidelines. Not only is there a sentence *range* for each particular offense score and criminal history combination, judges can make upward or downward departures from that range. Furthermore, in the 2005 Supreme Court case *United States v. Booker*, the Court decided that the guidelines were no longer to be considered mandatory but only advisory. This decision was predicted to enhance judicial discretion, further working against the guidelines' initial objective of trying to reduce such discretion. In all, these flexibilities have allowed economists to examine the role of sentencing guidelines, both pre- and post-*Booker*, in affecting judicial bias in sentencing.

Economic Analysis

The stated goal of the sentencing guidelines is to reduce the incidence of judicial bias. Has this goal been met? To determine if judges display bias even when constrained by the guidelines, one study (Mustard 2001) takes advantage of a huge data set that is made up of more than 77,000 individuals sentenced under the guidelines between October 1991 and September 1994. A total of forty-one categories of crimes are taken into account, from the most frequent crimes of drug trafficking, fraud, and larceny to the less frequent crimes of murder, manslaughter, and kidnapping, and many others including civil rights violations, pornography, counterfeiting, and antitrust violations. The study has data pertaining to each defendant's offense level, criminal history, race, education, income, number of dependents, and citizenship (US or not), and uses these data to explain variation in sentence lengths.

At first blush, the data depict substantial racial and gender discrimination in sentence lengths. For example, the average sentence (in months) for blacks is 64.09, which is double the average white sentence of 32.06. Even more pronounced is the gender gap, with the average male sentence of 51.52 nearly three times as large as the average female sentence of 18.51. It is discrepancies like these that often have critics denounce the flagrant bias observed in judicial sentencing decisions, especially with respect to race. But a first blush look at the data does not always tell a complete story.

The two most important factors that explain sentence lengths are a defendant's offense level and criminal history score, and it is a fact that these scores vary by race and gender. For example, the study finds that the average black offense level is 19.01 compared to the white level of 15.48, and the average black criminal history score is 2.37 compared to the white score of 1.81. For men, the average offense level is 18.30 compared to 13.11 for women, and the average criminal history score is 2.10 for men compared to 1.37 for women. One can question if these scores are themselves calculated with bias, but to the extent that objective measures are used to determine these scores, higher scores necessarily lead to longer sentences.

It is worth reiterating a point that was discussed in chapter 12. Precisely *why* offense levels and criminals scores vary by race and gender is an important, and complicated, issue. Understanding the "why" can only help better inform the debate on, and improve the implementation of, social policy options in reducing crime. But for the purposes of sentencing under the guidelines, the offense level and criminal history score for each defendant must be taken as given, *regardless* of the underlying reasons these scores may vary across demographic categories.

So now we can ask: do sentences vary largely due to differences in criminal behavior across race and gender, or to judicial bias? After controlling for defendants' offense level and criminal history, and for the district court in which they are tried, the study finds that large disparities in sentence length do exist on the basis of race and gender, as well as other factors that the guidelines are supposed to rule out such as education, income, and citizenship. The study finds that, on average, blacks face harsher sentences than whites, men face harsher sentences than women, defendants with low levels of education and low levels of income face harsher sentences compared to better educated and wealthier defendants, and non-US citizens face harsher sentences than US citizens.

The study is also able to examine if sentence differences stem from variations within the guideline sentence ranges or from judges departing from the ranges. In 72.9 percent of the cases, no departure is made from the guideline's ranges; in the remaining cases, upward departures are made 1.2 percent of the time, and downward departures are made 25.9 percent of the time. If judges depart from the ranges, they are susceptible to appellate review, which helps explain the adherence rate of almost three-quarters. When departing, it is far more common to observe downward departures than upward ones, but almost one-third of the downward departures are due to assistance to the prosecution, such as when defendants provide information about other cases. Still, this leaves departures (excluding assistance) occurring in nearly one-fifth of all cases.

What can be said about departures from the ranges and judicial bias? Blacks are more likely to receive upward departures than whites, and less likely to receive downward departures. Men are more likely to receive upward departures than women, and less likely to receive downward departures. When downward departures are given, blacks receive smaller departures than whites, and men receive smaller departures than women. Similar biases in departures are also found against defendants who are less educated, have lower income, and are not US citizens. In all, if the introduction of the sentencing guidelines in 1984 did reduce judicial bias, the results of this study suggest that they certainly did not eliminate it.

In an updating of the previous study (and similar ones not discussed here), one study (Sorensen, Sarnikar, and Oaxaca 2012) applies a different estimation strategy to determine if judicial biases exist even when judges are "constrained" by the sentencing guidelines. The study demonstrates that judges consider factors that the guidelines expressly prohibit. For example, for both white and black men, lower sentences are associated with being married, having dependents, and having a privately hired defense attorney. In terms of racial and gender biases, the study considers three groups— white women, white men, and black men. The results are that black men face higher sentences than white men, who face higher sentences than white women. Thus, for similar crime severity and criminal history, black men are the most, and white women are the least, severely punished.

One ambitious study (Rehavi and Starr 2014) addresses an important, and largely overlooked, question: how much of the racial disparities found at sentencing are attributed to racial disparities found in the initial charges that prosecutors bring? If judges are sentencing in large part as a reaction to the initial charges that prosecutors bring, and if these charges are racially biased, the true source of sentencing disparity can be traced back to an earlier stage—the prosecutorial stage. Prosecutors have a tremendous amount of power in determining precisely how to initially charge a criminal. The facts of any individual case can provide several options for potential charges. The study offers a nice illustrative example:

> For instance, if a gun is found in a car that transported a defendant to a burglary, the prosecutor must decide whether to allege that the burglary legally qualified as a "crime of violence" . . . , that the gun qualified as a "firearm," and that the defendant "carried" it "during and in relation to" the burglary—all of which are necessary to trigger a 5-year mandatory minimum sentence . . . which would run consecutively to the burglary sentence. A lenient prosecutor might choose to "swallow the gun" and just charge burglary. (1324)

This flexibility in prosecutorial discretion can lead to potential biases in deciding how to charge various defendants.

There is a fairly large scholarly literature on what motivates prosecutorial decisions. The initial charge is only the start of what can be a long process to the sentencing stage, and prosecutors are typically concerned with many factors in determining that charge. These include the likelihood of a case going to trial; the likelihood of conviction if the case does go to trial; the severity of the potential punishment; one's reputation among defense attorneys and judges; a sense of fairness; and, possibly, personal biases involving race, gender, and other demographics of defendants.

The study uses a very rich data set of federal cases from 2007 to 2009, with male defendants who are US citizens, who are either black or white, and who have been arrested for various property or violent crimes. The first step in the analysis is to determine if there are racial disparities in how defendants are charged, after controlling for a wide variety of factors that include type of crime committed, criminal history, demographics such as age and education, economic factors, and defense counsel type. The results demonstrate that black men are charged more severely than white men, especially with charges that carry mandatory minimum sentences. Quantitatively, black men are twice as likely as white men to face a mandatory minimum sentence charge.

The next step in the analysis is to determine if the initial charge disparities affect sentencing. The study demonstrates that racial gaps in sentence length, for defendants arrested for the same crimes and having the same criminal history, are largely attributable to prosecutorial discretion. Most important, it is the disparate use of mandatory-minimum-sentence charges against black men that leads to sentences that are, on average, approximately 10 percent longer for them. While the study cannot rule out the possibility that judges may still be biased against blacks when sentencing, it correctly argues that *just* considering judicial discretion independent of prosecutorial discretion is too narrow a focus.

A related study (Starr 2015) examines gender disparities in sentencing, again arguing that prosecutorial discretion plays a significant role in explaining judicial sentencing gaps. In this case, the sentencing gaps are substantial, with men receiving approximately 63 percent longer sentences than women arrested for similar crimes, with similar criminal histories, and controlling for other factors. Furthermore, women are less likely to be charged at all, less likely to be convicted if charged, and more likely to avoid prison if convicted. Combining the results of both studies, a bleak picture is painted for black male defendants—they face sentencing disparities for being black *and* for being male. These disparities are largely explained by prosecutorial discretion, although judicial bias remains an important concern.

Yet one other related study (Starr and Rehavi 2013) examines the impact of the 2005 *Booker* Supreme Court decision on racial disparities in federal sentencing. The *Booker* decision changed the status of the sentencing guidelines from mandatory to advisory. To the extent that the guidelines did constrain judicial sentencing, there was a concern that making the guidelines advisory would exacerbate the problem of racial discrimination in sentencing. In fact, the United States Sentencing Commission, in a 2012 report specifically addressing this concern, found that the post-*Booker* sentencing gaps for black men versus white men, and men versus women, *increased* relative to the pre-*Booker* sentencing gaps.

The study challenges the credibility of the Sentencing Commission's findings primarily for two reasons. First, as argued above, judicial sentencing disparities may largely be due to prosecutorial charging disparities. Without explicitly taking this factor into account, empirical results that focus solely on the sentencing stage are not likely to be telling a complete story. Second, and importantly, the Sentencing Commission's study does not consider other factors that may be accounting for sentencing disparity differences pre- and post-*Booker*:

> The Commission found that disparities after *Booker* (averaged over a period of years) were larger than disparities before it. Even assuming that were true, it would still be a huge logical leap to conclude that *Booker caused* this increase—a classic confusion of correlation and causation. Many things change over time—for instance, the mix of cases, the composition of the bench and of U.S. Attorneys' and public defenders' offices, substantive criminal legislation and case law, and the Department of Justice's enforcement priorities and internal policies—and any of these changes could have racially disparate impacts on sentences. The greater disparity in the post-*Booker* period, therefore, could easily have nothing to do with *Booker*. Indeed, even if *Booker* had *slowed* an underlying trend to increasing disparity, the Commission's methods would incorrectly imply that *Booker* led to greater disparity. (8)

The study's reasonably complicated approach to dealing with these issues, in brief, does not yield evidence that *Booker* had an adverse impact on the sentencing of black versus white defendants.

There is other economic research that examines the role of bias in sentencing outside the influence of sentencing guidelines. One study (Glaeser and Sacerdote 2003) examines the role of victim characteristics in affecting the punishment of drivers convicted of vehicular homicide. Such crimes are largely caused by drivers who are under the influence of alcohol or drugs, and as a result have more in common with accidents than they do with intentional acts of violence. This allows us to think of the victims of vehicular homicide to be largely determined at random, especially when compared to victims of other violent crimes.

The cleverness behind the study stems from the fact that the more complicated the relationship between criminal and victim, the more factors exist that may affect punishment. In general, differential punishments need not imply bias in sentencing, but controlling for the many factors that affect sentencing can be a difficult task. With randomly selected victims, however, the relationship between criminal and victim is far less complicated. If victims of vehicular homicide can truly be thought of as being randomly selected, differential punishments can more confidently be attributed to the presence of bias.

The study's main result in terms of racial bias is that drivers who kill blacks receive sentences that are approximately 60 percent shorter than the sentences received by drivers who kill whites. In terms of gender bias, drivers who kill women receive sentences that are approximately 60 percent longer than those received by drivers who kill men. The study concludes that bias appears to be an important contributing factor in the determination of punishment. How does the study account for this bias? "One proposed explanation . . . is that sentence lengths are driven, in part, by a taste for vengeance. Since this taste may be operating at a subconscious level, it would not be surprising if victim characteristics still motivate this taste, even when the victim is random" (365). Although the study finds evidence of bias in sentencing, it also notes that sentences are not determined *only* by bias, but also by other factors that fit well with the rational crime model discussed in chapter 10.

One study (Ayres and Waldfogel 1994) examines racial bias in the criminal justice system by determining if there is a difference in how bail is set for minority (black and Hispanic) versus white defendants. The primary role of bail is to ensure that the defendant appears in court when required. If a defendant does not appear, the bail is forfeited, either directly by the defendant or by a bail bondsman. Thus, the reasoning goes, the greater the amount of bail, the greater the incentive for the defendant to appear in court, or for the bail bondsman to guarantee that the defendant appears in court.

One objective an unbiased judge may have is to set bail to secure a particular level of *flight risk* that is constant across all defendants. Let's say that particular level of flight risk is 10 percent, and the judge sets bail at $5,000 for each of two defendants. If one defendant has a 20 percent flight risk at this amount, and the other has a 10 percent flight risk, the judge's objective is not met—the first defendant has too high a flight risk. To achieve the objective, then, bail must be set higher than $5,000 for the first defendant only, say at $7,500. Thus, to achieve equal flight risks, the two defendants must face different bail amounts. If the first defendant is black, and the second is white, the different bail amounts may have the appearance of being racially motivated, but that would be incorrect. Because the judge is assumed to be unbiased, the different bail amounts are only due to the defendants' different propensities to flee when the bail amounts are identical.

Instead, what if the judge is racially biased? Part of the bail amount for the black defendant would reflect that bias, so possibly bail would be set at $10,000 instead of $7,500. The additional amount can no longer be explained by trying to assure a flight risk of 10 percent. In fact, with a bail amount set at $10,000, that defendant's flight risk will be less than 10 percent—the greater the bail amount, the lower the flight risk, as the defendant (or the bail bondsman) has more to lose with flight.

To determine if bail amounts are affected by the race of the defendant, the study uses data from criminal cases in New Haven, Connecticut, for the year 1990. The study finds that race does statistically significantly affect bail, even after controlling for several other factors relating to the nature and severity of the crime. Quantitatively, black men face (on average) 35 percent higher bail than white men, and Hispanic men face (on average) 19 percent higher bail than white men. The problem with these empirical results, however, is that there are still many other factors that could affect the determination of bail, but due to data limitations these factors are not considered. Such factors include the weight of the evidence against the defendant, the defendant's prior criminal record and prior court appearance record, and the defendant's employment record. The fewer relevant factors that the study can consider, the less confident it can be that differences in bail amounts can be attributed to racial bias.

To circumvent the problem of not being able to consider many relevant factors, the study offers a novel solution. Instead of looking at differences in bail amounts to test for racial bias, they look at differences in bail bond *rates*. A defendant who uses the services of a bail bondsman agrees to pay a percentage rate of the bail amount to have the bondsman put up the bail. If the defendant does not appear, the bondsman forfeits the bail amount (or in some cases, a portion of the amount). This provides the bondsman with an incentive to ensure that the defendant does not flee. The more likely a defendant is to flee, then, the costlier (in terms of flight risk) it is for the bondsman to put up the bail for the defendant.

Although there are regulations that govern the setting of bond rates, bondsmen do have the opportunity to vary rates across defendants. If we assume that the bail bonds market is fairly competitive and that individual bondsmen face similar costs in operating their businesses, we can expect the differences in rates to be largely due to differences in flight risks. Quite simply, defendants who have higher flight risks are expected to face higher bond rates than defendants who have lower flight risks. The study finds that minority defendants face *lower* bond rates than white defendants, and this must be because minority defendants have lower flight risks. Why is this so? If there is judicial racial bias in the setting of bail, minority defendants may face a higher bail amount than necessary to secure a target flight risk. The higher bail amount leads to a lower flight risk, and this leads to a lower bond rate.

What is especially clever about this study is that it examines the bail bonds market to identify potential *judicial* bias. Trying to sort out why judges do what they do can be an empirical mess, especially to the extent that subjective values affect judicial decisions. By focusing on the bails bonds market instead, competitive bondsmen must survive by setting bond rates that are neither too high nor too low relative to their rivals (and the study presents evidence that the bail bonds market in New Haven is competitive, especially compared to other Connecticut towns). If competitive market conditions force bond rates to vary primarily due to differences in flight risks, and these differences are primarily due to differences in bail amounts, more confidence can be placed on this approach in identifying judicial racial bias. Of course, there still may be other factors accounting for the differences in bond rates that are not due to judicial bias, as the study readily admits.

As an example, another study (McIntyre and Baradaran 2013) examines potential racial bias in the judicial decision to release or hold a defendant pretrial. One important determinant of this decision is the judge's assessment of the defendant's likelihood of being rearrested for another crime *before* the trial takes place. Using a large data set covering the years 1990 to 2006, the study finds that (approximately) 43 percent of black male defendants are held, while only 34 percent of white male defendants are held, pretrial. At first glance, this difference points to racial disparities in judicial decisions. However, when the probability of rearrest is taken into account, the study finds no difference in the likelihoods of black and white defendants being held. Furthermore, again when rearrest is taken into account, the study finds no difference in bail amounts between black and white defendants. Just as sentence gaps are often largely, but definitely not only, explained by difference in crimes and criminal history, what appears to be racial discrimination in how the defendants are treated pretrial, may largely be explained by a nondiscriminatory factor—the potential for criminal behavior with pretrial release.

So, are judges racially biased? To answer this question, a researcher is required to sort through many complicating factors. Just using average sentence data across race and gender does not even scratch the surface of providing an adequate response. While the evidence is mixed, and certainly there must be a wide variation in how individual judges behave, there exists a body of evidence that firmly points to the possibility of judicial discrimination. But even with a belief that such discrimination exists, what is most interesting from a public policy perspective is the question of how to rectify such behavior.

The federal sentencing guidelines offer one approach, but the studies presented in this chapter tend not to support the idea that these guidelines have a significant impact on behavior. Either because the guidelines allow for too much wiggle room within sentence ranges or because judges often depart from the recommended ranges, sentencing guidelines do not appear to be an obvious cure-all. Or perhaps they are nothing more than a solution to a problem that doesn't exist, especially if the heart of the problem lies elsewhere, such as at the prosecutorial stage. One thing is for certain—racial discrimination continues to be one of the most serious public policy issues the criminal justice system must confront.

Discussion Questions

1. If sentencing differences across race and gender are largely a result of prosecutorial discretion in charging, is the solution to design policies that restrict such discretion? Propose and evaluate such potential policies.

2. If judges do discriminate when sentencing, and sentencing guidelines appear not to be able to adequately curtail such discrimination, how else can judicial discrimination be controlled? Evaluate these other controls.

3. One other important part of the criminal system in which racial discrimination may play a role is with juries, and there are two main avenues in which bias can occur:

   a. *Jury selection*. Both prosecution and defense attorneys have discretion in choosing which jurors to seat. *Peremptory challenges* allow each side to strike jurors without (at least traditionally) providing any explanations. In other words, these are not strikes for cause; these are completely at the discretion of the attorneys. (Although to help control racial bias, attorneys may face what is known as a *Batson challenge* that requires them to provide some explanation if the strike appears to be racially motivated. It is usually not difficult to provide some alternative explanation, however, so a *Batson* challenge may not be highly constraining.)

b. *Jury deliberation.* Individual jurors undoubtedly have their own biases that may affect not only their own decisions but the decisions of other jurors through the deliberation process.

Propose and evaluate public policy proposals that can help alleviate the potential biases associated with juries.

References

Ayres, I., and Waldfogel, J. 1994. "A Market Test for Race Discrimination in Bail Setting." *Stanford Law Review* 46:987–1047.

Glaeser, E. L., and B. Sacerdote. 2003. "Sentencing in Homicide Cases and the Role of Vengeance." *Journal of Legal Studies* 32:363–82.

McIntyre, F., and S. Baradaran. 2013. "Race, Prediction, and Pretrial Detention." *Journal of Empirical Legal Studies* 10:741–70.

Mustard, D. B. 2001. "Racial, Ethnic, and Gender Disparities in Sentencing: Evidence from the U.S. Federal Courts." *Journal of Law and Economics* 44:285–314.

Rehavi, M. M., and S. B. Starr. 2014. "Racial Disparity in Federal Criminal Sentences." *Journal of Political Economy* 122:1320–54.

Sorensen, T., S. Sarnikar, and R. L. Oaxaca. 2012. "Race and Gender Differences under Federal Sentencing Guidelines." *American Economic Review: Papers and Proceedings* 102:256–60.

Starr, S. B. 2015. "Estimating Gender Disparities in Federal Criminal Cases." *American Law and Economics Review* 17:127–59.

Starr, S. B., and M. B. Rehavi. 2013. "Mandatory Sentencing and Racial Disparity: Assessing the Role of Prosecutors and the Effects of *Booker*." *Yale Law Journal* 123:2–80.

US Sentencing Commission. 2012. *Report on the Continuing Impact of United States v. Booker on Federal Sentencing.*

PART V

Behavioral Law and Economics

CHAPTER FOURTEEN

How Does Behavioral Economics Contribute to the Economic Analysis of Law?

A Brief Introduction to the Marriage of Economics and Psychology

Background

Just as economic analysis in the 1970s began to present challenging new ways to think about the law, especially when compared to more traditional legal scholarship, more recently *behavioral economics* began to present challenging new ways to think about economic analysis:

> Over the last decade or so, behavioral economics has fundamentally changed the way economists conceptualize the world. Behavioral economics is an umbrella of approaches that seek to extend the standard economics framework to account for relevant features of human behavior that are absent in the standard economics framework. Typically, this calls for borrowing from the neighboring social sciences, particularly from psychology and sociology. The emphasis is on well-documented empirical findings: at the core of behavioral economics is the conviction that making our model of economic man more accurate will improve our understanding of economics, thereby making that discipline more useful. (Diamond and Vartiainen 2007, 1)

Behavioral economists study a wider variety of personal objectives than just wealth maximization, the leading objective assumed throughout this book. Furthermore, humans are quirky and flawed, and behave

in ways that obviously appear to violate the assumption of perfect ratio-
nality. It is not that behavioral economics posits an *irrational* economic
individual, but rather a rational individual who faces a number of complicated constraints that challenge the traditional economic assumption that
people typically make cognitively sound decisions.

This chapter will provide a (very) brief introduction to some behavioral economics issues that directly relate to topics previously covered
earlier in this book. The goal is modest—to provide a taste of how behavioral economists can approach a familiar topic though a fairly new lens.
One thing that will not be done is to provide a serious comparative discussion of traditional versus behavioral approaches to the law. As fascinating
and important as that would be, that analysis goes far beyond the scope of
this book. Other than some brief concluding comments, the focus here is
on five examples, each identified by a specific topic that was discussed in
an earlier chapter.

Alleviating the Kidney Shortage

Chapter 1 focused on the development of a market for kidneys to help alleviate the severe shortage of kidneys available for transplant. Behavioral
economists consider another approach to alleviate the problem, known as
presumed consent. Under the current system of donation only, the *default*
is that no one is a kidney donor: you have to make an explicit choice to
become one. Under presumed consent, the default is changed so that everyone is a donor: now you have to make an explicit choice *not* to be one.
The behavioral argument is that by changing the default, the supply of kidneys available for transplant will increase. Why is this so?

Defaults provide an interesting setting in which to study how social policy can be designed to take advantage of what is considered to be a quirk
in human behavior—the tendency of some people to stay put regardless of
what "staying put" entails. Let's say you want to be an organ donor. Under
the current system of donation only, the default is that you are not a donor,
so you must choose to opt in to the program. If the default is changed under
presumed consent, then you must choose not to opt out of the program.
In either case, because you want to be an organ donor, the default has no
impact on your ultimate decision.

But what happens if you don't want to be an organ donor? Under the
current system, you don't have to do anything. If the default is changed

under presumed consent, you must choose to opt out of the program. Once again, in either case, because you don't want to be an organ donor, the default has no impact on your ultimate decision. But there is a twist to consider in this scenario. The important question a behavioral economist will ask is, precisely why under the current system are you not an organ donor? Is it because you truly don't want to be, so if the default does change you will maintain that preference and opt out? Or is it because you stick with the default, *regardless* of what the default is? In this latter case, changing the default *will* matter.

Sticking with a default, regardless of what the default entails, is a phenomenon known as *status quo bias* (see Camerer et al. 2003). Why do some people always choose to stay with the status quo? One explanation may be that the costs of switching are too high. If you have to do something specific to switch, such as fill in paperwork or go to some place to apply, you may find it best to stick with the default and save on those costs. Or even if you are willing to incur the switching costs, perhaps you are a procrastinator— you have the intention of switching away from the default, but you just never seem to get around to it. Related to this explanation, it may not be the physical costs of switching that matter but instead the information costs. Perhaps you don't realize that there is another option or that there is even a default to begin with. In countries that use presumed consent, do all people realize that they are organ donors with the ability to opt out of the program? In many cases, however, even when switching costs and information costs are very low, the status quo bias exists.

Another explanation for status quo bias involves what is referred to as the *omission/commission bias*. In this case, people may care more about making errors of commission (they regret choosing an option other than the default) than they do about making errors of omission (they regret choosing an option that was the default). What this means is that people are more upset when they explicitly choose something that doesn't work out than when they stick with a default that doesn't work out. Experiencing regret through action or inaction is simply rationalized differently.

Regardless of why people tend to stick with defaults, the tendency to do so can be taken advantage of by policy makers. This is the idea behind presumed consent in organ donation. If being a donor is the default, behavioral economists believe that more people will be donors and the supply of kidneys available for transplant will increase. But this simple prediction may involve some complications.

First, the status quo bias must actually exist for the default to make a difference. It may be the case that everyone who chooses the default under the current system may not choose the default under presumed consent, leaving the number of organs available for transplant the same. Second, changing the default may have an impact on how people feel about the system. You may want to be a donor when you have to make the explicit choice to be one, but you may protest against a system that makes you a donor by default, so you choose to opt out. This can actually lead to fewer kidneys being available for transplant under presumed consent. Finally, and most important, presumed consent does not always involve a well-defined property right for doctors to harvest organs for transplant. In some countries where presumed consent is the default, it is often the case that family consent is sought out, and the family may have the opportunity to prevent the organs from being harvested. Thus, it is an empirical question as to whether presumed consent actually increases the supply of organs for transplant.

One study (Bilgel 2012) offers an extensive cross-country comparison of presumed consent versus *informed consent* (another way to describe donation only). Of the twenty-four countries included in the empirical analysis, fifteen use presumed consent and nine use informed consent. At first, using a simple approach that does not take into account confounding factors, the study confirms a result that is reasonably common in the literature: presumed consent does not have much impact on increasing the supply of organs for transplant. This result, however, likely has more to do with the various institutional settings found in different countries, as opposed to presumed consent in and of itself.

The study finds that presumed consent is likely to have its greatest impact under two particular institutional settings. In the first, family consent is *not* sought. This means that presumed consent places the property right of the organs with the doctors, as long as the donor did not explicitly opt out of the system. In the second, family consent is sought, but only if the donor is explicitly identified as a donor through a national registry. This setting requires more explanation.

Consider parents whose (adult) child has just died in a presumed consent country, and the child did not opt out of the system. Technically, the child's organs can be harvested for transplant. If the doctors seek permission from the parents, however, they may not know if their child truly wanted to be a donor, or simply never opted out of the default. In this case, the parents may not permit the organs to be harvested. By allowing the child, even under presumed consent, to explicitly register as an organ donor, the true wishes of the deceased can be publicly verified. The parents, then, may be more confident in their child's wishes to be an organ donor, and grant their permission.

In settings in which family consent is sought but a national registry is not maintained, the study finds that presumed consent has only modest impact on donation rates. What this demonstrates is that for the state to take advantage of the behavioral quirk associated with status quo bias, not only must the default be chosen to "nudge" people in the socially appropriate direction (see Thaler and Sunstein 2008, chap. 11), but other institutional factors must be taken into consideration. Of course, one important concern governing defaults is to clearly define what the "socially appropriate direction" actually is, and this will always be a contentious issue regardless of the default chosen.

Eminent Domain, Subjective Value, and Private Takings

In 2005, the Supreme Court ruled in *Kelo v. City of New London* that the government could take private property under eminent domain with the intention of eventually transferring it to private developers. The Court argued that the "public use" requirement of the Fifth Amendment allowed takings that promoted economic development. *Kelo* is very similar to *Poletown* (from chapter 3), with one interesting exception—the degree of public outrage that followed the decisions. The Poletown decision certainly outraged a great number of people, including those directly affected by the takings, legal and public policy analysts, and many individuals who simply dislike governmental takings power. But as Nadler and Diamond (2008, 714) noted, *Kelo* seemed to create a backlash that swept over the public at large:

> Rarely has a single Supreme Court decision triggered a groundswell of popular outrage, a news frenzy, and immediate legislative response. In testimony before Congress, property scholar Thomas Merrill commented that *Kelo* "is unique in modern annals of law in terms of the negative response it has evoked." A multitude of reform laws in many states followed quickly on the heels of the decision, with the declared purpose to limit the government's ability to exercise its power of eminent domain. . . . The effect of post-*Kelo* reform efforts is not yet clear, but it is clear that the reform efforts were invigorated by the public opinion backlash that was unleashed following the Court's announcement of the decision in *Kelo*.

The study uses the public response over the *Kelo* decision as a jumping-off point to examine precisely what it is about eminent domain power that outrages ordinary citizens. One reason for outrage is the often-discussed belief that just compensation typically undercompensates true subjective value. Homeowners can have several reasons for attaching significant value to their property that would not be reflected in a calculation of fair market value. These attachments may lead either to a willingness-to-sell price that far exceeds fair market value or to a refusal to sell at any price.

Another reason the study identifies is referred to as a *dignitary harm*. This form of outrage addresses emotional reactions property owners may have to governmental takings power. For example, as eminent domain power is invoked in a broader range of settings that go beyond what property owners view as being traditional (such as building highways or airports), an enhanced state of distress may exist due to a belief that the likelihood of property being taken has increased. In addition, resentment may exist if property is taken and then transferred to another private owner, creating distrust in the "public use" justification for a taking. This specific resentment may be exacerbated when the government transfers the property at a ridiculously low price, as seen in *Poletown* with GM and as seen in *Kelo* with the developer that was to be given a ninety-nine-year lease on the property for only $1 per year. Finally, one other dignitary harm may simply be associated with the use of eminent domain to take someone's *home*, as there may be stronger anti-taking feelings associated with homes than with other types of property.

The study undertakes two experiments in an attempt to gauge the reaction of property owners to different eminent domain settings. Briefly (see Nadler and Diamond 2008, for the complete experimental design), in the first experiment it is the government that approaches the property owner in an attempt to undertake a voluntary transaction, but with the *explicit* threat known at the time of transacting that eminent domain can be invoked if the transaction does not go through. In the second experiment, it is a private developer that approaches the property owner in an attempt to undertake a voluntary transaction, and there is no indication at that time that eminent domain power can ever be invoked. *After* the initial proposal is considered by the property owner, if the transaction does not go through, then the threat of eminent domain does become known.

In each experiment, the study examines the impact on the willingness-to-sell value of two main factors: how long the property owner has owned the property, and the proposed use of the property being taken. The length of time of ownership takes on two values—two years, or one hundred years. There are three proposed uses of the property being taken—to build a children's hospital, to build a shopping mall, or no use specifically stated. Thus, there are several experimental scenarios possible, and each subject was presented with a questionnaire involving one particular scenario.

The main result of the study is that the length of ownership has a much stronger impact on the willingness-to-sell value than does the proposed use of the property. There was even a reasonably large response indicating a refusal to sell at any price—approximately 9 percent in experiment 1 and 15 percent in experiment 2—suggesting an enhanced reluctance due to the initial contact's being made by a private developer. Only slight evidence suggests that the proposed use of building a children's hospital affected (lowered) the willingness-to-sell value compared to the other uses, and there appears to be no difference in how the subjects responded to the building of a shopping mall compared to no specified use.

In addition to measuring willingness-to-sell values, the study also asks subjects about their attitudes (across several dimensions) toward eminent domain under the different scenarios. In short, while attitudes toward eminent domain are more negative the longer the length of ownership, and with the use of the property being for a shopping mall or not specified, the most hostile opposition is found in experiment 2. Once it becomes known that the government will step in to aid the private developer through the use of eminent domain power, subjects typically vehemently oppose the taking (but this effect is not found to affect willingness-to-sell values).

One can question what these behavioral results truly add to the eminent domain scholarly debate. Conventional economic analysis has long established that just compensation is likely to underestimate true subjective value, possibly leading to inefficient takings. If you are reluctant to sell your property and eminent domain power needs to be invoked, does it really matter *why* just compensation doesn't fully compensate you? You've lived in your home for decades; you don't like the proposed use of the land being taken; you don't like the identity of the taker. For all of these reasons, just compensation may undercompensate you, and eminent domain power may be inefficient.

So what does behavioral economics add in this setting? The results of the study may allow for a more nuanced approach when considering reforms to discourage the inefficient use of eminent domain power. For example, a common reform suggested post-*Kelo* is to inflate just compensation, such as with a 25 percent premium over fair market value. While this reform addresses the tendency of just compensation to undercompensate subjective value, it does not account for differences across eminent domain settings. What if we consider some alternative reforms?

One other reform suggests that just compensation should vary with the number of years the property has been in the possession of the owner: the longer you have lived in your home, the greater will be your compensation. Or, just compensation should vary with the proposed use or with the identity of the taker: uses and takers that foster outrage in property owners should involve greater compensation. In the end, if behavioral economists can distinguish between different eminent domain settings in novel ways, the efficacy of public policy reforms can also be evaluated in novel ways.

Efficient Breach, Morality, and Liquidated Damages

Chapter 5 explored the concept of efficient breach. While moving resources to a higher-valued use is a standard economic objective, there are many who feel that a contractual breach often violates a moral code of behavior. Thus, breach, especially opportunistic breach mainly for profit, should be strongly discouraged by the law. An economic counterargument to this point is that if a contract is fully specified, breach is not immoral because it is a contingency that is already taken into account by both parties. If a contract is not fully specified, as long as the court's damage remedy matches what the parties *would have* agreed on, the breach is also not immoral. And, so goes the final part of the argument, the expectations remedy is a monetary remedy that both parties, in theory, typically prefer over other monetary remedies.

In terms of encouraging efficient *and* moral breach, then, a fully specified contract is often considered to be equivalent to an incomplete contract that is subject to the expectations remedy in case of breach. One study (Wilkinson-Ryan 2010), however, adds an interesting behavioral twist to this thinking. From a psychological perspective, is it the case that contracting parties think of breach *independent* of how damages are imposed? That is, if both ways to determine damages yield identical monetary amounts, are the parties indifferent to liquidated damages and the court-imposed expectations remedy?

To address this question, the study develops several experimental scenarios that the test subjects are asked to consider. For example, assume that you are one of the subjects. In one scenario you are asked to imagine that you are the owner of a restaurant, and you are considering renting out your restaurant for a private party for one night at a price of $1,000 (to be paid on the night of the party). The people renting the restaurant, the Wilsons, are getting an excellent deal, as the rental price for similar venues is $2,000. The reason you can offer such a low price is that on this particular night, you would have been closed otherwise. So, for the sake of this example, you can consider the $1,000 as pure profit. The contract includes a liquidated damages clause that if the restaurant becomes unavailable for any reason, the Wilsons will be compensated for the breach at the amount of $1,000.

The next part of the story is that two weeks before the Wilsons' party, you hear from another renter interested in renting your restaurant on that same night. They are a well-known rock band, and your restaurant is very close to where they are going to be performing, so they are willing to pay a substantial amount to rent your place. If you decide to rent to the rock band instead of the Wilsons, the liquidated damages clause in the Wilsons' contract will be enforced. You are then asked to consider the following question: "You were expecting a $1000 profit for this night. The band is willing to offer you much more. Given that you have to pay the Wilsons $1000, what is the smallest amount the band could offer such that you would accept their offer?" (657). In another scenario involving the identical setup, there is no liquidated damages clause included in the contract. Instead, in the event of breach, the courts would require you to pay the Wilsons $1,000 in compensation.

This experimental scenario is purposely designed to focus on, as closely as possible, the breaching party's motivation for *efficient* breach. The Wilsons are informed in plenty of time (two weeks before their party) to book another venue that will cost $2,000. Thus, the damages of $1,000, either stipulated in the contract or determined by the court, plus the original $1,000 they were going to pay will allow them to pay for the more expensive venue without any subjective loss in value. For you to breach the contract, you need *at least* $2,000 from the rock band. You must be compensated for the $1,000 profit you will no longer get from the Wilsons and for the additional $1,000 in damages you have to pay, again either through the contractual agreement or determined by the court. If you do decide to breach, then, the rock band will value renting your restaurant at more than $2,000, whereas the Wilsons only value *your* restaurant at a maximum of $2,000 (noting that the Wilsons can go elsewhere for $2,000).

So, precisely what is this experimental design trying to determine? If, as the breaching party, all you care about is profiting from the breach, you should be indifferent to liquidated damages or expectations damages of $1,000. You will breach if the rock band pays you a minimum of $2,000 under either scenario. If, however, you have reservations about breaching the contract for whatever reasons, you may require a minimum that is greater than $2,000. More important, if a fully specified contract has a different meaning to you than one that is incomplete and governed by the expectations remedy, you may require different amounts to breach.

For example, you may feel that breaking a promise is somewhat immoral, which leaves you with a reluctance to breach just to earn additional profit. How much additional profit must you earn to overcome this reluctance? The study hypothesizes that the more distaste you have for breaching the contract, the more profit you will require to breach. Furthermore, liquidated damages that are negotiated between the parties prebreach have the potential to reduce your distaste for breach, thus requiring less profit to breach when compared to an incomplete contract governed by the expectations remedy. The study offers an explanation as to why this may be so:

> Liquidated damages are a means of making the sanction for breach explicit within a contract. Decision researchers have found experimental evidence that, when social norms are in conflict with efficiency incentives, a more explicit incentive structure leads to more self-interested behavior. Even when the law of contracts is arguably clear itself on the legal remedy for breach, moral intuition differentiates between a background law like the rule of expectation damages and an obligation to pay damages included as a clause in the body of the contract. When parties stipulate damages, they clarify the respective expectations of the parties, permitting efficient breach without repudiation of the mutual understanding. (636)

In short, less specified or less formal contracts may be associated with a greater moral urgency not to breach than are more fully specified or more formal contracts.

As discussed in chapter 5, the concept of breach is not easily associated with a fully specified contract. If the terms of the contract specifically allow for liquidated damages when, for example, property is not conveyed to the original buyer, the contract is not technically breached when such damages need to be paid. *Any* contractual clause that is upheld, be it a conveyance of property or a payment of damages, satisfies the terms of the contract. In these cases, the immorality of breach may not be considered too serious an issue for the contracting parties. But with incomplete contracts, the immorality of breach may be an important factor. Social norms may be more at play now, and because specific breach contingencies are not accounted for in the contract, upholding the contract is more directly associated with the morality of keeping of a promise.

To test this hypothesis, the study compares the amounts you would need to breach under the two different scenarios. We know that you need a minimum of $2,000 to make it financially worth your while to breach, but how much more than $2,000 do you need to possibly compensate for your distaste to breach? The study predicts that you will need more to breach when your contract is unspecified and damages are governed by the expectations remedy than when your (identical) damages are stipulated in the contract.

The results of the study support its hypothesis. The average amount needed to breach the contract with the liquidated damages clause is approximately $2,800, while the average amount needed to breach the contract governed by the expectations remedy is approximately $3,900. This difference of $1,100 is interpreted as meaning that subjects who saw a contract with a liquidated damages clause are *more* willing to breach compared to those who do not see such a clause.

To further emphasize the difference between liquidated damages and the expectations remedy, the study examines another scenario that is identical to the previous one, with only one important difference—the liquidated damages clause is now a penalty clause. Specified in the contract is a clause that requires you to pay the Wilsons $1,100 if you breach for any reason, yet the expectations remedy scenario remains at damages set at $1,000. Thus, it is more expensive to breach the contract with the stipulated damages clause, suggesting that you may be less willing to breach relative to the contract that has the lower court-determined damages.

The results for this scenario are very similar to the previous one. The average amount needed to breach the contract with the penalty clause is approximately $3,000, while the average amount needed to breach the contract governed by the expectations remedy is approximately $3,700. This difference of $700 is interpreted, once again, as meaning that subjects who saw a contract with a penalty clause are *more* willing to breach compared to those who do not see such a clause, even if breach costs them $100 more with the penalty.

The results of this study lead to two main conclusions. First, the breaching party does not consider a contract that is fully specified to be identical to a contract that is incomplete, even when both contracts ultimately lead to the same amount of damages being enforced. There is a greater distaste for breach when the contract is governed by the expectations remedy than when it includes a liquidated damages clause. Second, regardless of whether the contract is fully specified or incomplete, the breaching party exhibits a similar distaste for breach. This can be seen by the premium required for breach being larger than $2,000 (the minimum needed for financial gain) in each case.

Thus, breaching parties may not breach even when it is profitable for them do so from a purely monetary perspective. This is a strong result in that it is the breaching party who has most to gain from breaching. Arguing that a breached-against party has a distaste for breach, even when adequately compensated, is important to recognize, but it is a more obvious observation than arguing that a breaching party has a distaste for profitable breach. In short, both liquidated damages and the expectations remedy that make the breached-against party whole may still, nevertheless, not encourage efficient breach because of the breaching party's reluctance to breach.

One important implication of this result is that using as a benchmark what the parties *would have done* had they fully specified their contract to justify the use of the expectations remedy may now be problematic. When a breach occurs (as in the book example from chapter 5), the conventional economic argument is that the seller should be held to the expectations remedy for two reasons: that remedy is efficient in terms of breach, and it is a (monetary) remedy that both parties could have agreed to specify. Thus, the expectations remedy mitigates the immorality of breach. But how the parties feel about breach with an unspecified contract subject to the expectations remedy may be completely different from how they feel about a fully specified contract that includes expectations damages. The behavioral argument advanced here is that it is liquidated damages (not the expectations remedy) that mitigates the immorality of breach. An implication of this result is that public policy may be better directed at encouraging liquidated damages prebreach than at having the courts enforce the expectations remedy postbreach, at least to the extent that the immorality of breach matters from a social perspective.

The Negligence Rule and Implementation Costs

In chapter 7, we compared tort no-fault liability rules, like strict liability, to fault rules, like negligence, using several criteria. With respect to care levels, negligence is an efficient liability rule in that it provides the incentive for the injurer to take due care to avoid liability, and simultaneously for the victim to take due care to optimize on the margin. Strict liability can be efficient in a unilateral care setting, but it is not efficient in a bilateral care setting because it does not provide the fully compensated victim with the incentive to take due care. The negligence rule, however, is difficult to apply because of the information costs incurred in finding the injurer's due care and actual care levels.

Traditional economic analysis has long recognized this shortcoming of the negligence rule, leading many scholars to argue in favor of using strict liability due (at least in part) to its ease of application. While it is well accepted that negligence is a difficult rule to apply, most traditional analyses basically stop at simply identifying this problem. Behavioral economists, on the other hand, delve deeper into the "black box" of the negligence rule, attempting to look at specific aspects of these difficulties. One such specific aspect is known as the *hindsight bias*, nicely described by Kamin and Rachlinski (1995, 90): "Ignoring a known outcome while recreating a decision is a difficult cognitive task. In making such judgments, people overestimate both the probability of the known outcome and the ability of decision makers to foresee that outcome. . . . When trying to reconstruct what a foresightful state of mind would have perceived, people remain anchored in the hindsightful perspective. This leaves the reported outcome looking much more likely than it would look to the reasonable person without the benefit of hindsight." A return to the numerical example introduced in chapter 7 will help further explain this concept.

A (potential) injurer has to decide if she wants to salt the sidewalk in front of her house. If she doesn't salt, a (potential) victim has a 10 percent probability of slipping. If she does salt, the probability of slipping is reduced to 2 percent. If the victim slips, he will suffer damages of $100. Salting the sidewalk, then, leads to an expected savings of $(.10 - .02) \times$ $100 = \$8$. If the cost of salting is less than $8 (in the original example it is $3), it is efficient for the injurer to salt. But if the cost of salting is greater than $8, it is not efficient for her to salt. Let's now assume that the cost of salting is $9, leading to a due care level of *no* salting.

If the injurer's behavior is governed by the negligence rule, she efficiently has no incentive to salt the sidewalk as long as the rule is correctly applied. The injurer avoids liability by taking due care, which in this example is to not salt the sidewalk. But what if the victim slips and still decides to sue the injurer for damages? A jury that correctly perceives that the victim had a 10 percent chance of slipping when the injurer did not salt the sidewalk will not hold the injurer liable for damages. With hindsight bias, however, the jury may misperceive the probability of slipping and hold the injurer liable.

When the jury consider this case, it is with the knowledge that an accident has occurred. That is why there is a case in the first place. With a known outcome, when the jury is asked to consider what the probability of the accident's occurring was *before* it occurred, the potential for the hindsight bias arises. The jurors are affected by the fact that the accident has occurred, and this leads them to assess the prior probability at a level higher than the true one of 10 percent. For example, let's say they believe the probability of the accident's occurring without salting was 50 percent. With this hindsight bias, the jury believes the injurer was not acting reasonably by not salting. The jury would find her negligent and hold her liable for damages even though she was taking due care.

The hindsight bias can weaken the incentive for the injurer to take due care. In this example, if the injurer does not salt, she bears no liability when the negligence rule is applied correctly. But if she is mistakenly found liable when not salting, her expected loss is $.10 \times \$100 = \$10$. If she decides to salt the sidewalk to avoid liability, it costs her $9 to do so, and it is worth spending $9 to save $10. Just as we saw in chapter 9 when discussing defensive medicine, under a misapplied negligence rule, the injurer may take more than due care to avoid liability. This is the safer, but less efficient, act.

It should be noted that the injurer will not take more than due care in this setting if her behavior is governed by strict liability instead of the negligence rule. If the injurer spends $9 to salt the sidewalk, this lowers her expected liability, but it does not eliminate it. Salting reduces the probability of the accident from 10 percent to 2 percent, thus saving the always liable injurer $(.10 - .02) \times \$100 = \$8$, which is not worth spending $9 to do. Thus, the hindsight bias can be used as an argument in favor of adopting strict liability over the negligence rule in terms of providing the injurer with the incentive to take no more than due care, at least in this unilateral care example.

The study examining hindsight bias (Kamin and Rachlinski 1995) cited above provides experimental evidence of its existence. Using a hypothetical scenario (loosely based on the Second Circuit case *Petition of the Kinsman Transit Co.*, 1964), researchers asked some subjects to consider facts from a perspective of foresight and others to consider them in hindsight. In the foresight portion of the experiment, subjects were told that a city had built a drawbridge and was now deciding whether to hire an operator during the winter months, when there was no boat traffic that necessitated the raising of the bridge. The operator would be able to monitor weather conditions and raise the bridge in case of a flood, which would help alleviate some of the damage that might be caused by the flood. Subjects were asked to consider whether a flood was sufficiently probable to warrant the city's paying for a bridge operator to be present twenty-four hours a day.

In the hindsight portion, added to that story was an adverse outcome. Subjects were told that the city decided not to hire an operator, and as a result there was no one present to raise the bridge during one winter when debris got stuck beneath the bridge. The debris caused flooding to occur, and this would have been completely avoided had the bridge been raised. The flood damaged a neighboring bakery, and the owner sued the city for damages. Subjects were instructed to hold the city liable if the flood was sufficiently probable that the city should have hired an operator to monitor weather conditions and prevent the flooding.

The study used a fairly elaborate experimental design that involved audiotapes, visual slide shows, and actors (see Kamin and Rachinski 1995, 94–98, for a full description of the design). The foresight group heard a reproduction of a planning committee meeting discussing the pros and cons of hiring an operator before any outcome had occurred. The hindsight group was given the same information, but presented in a trial setting after the adverse outcome had occurred. The experiment was designed to compare the behavior of the two groups: "The primary hypothesis was that the participants in the foresight condition would be less inclined to take the precaution than participants in the hindsight condition would think they should have been. We expected these decisions to correspond with higher probability estimates generated by participants in the hindsight conditions" (93). The hypothesis was confirmed: 24 percent of those in the foresight group chose to hire the operator, while 57.7 percent of those in the hindsight group believed that the operator should have been hired. Furthermore, the hindsight group had a higher estimate of the likelihood of the flood compared to the estimate made by the foresight group.

A similar study verifies the hindsight bias in a medical malpractice setting that involved the duty of therapists to determine the potential dangerousness of their patients: "The well-known *Tarasoff* decision states that when a therapist determines that a patient may be dangerous, the therapist has a duty to take steps to protect the potential victim (*Tarasoff v. Regents of the University of California*, 1976). If the therapist does not use reasonable care in the assessment or management of dangerousness, the therapist may be found liable for negligence" (LaBine and LaBine 1996, 501). Using hypothetical scenarios involving the potential for patient violence and the therapist's actions prior to the violent outcome, the study finds that respondents who were informed of a violent outcome were more likely to find the therapist negligent and the violence more foreseeable, compared to respondents who were given identical scenarios but not informed of the violent outcome.

At this point, you may consider the hindsight bias an impediment to implementing the negligence rule, suggesting that a different rule may be preferable. Or, you can think about ways to *debias* the negligence rule. Debiasing involves developing ways to minimize the impact of hindsight bias (or any other bias) while maintaining the negligence rule. For example, in Kamin and Rachlinski's (1995) study, a third group of participants face the same scenario as the hindsight group, with one key difference — they are exposed to a debiasing procedure. In this particular case, the debiasing procedure includes (in part) a final admonishment from the judge: "Making a fair determination of probability may be difficult. As we all know, hindsight vision is always 20/20. Therefore it is extremely important that before you determine the probability of the outcome that did occur, you fully explore all other possible alternative outcomes which could have occurred. Please take a moment to think of all the ways in which the event in question may have happened differently or not at all" (97). The study finds, however, that the hindsight group with the admonishment behaved almost identically to the hindsight group without it. While there is mixed evidence of the effectiveness of admonishments and other debiasing procedures in reducing hindsight bias (for a discussion, see Smith and Greene 2005), the idea of debiasing illustrates the potential for behavioral economists to add new policy ideas to the debate on fault versus no-fault tort-liability rules.

The Deterrent Effect of Prison

In chapter 11, evidence was presented concerning the deterrent effect of prison. While a number of studies find that prison reduces crime through incapacitation *and* deterrence, it was not uncommon for studies to also find that the resource cost of imprisonment can be quite large relative to its crime reduction benefits. Is it possible, however, to enhance the deterrent effect of prison *without* incurring much greater costs? It may be, depending on how prison sentences are *framed*.

A person's preferences over options that are (to a large extent) identical may depend on how these options are framed. For example, how would you answer the following question: would you travel for ten minutes to be given $5? Now consider two different ways to frame the same question (from a thought exercise presented in Thaler 1980, 50):

(a) You set off to buy a clock radio at what you believe to be the cheapest store in your area. When you arrive you find the radio costs $25, a price consistent with your priors (the suggested retail price is $35). As you are about to make the purchase, a reliable friend comes by and tells you that the same radio is selling for $20 at another store ten minutes away. Do you go to the other store? What is the minimum price differential which would induce you to go to the other store?

(b) Now suppose that instead of a radio you are buying a color television for $500 and your friend tells you it is available at the other store for $495. Same questions.

Although there are different possible responses to these questions, undoubtedly there will be those who go to the second store in part (a) but do not go to the second store in part (b). From a traditional economic perspective, this is unusual. If you can save $5 by traveling for ten minutes, why should it matter if you are saving $5 off a $25 price or a $500 price? If it costs you less than $5 to get to the second store, you should make the trip. This is the prediction of rational analysis. Behavioral economists, however, can make a different prediction.

In both part (a) and part (b), you will save $5 if you go to the second store. The difference is, however, that saving $5 off a $25 price seems to be a "big" savings (a 20 percent discount), while saving $5 off a $500 price seems to be a "small" savings (a 1 percent discount). The utility you get from the additional $5 appears to depend on the initial price. And if you did answer yes to both part (a) and part (b), we can take this example to an extreme and ask if you would still travel ten minutes to save $5 off the price of a new car? As the initial price gets higher, the utility associated with the $5 saving is likely to greatly diminish.

One clever study (Bushway and Owens 2013) applies this behavioral economics logic to a crime-and-punishment setting. Consider two criminals who are being sentenced for committing identical crimes. The first criminal is sentenced to five years in prison and ends up serving all five years. The second criminal is sentenced to ten years in prison but ends up serving only five years. How do these two sentences affect criminal behavior? With the incapacitation effect, both criminals are imprisoned for five years, so that impact is the same. With the deterrent effect, one would think that the second sentence must deter no less, and likely more, crime. The threat of a ten-year sentence, even if not fully served, is likely to involve a greater deterrence relative to the threat of a five-year sentence. But this is where the study introduces a behavioral twist.

The deterrent effect can be split into two components—general deterrence and specific deterrence. General deterrence involves deterring crime from the public at large, whereas specific deterrence involves deterring crime from criminals who have served prison sentences in the past. That is, specific deterrence attempts to reduce *recidivism*. The behavioral argument is that a five-year sentence that is fully served may be viewed as a harsher punishment than a ten-year sentence in which only five years are served.

As an analogy, think about a more common setting in which this type of framing issue matters. You can buy a new sweater for $100, which is the full retail price. Or, you can buy the *identical* sweater for $100, but the full retail price is listed as $200. How many of us feel happier in the latter case, even though we are still paying the exact same amount for the exact same sweater? The only difference between the two cases is that in the latter, we feel like we are getting a good deal. In thinking about the punishment settings, in both cases the criminal serves five years, but in the latter case the criminal may feel like he is getting off lightly, thus getting a good deal. The important, and unusual, point to notice is that a ten-year sentence in which only five years are served may have *less* of a specific deterrent effect than a five-year sentence that is fully served.

To test if the recidivism rate depends on the length of time served relative to the length of the sentence, the study takes advantage of a revision in the Maryland Sentencing Guidelines that was enacted on July 1, 2001 (also discussed in chapter 11). The guidelines revised offense scores for a number of crimes, increasing the recommended sentences in some cases and decreasing it in others. The criminal history scores for these crimes were not changed. This allows the study to compare criminals with identical criminal histories, committing identical crimes, but subject to different recommended sentence lengths depending on whether they happened to be sentenced before or after July 1, 2001. Thus, the study can compare postrelease criminal behavior for criminals who served identical sentences but faced different recommended sentences for no reason other than a change in the guidelines.

The study finds that for a given length of time served, the longer the recommended sentence, the greater the probability of recidivism. Thus, in terms of the specific deterrent effect, the longer recommended sentences lead to an increase in crime. The study does not find that the change in the guidelines has any impact on the sentences that judges passed down or on the actual time served. Furthermore, reverse causation is ruled out since the motivation behind the revisions has nothing to do with changing crime rates. Finally, the revisions are not found to affect general deterrence.

In most cases, when a sudden change in sentencing guidelines occurs, it is the "unlucky" criminals who confront the harsher recommended sentences. But in this study, it is the "lucky" criminals who face the harsher recommended sentences, because it allows them to view their time served relative to what time *they could have served*. These "lucky" criminals feel less punished, even when actually serving an identical prison sentence to other criminals who don't experience the same amount of time *not* served.

What is perhaps most interesting about these results is their policy implications: "The passage of legislatively mandated mandatory minimum punishments that are not implemented by prosecutors, judges, and parole boards may have perverse effects on recidivism. Our findings suggest that consistency in the threat and the action of the criminal justice system can make punishment more effective at reducing crime" (Bushway and Owens 2013, 326). If the psychological impact of the length of a prison sentence served depends on the length of the recommended sentence, recidivism can be reduced simply by reducing the length of the recommended sentence. The actual length of time served, where the resource costs of imprisonment are most prominent, does not have to be changed.

Behavioral versus Traditional Law and Economics: Final Thoughts

There is certainly a serious debate over the value of behavioral law and economics, especially concerning its *relative* importance over traditional economic analysis. To some scholars, this debate takes on an "us versus them" feel, as depicted by the following quote by pioneering behavioral legal scholar Russell Korobkin (2011, 1655):

> The battle to separate the economic analysis of legal rules and institutions from the straitjacket of strict rational choice assumptions has been won. The fundamental methodological assumption of rational choice economics, that individual behavior necessarily maximizes subjective expected utility, given constraints, has been largely rejected as an unyielding postulate for the analysis of legal policy. Yes, such an assumption, even if inaccurate, simplifies the world, but it does so in an unhelpful way—much in the way that it is unhelpful for a

drunk who has lost his car keys in the bushes to search under the streetlight because that is where the light is.

To others, however, there is a concern about the too rapid acceptance of behavioral law and economics, especially in terms of advising public policy, as expressed by legal scholars Joshua Wright and Judge Douglas Ginsberg (2012, 1087–88):

> While behavioral economics broadly, and behavioral law and economics in particular, are too new to support bold predictions about what future laboratory and field evidence might show, the theoretical and empirical infirmities plaguing the behavioral welfare claims suggest these faults will prove to be enduring limitations. Further, the chasm between the aggressive policy interventions proposed in the behavioral law and economics literature and the interventions (if any) warranted by existing behavioral economic theory and empirical evidence is a warning sign of a discipline far overextended.

While these quotes depict tension between the two approaches, this need not generally be the case.

Behavioral economics cannot exist in an economic vacuum. If you are going to develop models of behavioral quirks and flaws, for such quirks and flaws to have any real meaning they must depict behavior relative to rational behavior (that is, not quirky or flawed). Thus, much behavioral economics research explicitly builds on traditional models. Furthermore, for behavioral economists who are concerned with social welfare and advising public policy, it is the benchmark of rational behavior that is often used to motivate policy advice. That is, if the key question is whether we can get individuals to behave *as if* they are perfectly rational, behavioral economists *necessarily* must rely on rational models of behavior to further their interests.

One thing is certain—behavioral economics is no passing fad. The field in general has seen substantial development in the past twenty years or so. And specifically in law and economics, the field is developing very rapidly (for evidence of this, see Zamir and Teichman 2014). Daniel Kahneman, a psychologist, won the 2002 Nobel Prize in Economics for research (often conducted with his coauthor Amos Tversky) that had a substantial impact on economic thinking (see Kahneman 2011). Many well-respected economists have embraced the behavioral approach, and PhD economics students are being exposed to behavioral models early (and often) in their graduate training. In short, economists (and everyone else) have to get used to the fact that traditional and behavioral economics are going to coexist for a very long time.

When the law and economics movement began to develop in the 1970s, there was much debate over its relative importance to traditional legal analysis. Yet both approaches to the law have survived side by side ever since. Economists often espouse the value of competitive markets in the production of goods and services. The same can be said about the competition for ideas in the intellectual marketplace. Behavioral law and economics, whatever you believe its value, presents an approach to the law that only heightens this competition, likely to the advantage of *both* approaches.

There is one last point worth mentioning concerning the relative importance of behavioral economics to traditional economics. While there is no doubt that there is much interesting and important research in behavioral law and economics that is currently being, and has been, done, the exact same thing can be said about traditional law and economics research. The proof of that can be found by looking back at the many references found in the first thirteen chapters of this book, especially those representing research published in the new millennium. The study of law and economics, traditional *and* behavioral, is alive and well. On this point, there appears to be little room for debate.

Discussion Questions

1. One major policy implication of some behavioral economic models involves the notion of *paternalism*, that is, policies designed to protect people from themselves. Consider the following approach to enacting such policies:

   Paternalism treads on consumer sovereignty by forcing, or preventing, choices for the individual's own good, much as when parents limit their child's freedom to skip school or eat candy for dinner. Recent research in behavioral economics has identified a variety of decision-making errors that may expand the scope of paternalistic regulation. To the extent that errors identified by behavioral research lead people not to behave in their own best interests, paternalism may prove useful. But, to the extent that paternalism prevents people from behaving in their own best interests, paternalism may prove costly.

   Our purpose in this article is to argue that in many cases it is possible to have one's cake and eat it too. We propose an approach to evaluating paternalistic regulations and doctrines that we call "asymmetric paternalism." A regulation is asymmetrically paternalistic if it creates large benefits for those who make errors, while imposing little or no harm on those who are fully rational. Such regulations are relatively harmless to those who reliably make decisions in their best interest, while at the same time advantageous to those making suboptimal choices. (Camerer et al. 2003, 1211–12)

How would you evaluate the idea of asymmetric paternalism? To give your response specific focus, apply it to behaviors such as smoking, excessive drinking, overeating, or using drugs.

2. In the Bushway and Owens (2013) study, one policy implication of the results is that if recommended sentences are brought in line with actual sentences, crime can be deterred without incurring additional prison resource costs. But what other costs may be associated with this policy suggestion?

3. Many law and economics settings involve individuals who have to correctly assess risks in order to behave efficiently. For example, criminals must assess the probabilities of being apprehended and convicted, and injurers (and victims) have to assess the risks of accidents' occurring. One behavioral flaw is that these individuals are unlikely to be able to assess risks accurately, and possibly not even *remotely* accurately. This type of flaw is often at the root of serious criticisms concerning the economics of crime and punishment, and the economics of tort law. How would you evaluate these criticisms?

References

Bilgel, F. 2012. "The Impact of Presumed Consent Laws and Institutions on Deceased Organ Donation." *European Journal of Health Economics* 13:29–38.

Bushway, S. D., and E. G. Owens. 2013. "Framing Punishment: Incarceration, Recommended Sentences, and Recidivism." *Journal of Law and Economics* 56:301–31.

Camerer, C., S. Issacharoff, G. Loewenstein, T. O'Donoghue, and M. Rabin. 2003. "Regulation for Conservatives: Behavioral Economics and the Case for Asymmetric Paternalism." *University of Pennsylvania Law Review* 151:1211–54.

Diamond, P., and H. Vartiainen, eds. 2007. *Behavioral Economics and Its Applications*. Princeton, NJ: Princeton University Press.

Kahneman, D. 2011. *Thinking, Fast and Slow*. New York: Farrar, Straus and Giroux.

Kamin, K. A., and J. J. Rachlinski. 1995. "Ex Post ≠ Ex Ante: Determining Liability in Hindsight." *Law and Human Behavior* 19:89–104.

Korobkin, R. 2011. "What Comes after Victory for Behavioral Law and Economics?" *University of Illinois Law Review* 2011:1653–74.

LaBine, S. J., and G. LaBine. 1996. "Determinations of Negligence and the Hindsight Bias." *Law and Human Behavior* 20:501–16.

Nadler, J., and S. S. Diamond. 2008. "Eminent Domain and the Psychology of Property Rights: Proposed Use, Subjective Attachment, and Taker Identity." *Journal of Empirical Legal Studies* 5:713–49.

Smith, A. C., and E. Greene. 2005. "Conduct and Its Consequences: Attempts at Debiasing Jury Judgments." *Law and Human Behavior* 29:505–26.

Thaler, R. H. 1980. "Toward a Positive Theory of Consumer Choice." *Journal of Economic Behavior and Organization* 1:39–60.

Thaler, R. H., and C. R. Sunstein. 2008. *Nudge: Improving Decisions about Health, Wealth, and Happiness*. New Haven, CT: Yale University Press.

Wilkinson-Ryan, T. 2010. "Do Liquidated Damages Encourage Breach? A Psychological Experiment." *Michigan Law Review* 108:633–71.

Wright, J. D., and D. H. Ginsburg. 2012. "Behavioral Law and Economics: Its Origins, Fatal Flaws, and Implications for Liberty." *Northwestern University Law Review* 106:1033–88.

Zamir, E., and D. Teichman, eds. 2014. *The Oxford Handbook of Behavioral Law and Economics*. Oxford: Oxford University Press.

Case Citations

A&M Records Inc. v. Napster Inc., 114 F. Supp. 2d 896 (2000).

Acme Mills and Elevator Co. v. J.C. Johnson, 141 Ky. 718 (1911).

Anderson v. Cornejo, 355 F. 3d 1021 (2004).

Ewing v. California, 538 U.S. 11 (2003).

Fontainebleau Hotel Corp. v. Forty-Five Twenty-Five Inc., 114 So. 2d 357 (1959).

Helling v. Carey, 83 Wash. 2d 514 (1974).

Indiana Harbor Belt Railroad Co. v. American Cyanamid Co., 916 F. 2d 1174 (1990).

Jones v. Star Credit Corp., 298 N.Y.S. 2d 264 (1969).

Kelo v. City of New London, 545 U.S. 469 (2005).

Mapp v. Ohio, 367 U.S. 643 (1961).

Moore v. The Regents of the University of California, 249 Cal. Rptr. 494 (1988).

Moore v. The Regents of the University of California, 271 Cal. Rptr. 146 (1990).

Muller v. Light, 538 S.W. 2d 487 (1976).

Petition of the Kinsman Transit Co., 338 F. 2d 708 (1964).

Poletown Neighborhood Council v. City of Detroit, 410 Mich. 616 (1981).

Prah v. Maretti, 108 Wis. 2d 223 (1982).

Tarasoff v. The Regents of the University of California, 131 Cal. Rptr. 14 (1976).

United States v. Booker, 543 U.S. 220 (2005).

Voss v. Black and Decker Mfg. Co., 59 N.Y. 2d 102 (1983).

Williams v. Walker-Thomas Furniture Co., 350 F. 2d 445 (1965).

Index